CIRCLE
⚨ HOPE

About the author:

Perry Tilleraas is a recovering person with AIDS. He is the author of the Hazelden meditation book, *The Color of Light*, which has given many people touched by AIDS courage, strength, and hope. He is also a contributing writer to *PWAlive*, a newsletter by, for, and about people with AIDS.

CIRCLE ♀ HOPE

Our Stories of AIDS, Addiction & Recovery

PERRY TILLERAAS

HAZELDEN®

Editor's note:

Hazelden Educational Materials offers a variety of information on chemical dependency and related areas. Our publications do not necessarily represent Hazelden or its programs, nor do they officially speak for any Twelve Step organization.

The stories in this book are real. In all cases, names have been changed to protect the anonymity of all the people involved in these stories.

Various Twelve Step programs are mentioned in these stories. These programs are adaptations of Alcoholics Anonymous, which is a program designed for recovery from alcoholism. The other Twelve Step programs mentioned are patterned after the AA recovery program, but address other problems.

The following publishers have generously given permission to use extended quotations from copyrighted works: From *AIDS: Passageway to Transformation*, by Caroline M. Myss. Copyright 1987 by Stillpoint Press. Reprinted with permission. From *Keeping Hope Alive*, by Max Schneider and George F. Solomon, edited by Milan Korcok. Copyright 1988 by Manisses Communications Group, Inc. Reprinted with permission. From *Chemical Dependency and Intimacy Dysfunction*, by Eli Coleman. Copyright 1988 by the Haworth Press. Reprinted with permission. From *Journal of Substance and Abuse Treatment*, vol. 3, article by Larry Siegel. Copyright 1986. Reprinted with permission of Ablex Publishing Corporation. From "Voodoo Death, the Stress Response, and AIDS," by I. Cohen Sanford, in *Psychological, Neuropsychiatric, and Substance Abuse Aspects of AIDS*, edited by T. Peter Bridge, et al. Copyright 1988. Reprinted with permission of Raven Press. From Margo Adair, "Conscious Recovery," *Psychoimmunity and the Healing Process*, edited by Jason Serinus © 1986, 1987 by Jason Serinus. Celestial Arts, Berkeley, CA 94707.

I dedicate this book to the memory of Perry Ferguson, David Bergin, Mike Rooney, Tom Young, and Wil Garcia.

Contents

Dedication
Acknowledgments

Part One: Aids and Addiction, Healing and Recovery

Part Two: The Stories

Acknowledgments

I'm deeply grateful to the following people with AIDS, ARC, or HIV antibodies who took time to talk to me and my tape recorder, but whose stories, because of space limitations, are not included in this volume. You are very much a part of this book — its creation and spirit. Thank you for opening your hearts and enriching my life.

Donald B.
Scott B.
Tina B.
Charlon
Kevin D.
Larry D.
Charlie H.
D.J.

Hank J.
Michael L.
Stephen P.
Jim R.
Don S.
John S.
Michael T.
Tom Y.

Special thanks to the following professionals who took time to be interviewed. Although only a few of you are quoted, all of you contributed to this book. Thank you for sharing your insights and hard-won understanding.

Stuart Altschuler
Pam Anderson
Peter Bell
Gregory Christian Bergh
Jeff Brown
John Cebuhar
Nada Cox
Rick Davis
Jack Devine
Dana Finnegan
Sally Fisher
Don Flavin
Stephanie Grant

Danny Jenkins
Samuel Kirshner
Mike Lew
Germain Maisonett, M.D.
George Marcelle
Emily McNally
Mary Alice Mowry
Mel Pohl, M.D.
Alan Rice
Donna Ruscavage
Bob Suazo
Ron Vachon

Thanks to my editors Becky Post and Tracy Brownson for sticking with this long project and never, ever complaining. Thanks to Susie Gilhoi and Diane Clough for your excellent transcriptions.

Thanks to Brother Louie Blenker, Larry Siegel, and my parents for their kind and timely support. Thank you Hank Jones and Don Johnson for putting me up, and putting up with me.

Special thanks to First Universalist Foundation of the First Universalist Church, 5000 Girard Avenue South, Minneapolis, and to its AIDS Task Force. Without your generous financial help, I would not have been able to complete this book. Bless your hearts, all of you.

To everyone who is quoted in Part One, or whose story is included in the main section of this book, thank you for being willing and able to carry the message.

PART ONE

AIDS AND ADDICTION, HEALING AND RECOVERY

Introduction

Not long ago, people thought chronic alcoholism was a hopeless malady. We alcoholics were destined to stumble in and out of hospitals until we died or were finally committed to insane asylums. Even today, most alcoholics and people addicted to other drugs do not recover. Most, but not all. Now we know that alcoholism and addiction can be treated and that recovery is possible. Although life threatening, alcoholism and addiction are neither hopeless nor universally fatal.

Neither is AIDS. Though life threatening, AIDS and AIDS-related conditions are not universally fatal or hopeless. More and more, AIDS is becoming a chronic, survivable illness.

For some reason, a huge percentage of people with AIDS, AIDS-related conditions, and people who test positive to HIV are chemically dependent. What's the connection? Is the fact that most people with AIDS also have some history of substance abuse — alcoholism and/or drug addiction — a meaningless coincidence? Or, might not this first, and some would say primary, disease have a causal relation to the development of severe immune deficiency? Is there a physical connection? Is there an emotional, psychological, spiritual connection?

I think there is. I think that if you read these stories with your heart open, you will realize there is a connection too.

As individuals and as a community, we must step out of the sea of denial that surrounds AIDS. We must start talking about alcoholism, other drug addiction, sexual compulsion, and untreated childhood abuse. We must start calling things by their right names. We must take all those topics that are "out of bounds" and place them "in bounds," inside the arena of what's acceptable to talk about.

Regardless of whether or not there is a causal relationship between AIDS and addiction, this fact remains: alcoholism and other drug addictions affect most people with AIDS and ARC, and most people who work with people with AIDS. Directly.

Powerfully. Without some form of recovery from the first disease, it is very difficult to recover from the second disease.

The Stories

Bill Wilson, in the book *Alcoholics Anonymous,* said that the bottle was only a symptom. What I think he meant was, drinking and drugging are just symptoms of a diseased belief system that says, I am alone, separate, different, and unacceptable. Acting on that belief system, we cut ourselves off from other people, from ourselves, and from spirit. We forget who we are.

That's why recovery starts in a group. We connect to other people and discover our similarities, our oneness. By listening to others, we begin to remember who we are. As other people tell us their stories, we become aware of our own stories, the truth of how it is for us, the truth of how it has been for us. Then, we begin telling our story, and our recovery begins.

This is a book of stories. Yours and mine. Our circumstances are always slightly different. Some of us have loud, dramatic stories. Some of our stories are quiet. Don't worry about the difference; listen for the feelings.

Circles

Around the country, people are pulling their chairs into circles of hope. AA meetings, NA meetings, Al-Anon meetings, AA and NA meetings with an AIDS focus, HIV positive anonymous meetings, AIDS Anonymous meetings, healing circles, therapy groups, and AIDS support groups. Because, of course, we can't do this alone. It's too hard. But what is impossible to do alone, is possible with help. The big first step for all of us — whether we are people with AIDS or not, alcoholics and drug addicts or not — is asking for help. Once we do that, the world turns, a path opens up, an empty place in the circle appears, we pull up a chair, and we begin our journey of healing and recovery.

One of the most wonderful things recovery is teaching me is how to be one person in a circle. I always wanted to be part of something, but I never felt part of anything. I either didn't belong at all, or I had to be in charge. Recovery has taught me to always look at what needs changing in myself. That's what makes me part of the circle; we are all recovering, needing to change, healing; we are all the subjects. There are no *thems,* only *us.*

So, when people who are working in AIDS separate themselves and make me a them, I get sad and angry. Sad, because they deny their own opportunity to heal. Angry, because as a person living with AIDS, I refuse to be separated from the rest of the world. Too many doctors, nurses, chaplains, priests, ministers, nuns, and caregivers working in AIDS separate themselves from us. "I'm fine; I'm the helper. You're sick; you're the patient, the client, the problem. There's nothing wrong with me, it's you."

Those of us familiar with the family disease of alcoholism recognize the belief system and the resulting behavior. It's called codependency. And it's rampant in this AIDS business. AIDS attracts codependent people, probably because there are so many alcoholic, drug addicted people with AIDS. How could it be otherwise?

So please, if you feel somehow connected to this AIDS scene, but worry that you don't qualify for healing and recovery because you don't have AIDS or aren't an addict, please just pull up a chair and have a seat in the circle. You are one of us because you are a human being, and all human beings have places in their lives that need healing. Everyone qualifies.

A Little Black Puppy

Occasionally I visit a wonderful, loving psychic named Diane. One day she told me that I had survived my childhood, my youth, and even my adulthood. "Relax," she said, "who you are survived, intact."

I believe that the reason I survived was that I placed the core of me, my essential self, what I have come to call my little child, little Perry, in a protected place with very thick walls.

I have a black-and-white photo of myself taken when I was maybe thirteen years old. We lived in the country in southern Minnesota and we raised sheep. In this photo, I'm standing next to a lamb that I am fitting for 4-H exhibition. Behind and around me the landscape goes on and on in a hazy kind of country dreariness — empty fields, nothing. My eyes are underlined with dark shadows; I look sad and lost. When I look at this picture, I am painfully aware that there was no one I could talk to about how it was for me, a young gay boy in Blooming Prairie. I didn't even know that I needed to talk to someone; I didn't know that getting support was an option.

During that time, our family dog was always having puppies that we would have to find homes for. We couldn't get rid of one of the puppies, from one of these litters. It was friendly, kind of dumb, black and white, and getting big.

I don't think I was told directly, I think I simply surmised my job, but I knew what I had to do. I whistled after the puppy and he followed me to the dump near our place, and I clubbed him to death.

In order for me to have done that, some part of me must have been buried very deep. Some important part of me was gone, lost in the fog, hidden behind thick walls of emotional numbness. I stayed gone, numbed out, disappeared, for the next twenty years.

I also have pictures of me taken when I was two years old. In one, I look angelic. It's amazing. In another, I'm willful, stubborn, determined, and angry. I got lots of strokes for sitting quietly with my hands folded in my lap, being the perfect angel. Even now, I often think that's how I "should" behave. That's why I'm so glad to have the other picture; it reminds me there's another side of me that deserves to be loved and appreciated

— what I call my glaring, pissed-off, two-year-old self.

Somewhere along the line, that little boy, the angel and the devil, went into hiding. It wasn't safe. The young boy who was left, the one who could kill a puppy, must have really hated himself. I believe the message I had internalized was that I should die. It wasn't just about getting rid of a puppy; it was also about a little boy. Luckily, that little boy didn't get killed, he just got buried. Luckily, by the time he became an adolescent, he found escape through alcohol. Without the booze, I might have had to die.

After awhile the booze stopped working, and twenty years later, I began uncovering the rubble of my past, looking for that little boy. Well, the angel can still smile, the other one is still really pissed off, and the one who got left behind, who had to kill the puppy, is needing a lot of love and attention. I need to spend time with all three and make sure that all those old leftover death messages are replaced with life messages.

It wasn't until I stopped drinking and drugging that I realized there *was* anyone to recover. My healing is about recognizing that yes, indeed, I am a survivor, and my essential creative self made it through. Part Two of this book contains recovery stories from twenty-four other survivors.

The Land of Denial

When I was drinking and using other drugs, I didn't like my condition — the state I was in. I had a nagging suspicion there was another way to be, but awareness of what the other way was kept eluding me. It was like trying to recall something just beyond my memory. That fuzziness is what I call living in the "land of denial."

I'm afraid that if I drink or drug again, I will forget that that's a condition I choose, that there is another way, and I will lose my self in the "land of denial" again.

The night of my last drunk and drug trip, when I finally got to bed, I looked up at the ceiling and saw myself wandering around in a white rats' maze. A voice said to me, "You've been playing around on the edge for a long time, always sure that, at the last minute, you could pull yourself back. But your time is up. You could get lost in this maze now and never find your way out."

The next day, help knocked at my door and I had enough willingness to open it. I took the warning seriously, and still do. I'm afraid of getting lost in the maze.

If you are lost in the maze of your own denial and can't remember the way out, perhaps the stories in this book can help. If you feel like you're living your own rats' maze nightmare, there is another way. If you've never been sober — not simply dry, but clean and sober — it may be hard to imagine why it would be worth giving up your chemical, especially if you are faced with some aspect of AIDS.

Trust us on this one. There is another way to be. It is your birthright. You do have a memory of it. Somewhere in your cells you know that in your natural state, you are an empowered, a sober, happy, child of the universe.

The problem is, in the land of denial, the fog is too thick; the rats' maze too convoluted; you can't get out by yourself. You have to ask for help. Fortunately, a little bit of willingness is all you need, and a hand will reach out to guide you. We promise.

At first, I wasn't sure if I was honestly willing. Then someone told me that I didn't need to be sure and I didn't need much willingness; I just needed to be willing to be willing. I wasn't sure I had that much willpower, but I thought I could honestly be willing, to be willing, to be willing, to be willing...That's all it took. That's all it will take for you.

I invite you to read the stories in Part Two of this book. They are true stories, based on tape recorded interviews. They are presented here almost exactly as they were told to me. I have changed names and other details to protect each person's anonymity, but I've made every effort to preserve the voices and the sound of the stories. The circumstances may be different than your circumstances; the details will not be the same; yet, if you listen for the feelings, you will find that these people are very much like you. They know how you feel, how it is for you. What worked for them may also work for you.

And if you are like many of us, by listening to these people tell their stories, you will remember more of your story, the details of your life, the truth of your experience. You will recover lost parts of yourself. You will find an essential self, a little child who survived.

CHAPTER ONE

AIDS and Addiction

Some of the promotional literature that we've seen around here, in trying to get people to focus back on alcohol and drugs, is saying that AIDS is the second epidemic killing gay people. I'm getting to the point where I believe it's the same epidemic. So many of the gay men who come to us who are alcoholic or addicted to other drugs are HIV positive, have ARC, or have AIDS. I mean, it's the rare individual who doesn't have HIV, or ARC, or AIDS. From where we are, it's overwhelming.

— STEPHANIE GRANT
Project Connect, Gay and Lesbian
Community Services Center, New York, N.Y.
(personal interview)

This is just anecdotal evidence, but because of my job and because I'm gay, I've been in touch with a lot of people with AIDS, and I have this guesstimate in my head that at least 90 to 95 percent of these people have abused drugs and have abused alcohol, and many of them were or are alcoholics, and were or are hooked on drugs.

— RON VACHON
Director of the Office of Gay
and Lesbian Health Concerns
The City of New York, Department of Health
(personal interview)

It's got to be at least 98 percent of people with AIDS who have a history of substance abuse. It's got to be. I mean, if you can find 2 percent in this population who don't have a history, I would be surprised.

— NADA COX
Clinical Supervisor at Our House,
A Los Angeles residential
treatment facility for people with AIDS
(personal interview)

In my experience, I have not seen an AIDS patient that did not have a history of problematic use of alcohol or drugs ever — not one. The flip side is that I have never seen an AIDS patient in long-term recovery [from AIDS] who is continuing to use alcohol and drugs.

— LARRY SIEGEL, M.D.
in *Alcoholism & Addiction*[1]

The Centers for Disease Control (CDC) has not been keeping track of the numbers of people with AIDS who have a history of high-risk substance use and abuse — only IV drug users. Yet, whether the CDC recognizes it or not, whether AIDS doctors pay attention to it or not, whether the media ignores it or not, the connection is there. Those of us who know a lot of people with AIDS, or work with people with AIDS, *and* are sensitive to chemical dependency, know it. The fact is, a huge percentage of people with AIDS, ARC, or some kind of AIDS-related illness are also chemically dependent or have a history of drug and alcohol abuse.

What about Cofactors?

Since 1984 when HTLV-III and LAV were discovered, and we were *told* that this virus was the sole cause of AIDS, little by little, media attention, public health attention, and research money have focused on this virus, now called HIV. In fact, what has happened is AIDS, a disease of the immune system, has become HIV disease.

Questions such as, What are the factors that make a person open to infection in the first place, and susceptible to disease in the second? — are ignored. What used to be a very important question — Why do some become ill and others remain healthy? — has been dismissed by simply projecting that everyone who has HIV antibodies will eventually get sick. That projection is not backed up by good epidemiology and seems to be a kind of "wishful thinking" on the part of sections of the AIDS establishment — an easy way to dismiss a difficult question.

However, even Robert Gallo — who claims to have co-discovered the HIV virus, and who once responded to a question about cofactors by saying, "You don't need cofactors when you're run over by a truck," now is suggesting that, in addition to HIV, another one of his viruses may be needed to "cause" AIDS. In the quotes to follow, other people are more clear and direct about cofactors:

> The presence of something in addition to the HIV virus exposure seems to be required to acquire the virus and become ill from it. One or more cofactors must exist. A variety of such cofactors have been proposed (Seligmann et al., 1984), including repeated exposure to the HIV virus, nutrition, and other coincident infections. In spite of this, very little investigation has been done of some of the more obvious cofactors, such as the use of ethyl alcohol and other drugs by people who get AIDS.
>
> — LARRY SIEGEL, M.D.
> in *Journal of Substance
> Abuse and Treatment*[2]

However, it is widely recognized that only about 10 to 30 percent or so of those individuals who have evidence of being exposed to or infected with this virus (i.e., high-risk group showing evidence of antibody to the virus or virus antigens) have to date developed overt AIDS. Thus, it is felt that there must be co-factors involved along with the virus for full development of the syndrome, including collapse of the immune system. . . .

Recently some studies on possible cofactors important in virus infection, especially substances or agents that increase the susceptibility to viruses and their effects, have focused attention on drugs considered "drugs of abuse" used for "recreational" purposes in this country and elsewhere.

— HERMAN FRIEDMAN, ET AL.
in *Psychological, Neuropsychiatric, and
Substance Abuse Aspects of AIDS*[3]

According to the public health model definition, alcoholism and AIDS are diseases which require an interaction between the host, the agent, and the environment. Everyone who uses alcohol, heroin, cocaine, or marijuana does not come down with "drugism." The reasons they do, or don't, depend on heredity and many other factors.

But the amount of agent (or drug) a person is exposed to does have something to do with it, and this is often related to the environment. For instance, not everyone who is exposed to the tuberculosis bacillus comes down with tuberculosis. . . .

This also is true of AIDS. Not everyone who is exposed to the HIV virus becomes infected or comes down with AIDS. It's not known why this is so, but it's possible that there are co-factors. The use of mind-altering drugs may be one of the co-factors.

Mind-altering drugs change brain chemistry. And most people believe that when the high goes away, the chemical or organic brain syndrome they have created will also immediately disappear. That's not so. The evidence is quite clear that continued drug use depletes neurotransmitters of needed chemicals.... After chronic use of alcohol, it may take up to three years before neurotransmitters are back to normal.

Recent studies reported in the journal *Alcoholism* show that cognitive defects may exist for ten years after drinking stops.

— MAX SCHNEIDER, M.D.
in *Keeping Hope Alive*[4]

I think it's time that, on a national public health level, we reopen the possibility of cofactors, or contributing causes, to AIDS. One of the most obvious choices for a cofactor is the use and abuse of chemicals.

Denial and the Medical Model

A basic tenent of modern Western medicine is the "germ theory" of disease. According to this theory, the most important factor in the development of disease is the germ. Coupled with a tendency to divide the body into various separate and unconnected parts (specialties), the germ theory is the basis for AIDS research and public health policy. The germ theory is the reason AIDS became HIV disease without so much as a by-your-leave.

This model makes life easier in the laboratory, but it doesn't work very well in the world of human beings. It doesn't account for the person, the whole person, whose immune system is connected to his or her nervous system, endocrine system, and on and on. It doesn't account for a person's past history except as that relates to one thing — contact with the germ, in this case, "the deadly AIDS virus."

The medical model does serve some human function. It allows people to stay in denial. As long as AIDS is just about a germ, then the only thing to concern yourself with is whether or not you come in contact with the germ.

The result? Nobody needs to look at himself or herself. No need for self-examination, no need to question how society works, no need to worry about how the environment might affect our immune systems, no need to make any changes, everything is fine. "I'm not one of those homosexuals or IV drug users; it's their problem, not mine. They came into contact with the germ, not me." We become alienated from each other.

Another problem with the medical model is that everyone who does come in contact with the germ is encouraged to stay a victim. "The world happens to me; there's nothing I can do. I have no power. The best I can hope for is to be rescued by science." On the basis of this model, there is no point in making any lifestyle change. No reason to protect, build, or strengthen your immune system. Because once the germ hits you, there's nothing you can do. We become alienated from self.

Modern Western medicine and the medical model encourage victim thinking. From medical research to the hospital experience itself, the model is *helpless patient/powerful rescuers.*

This victim thinking is also classic alcoholic thinking: "Oh poor me. The world is unfair. I can't trust people. It's not my fault; if only other people were different...." And on and on.

> If self-pity is an emotion you allow yourself, you are taking the position of being victimized by something happening to you; a posture of total powerlessness is something you cannot afford. To whatever degree you disidentify with what is happening to you — to your body, or any aspect of yourself — you give up part of your power. As your consciousness is an integral part of yourself, it too must be engaged in healing. It is not enough for it simply to react to what is happening. When you have any life-threatening illness you need to dedicate your whole self to the healing process —

every thought, every feeling, every cell of your body must be involved in the discovery of health. [Emphasis added.]
— MARGO ADAIR
in *Psychoimmunity and the Healing Process*[5]

Sounds like the process of recovery from alcoholism and drug addiction. When an addict steps out of self-pity and victim thinking and starts taking responsibility for his or her life, recovery begins. And then, every effort is directed toward getting better.

Alcoholism and the Whole Person

The people who started Alcoholics Anonymous adopted the theory that alcoholism is a disease, and then they came up with a holistic model for treating it. They helped alcoholics see that they were not helpless victims, but active agents in their own lives. It was brilliant, and it worked. Lucky thing. If we left our addictions up to modern medicine, very few of us would ever get better.

The Twelve Step model involves the whole person, "every feeling. . . every cell." For example, more and more, we are coming to understand how important our family history is in the development of our addictions. We are beginning to understand that abusive childhoods make us susceptible to relying on alcohol and other drugs for positive feelings about ourselves and for escape from pain. That doesn't mean that at a certain point we don't develop a physical disease. It simply means we are recognizing what made us susceptible to disease in the first place.

Susceptibility and a Holistic Alternative

As the AA founders realized, there is an alternative to the medical model of one germ one disease. That is the holistic

17

model that understands that the "soil" — the whole person — is more important to the development of disease than the germ.

It wasn't until the 1870s that Louis Pasteur popularized the germ theory. In the long history of medicine, it's still a new concept. It was Hippocrates who said that if we are to understand the illness, we must know the person. Today, there are people repopularizing this older, broader understanding of disease. The popularity of Bernie Siegel's books makes me confident that, as a culture, we are becoming conscious of what we've always known on a deep level: our person is a whole, connected, unified entity, and if something is wrong with one part, we must engage the entire entity — body, mind, and spirit — for healing.

Healers and shamans have always understood that attitudes, beliefs, and emotions affect healing and disease. Now, the science of psychoneuroimmunology (PNI) is teaching us exactly why. Researchers are learning how the brain, the mind, and the immune system are connected. Scientists are able to explain how a positive attitude aids recovery from physical disease and why low self-esteem makes one susceptible to illness.

Using a holistic model of disease, what we do, think, and say has a lot to do with whether we are sick or not. Not only our actions, but also our attitudes and beliefs can make us susceptible to developing disease.

Happily, the converse is also true. Our attitudes can help us heal. And, we have total control over our attitudes. Within a moment, we can change our attitude. We can choose to express, rather than repress, emotions. We can find our beliefs, and if they are not life supporting, we can change them.

When we understand our inner connectedness, we understand that we are not helpless victims of a hostile, germ-filled environment. When we open to learning what makes us susceptible to illness, we open to the possibility of self-healing.

Alcoholism, Addiction, and AIDS

The point of all this is simple: Using the "germ" model of disease, AIDS is no longer a disease of the immune system; it becomes HIV disease. The best we can hope for with HIV disease is to either avoid HIV, or if we have been exposed, pray for a cure from medical science. There is nothing *we* can do.

Using the "soil" model, AIDS is a disease of the immune system, a system that is connected to the endocrine system, the lymphatic system, the nervous system, and the brain. Therefore, we need to enlist all our own internal efforts to guard our health, or regain our health — "every thought, every feeling, every cell."

Using the soil model, we must pay attention to those things that make us susceptible to disease in the first place. We understand that not everyone who comes in contact with any virus, bacteria, or disease-causing agent gets sick. If that were true, we'd all have colds all of the time. Only when we are susceptible is a virus able to "make us sick." The soil has to be ready.

I think alcoholism and drug addiction contribute to susceptibility to AIDS.

First, alcohol and other drugs are immune suppressive.

Second, the lifestyle associated with heavy drinking, drugging, and other compulsive behaviors like sexually acting out, is immune suppressing. While abusing drugs, you're not likely to eat regularly or well, sleep regularly or well, or exercise. You're likely to be stressed out more often than not. Substance abuse contributes to craziness in relationships, job upheaval, money problems, and constant anxiety.

Third, substance abuse cuts us off emotionally and spiritually. Not only are we unable to connect to our own feelings and form intimate relations with other people, while using, we cut ourselves off from a higher purpose and a spiritual sense of self. We live in a world of fear and loneliness. Our self-esteem plunges lower and lower and our self-hate manifests in self-neglect. We become despairing and hopeless.

19

Finally, alcoholism and other addictions feed a belief system that tells us the world we live in is a place where bad things happen, and we deserve to have them happen to us.

Those are the messages circulating through our entire connected organism. Those are the messages that lodge in our cells. What a setup for illness: we compromise our immune system with the chemicals; we put ourselves in dangerous, stressful, high-risk situations; we expect bad things to happen; we believe we deserve them.

The danger from alcohol and drug use is not simply that we lose our inhibitions. The danger is we become susceptible to disease psychically, spiritually, emotionally, mentally, and physically. We make it easy to acquire immune dysfunction.

CHAPTER TWO

Voodoo Hexes and Other Death Messages

So-called voodoo or hex death is a classic example of bio-psychosocial interaction. It is a dramatic demise that occurs when a person feels cursed by another believed powerful enough to kill or powerful enough to create a feeling of hopelessness. The victim has to believe that the hex works and that he cannot control it. The role of the community and family is crucial. If a hexed person resists his fate, the community, including the family, withdraws support. The hexed feels cast out, isolated, alone. He sees death as the only escape from an intolerable loneliness. Only when he accepts the in-evitability of death does the community return and act in various ritual ways suggesting death positively.

It has been frequently noted that a person's belief that he has been subjected to sorcery and is condemned to death will result in his death.

— SANFORD I. COHEN
in *Psychological, Neuropsychiatric,
and Substance Abuse Aspects of AIDS*[1]

Childhood Abuse

This chapter is about what I have come to call "death messages." They are judgments we made about ourselves, usually when we were children, based on beliefs that we accepted from others, or decided were true on our own because of the things that happened to us or around us. The actual events are long past and often forgotten. Unless replaced, however, the judgments we made are still operating in our unconscious, telling us that we will never be happy; we don't deserve to exist; the world is not safe; it would be better for everyone if we were invisible or dead.

Healing and recovery mean replacing the voice that tells us we are bad and deserve to die with a voice that tells us we are good and deserve happiness, abundance, long life, and love.

It can be painful to remember or re-create the events in our lives that caused us to judge against ourselves because we often discover a small child we left behind — a child who didn't understand what was happening and made some mistaken assumptions about him- or herself — a child suffering from abuse or neglect.

When I started collecting the stories for this book, I soon discovered that there was another component to this AIDS and addiction issue — abuse. Everyone I talked to had suffered from childhood abuse in one form or another. I think the incidence of some form of traumatic childhood abuse or neglect among people with AIDS is as high as the incidence of alcoholism and addiction.

For some time now, people have been asking women who enter alcohol and other drug treatment centers about childhood abuse. The percentages of women who are aware of their abuse is very high. Now, in a few treatment centers, chemical dependency professionals are asking men who enter these treatment centers about their histories. If they ask the right questions, they find that boys are also victims of incest and other abuse.

Not only is that important information to have for treating alcohol and other drug addictions, it is, as we'll discuss in Chapter Three, critical information if you want to help someone step out of the insanity of sexually compulsive behavior.

The message a little child gets from abuse, whether it's

incest or other sexual abuse, physical abuse, or neglect, is that he or she is bad and not worth very much. The message we carry around in our heads is that the world would be better off if we were dead. The message is that the family secret is more important than we are, that we're not worth much if we're not worth more than a secret.

The voices say I'm ugly; the voices say I'm stupid; the voices say I'm incompetent; the voices say I carry a dangerous secret, and if I tell anyone, I'll release a tremendous destructive force.

When a child is attempting to make sense of the universe, and the people he turns to for information — the people closest to him — are actively abusing him, he gets some very specific messages about the world and about himself. One is that there's something wrong with him.

This translates into adulthood as a negative body image, negative self-image, isolation, difficulties in interpersonal relationships — all sorts of addictive and compulsive behaviors. Behaviors ranging from the ones that are censured by society, like sexual promiscuity or sexual addictions, eating disorders, drug addiction, and alcoholism, to forms of compulsions that are rewarded by society, like workaholism, compulsive body building, marathon running.

— MIKE LEW
Author of *Victims No Longer:*
Men Recovering from Incest and
Other Sexual Child Abuse,
and Boston area therapist
(personal interview)

Victim Thinking

Children who are abused or neglected are victims. They are helpless. Unfortunately, children who survive into adulthood, unless treated for their childhood abuse, will most likely continue to act and think like victims. No matter how big you are, how much money you have, how strong you are, the world is still a terrifying place, and everyone looks bigger than you.

With both childhood physical abuse and childhood sexual abuse, there's a belief about being trapped. In the case of sexual abuse, even if not forced, there's a sense the child has of being trapped. There's not a lot they can do, and so their beliefs generalize out of that. In the field we call it *external locus of control*. The concept is, I look outside myself and I don't have any choices for myself. My choices are made by other people and there's not a lot I can do. Things happen to me and I have to put up with them, negotiate as best I can, and hope things come my way.

— JEFF BROWN
Minneapolis therapist in
private practice
(personal interview)

People who internalize the message that their only worth is as a sexual object, or a plaything, or a victim, won't learn how to protect themselves and may continually find themselves in physically dangerous environments.

There's more and more evidence now that people who fight illnesses have a better survival rate than people who don't. If people feel they are worthless, or wish they were dead, or believe they deserve to die, certainly their chances of fighting and surviving are diminished.

But the people who I work with are survivors. A lot of men who were abused don't survive. They die in any number of ways: with needles in their arms, in car crashes, suicide. These are the people who didn't make it through, who did fall victim. Lots of suicides just couldn't take the pain anymore. When men start doing recovery work, they have a long history of being fighters; they are survivors. It's incredible strength that's brought them to the point of beginning the recovery process and determining they will go through what they know will be exceedingly painful. It's not easy to recover. Given that, it's been my experience that the men and women in my practice are extremely power-ful fighters.

— MIKE LEW
(personal interview)

And so are the men and women whose stories are recorded in this book. Chances are, so are you. Many of the people in this book were able to go back to their childhood and reclaim that little child. They are now parenting and teaching their child new beliefs: that the world is safe, that they are worthwhile, loveable, beautiful, capable, creative, worthwhile, deserving, strong, able to say no, able to protect themselves.

They are replacing death messages with life messages; they are exchanging victim thinking with empowerment.

It used to be that people didn't want to talk about abuse. It was a taboo subject, even in Twelve Step groups. And few therapists were prepared to deal with it. Thankfully that is changing. You may have to search for help, but it is there.

Relapse

Recovery from my childhood has been an ongoing process. It started when I got clean and sober. That allowed me to get honest and begin to remember. Later, I had brief incursions of memory that helped me put puzzle pieces together and get a picture of what happened to me, what my childhood was like. My story is not terribly dramatic; at least I don't think so. It would not have made the newspaper. Nevertheless, the beliefs I internalized about myself were devastating.

The professional help I received, and the support I had from my friends, enabled me to stay clean and sober while dealing with the past. I have been lucky. Many of us relapse — go back to using — because of memory incursions. The chemicals kept the memories at bay; when the chemicals disappear, the memories appear. That's why I think it is critical to address this issue — in our Twelve Step groups, in treatment, in after-care, in our AIDS service organizations.

Voodoo Hex

It takes a lot of courage to be honest and face our feelings, to turn around and face our shadow. And the predominant culture does not support us in our quest for the truth. Society's rule is: Keep the secret; honor thy father and thy mother; better you die than challenge the system. Deny, deny, deny. The rules apply regardless of whether your family system is incest, physical abuse, neglect, or the family disease of alcoholism or another addiction. The community and the family support us in remaining compliant victims. The promise is that we will be accepted if we go along with the hex.

Homophobia

One Sunday morning, a priest at the Basilica — he used to be the monsignor — was in the pulpit discussing homosexuality. He said it was innately bad and totally against God's will — a grievous sin. So I got up and I told the priest that I wasn't listening anymore. I tore up my offering check and said, "If I wanted to be abused, I could go out onto the street. I came here for my spirituality; I didn't come here to be abused." And I walked out. I called up the rectory afterward, and I was told that he was an old priest. I told them that when I was a kid, I was taught by an old priest that blacks were the sons of Cain and that they were going to burn in hell. Being old priests gives them no right.

When we speak up, they say we're "oversensitive." But when people go home, they think it's all right to bash gay people because they heard it in church.

When my friend Terry Knutsen got killed in Loring Park, he didn't get killed by street people. He got killed by four boys from a very expensive private school. They were well educated and well-off, and they bludgeoned him to death with a baseball bat. The courts gave one of them six months and slapped the others on the hand. Where did those kids learn that from? They learned it in their homes and in their schools and in their churches. No one wants to discuss it. It's the same way this racism happened in Howard Beach, New York, when those kids forced this black person onto a highway. They should indict the schools, the churches, the parents.

If we let schools and churches continue to tell these lies, this is going to keep going on, and this next generation of children will be afraid to come out of the closet. The only time they'll come out is when they're drunk or stoned. They'll have the same death wish we grew up with.

They don't want you to talk about gay rights, or racism, or sexism. They don't want to deal with that. You've got to say, "I'm going to die first," and then they'll support you. "If you promise to die, then we'll support you, give you money, even to help you die — make it comfortable for us so we don't have so much guilt."

— MARK
A person with AIDS
(personal interview)

What was the message that gay people in Minnesota internalized the day the murderers of Terry Knutsen were let off? What were the messages internalized by a nation of gay men and lesbians when Dan White, the murderer of Harvey Milk, was acquitted?

What is the message you internalize as a kid when you know you are different, that you *are* a homo, a faggot, a sissy, and the worst thing any kid can be called is homo, faggot, sissy?

I think that the effects of growing up gay in this anti-sexual, anti-homosexual society are similar to the effects of growing up battered, abused, or neglected. The message we take with us into adolescence and adulthood is the same: we don't deserve to live. To varying degrees, that message gets lodged in the memories of every gay kid.

You know that who you are will never be acceptable. You know that you will never be able to talk about how you feel to anyone, even your best friend.

Just as adults who were abused as children often block their memories of childhood, so gay men and lesbians often block many of the painful memories of childhood and adolescence. We pass over questions about how it was for us with blithe answers or jokes. Denial is a wonderful coping skill, until that denial keeps you from changing your life, from changing the messages you internalized and "set" during childhood and adolescence.

I think that gay men and lesbians need to adopt the recovery process used by survivors of sexual and physical abuse. We need to go back and reclaim that little gay boy or girl who was left behind. Every time something happened, every time some-one made a joke, every time someone called us a name, every time we wanted to say something and couldn't, every time we wanted to express a feeling and didn't, we left a part of ourselves in unfinished business. The process of becoming whole is the process of going back and reclaiming ourselves, of having the feelings *now* that we didn't have then. When we do, we become bigger, stronger, more powerful. When we do, we take power away from the hex. The hex stops working when we stop believing that we ought to be invisible or dead.

Racism, Poverty, Sexism

There are other sources of a voodoo hex. Racism, poverty, and sexism also breed low self-esteem and victim thinking. The contradiction between the images of television and advertising and real life is ego smashing and demeaning: If I'm not like that, there must be something wrong with me.

For the voodoo hex to work, we must internalize the message, *and* our community, our society, must support it. The fact that every major social program since the New Deal and the Great Society has been smashed, decimated, or cut during the last decade is evidence that the people who run this society support the voodoo hexes.

AIDS and HIV

Feeling isolated, helpless, and alienated, together with being viewed as a pariah, may have similar effects on AIDS patients as having the "bone pointed" or being socially shunned or lacking social support so that death is felt to be their only recourse.

The phenomena may result from the AIDS patient's reactions to family's response, social and religious beliefs, and the response of the health care team, employees, and lovers. . . .

Many patients perceive or sense other people (family, health care staff, society) as wishing that the patient would disappear or die and not endanger them. This is clearly suggested by the suggestions to quarantine AIDS patients, i.e. . . . to remove them from society so they will not damn the rest of the community. . . .

The realities of the illness and the response of others to them lead many patients to feel they have lost any measure of control of their lives and that they are at the mercy of a community that wants them dead.

— SANFORD I. COHEN
in *Psychological, Neuropsychiatric,
and Substance Abuse Aspects of AIDS*[2]

For some reason, back in 1981 when very little was known about this new disease, the media and public health officials decided that AIDS was universally fatal — there would be no recovery. From then on, every article about AIDS promoted the myth that it was the one disease for which there was no hope.

In 1984 we were told that HTLV-III (now simply HIV) was the cause of AIDS. Within three years, public health officials and the media have turned a positive HIV antibody test result into a death sentence. Not able to explain why some people who are exposed to HIV develop AIDS and some don't, they simply say everyone will — sooner or later. That's a projection, a hex.

And it works. Healthy people who test positive for HIV are committing suicide, planning their funerals, and lining up for the very toxic chemotherapy AZT.

There are even some public health officials who would like to extend the hex to all gay men. Even if you test negative to the HIV test, they say, "You can't be sure; HIV is very mysterious. It's probably lying dormant in your body, waiting to kill you and someone you love." That is a hex.

Feeling hopeless negatively affects your body. Your attitudes affect your immune system. Hexes work. Luckily, a positive attitude also works. That's what this book is about: changing our attitudes, breaking the hex, exchanging a skull and crossbones hex for a circle of hope.

CHAPTER THREE

Sexually Compulsive Behavior

...the sexually compulsive individual does not simply depend on sex to survive and satisfy his or her body's need. He or she compulsively seeks out sexual activity in order to cope with, to forget about, to escape from, to anesthetize the pain of his or her life. Sex initially accomplishes those goals but inevitably loses its effectiveness and produces more pain, because of the negative effects caused by the compulsive drive. It is a pathetic, frustrated, hopeless search. Without recognition of the problem and redirection, the individual continues to suffer.

— Dr. Eli Coleman
in *Chemical Dependency and
Intimacy Dysfunction*[1]

Before I stopped drinking and drugging, I was unable to separate intimate behavior from sexual behavior. I believed that the only way to get close to someone was to go to bed with him. There was also a time when I consciously believed that if I was being sexual — never mind with who — I was doing the most important thing I could be doing.

Sometime, maybe a year or two after I got sober, I was having a terrible time staying out of the bars. I couldn't stop cruising. A good friend, someone who had been sober longer than I had, said to me, "Maybe you can't stop." That simple statement hit me like a ton of bricks. Just as I "couldn't stop" drinking, I "couldn't stop" acting out sexually. I needed help. That

moment was the beginning of relief for me. I stopped denying that I had a problem.

Not everyone affected by AIDS has a history of sexually compulsive behavior. But a lot of us do. We found in sex a way to
numb out and disappear. Sexually compulsive behavior usually
starts *with* shame, the shame of some childhood trauma. It continues *in* shame, the shame of acting out. Now, in the age of
AIDS, the shame and pain can be excruciating. Nevertheless,
many people decide that the pain of facing our traumatic
childhoods, and actually experiencing the feelings we've been
trying to avoid all these years, is worse than the shame of acting
out. Avoiding the pain is worth the risk of AIDS.

Certainly, with the help of alcohol or other drugs, it's easier
to make the "decision" to act out. But, like myself, many people find that their own compulsive sexual behavior does not
go away with sobriety. It is as painful and difficult, as cunning
and baffling, as any addiction to alcohol, narcotics, or nicotine.
And it doesn't go away with a hot and horny safe sex cam-
paign. Demonstrating the use of a condom is no substitute for
professional therapy.

I think that, for the behavior to change, it is necessary to
get treatment for the original trauma. The Big Book of
Alcoholics Anonymous explains that, for the alcoholic, the bottle is only a symptom. For the sexually compulsive, sex is only
a symptom. To try to change the symptom and ignore the
underlying cause is to stay in denial and protect the secret.

In her work as a therapist at Our House, an AIDS Project
Los Angeles (APLA) residential shelter for people with AIDS
who have substance abuse problems, Nada Cox found the same
thing. She told me:

> I would say that 90 percent of the people in the house
> were sexually molested as children.
>
> We are starting a group to deal with sexual com-
> pulsivity. That group is going to have to deal with
> childhood molestation issues.

Before I got here, I worked in child protection, so the connection between sexual compulsivity and childhood abuse is very clear for me. I think I'm one of the few who see it. The reason that I know so many people were molested as kids is, I asked. Most people don't ask.

— NADA COX
(personal interview)

Of course, treating past trauma isn't enough. We have to move on. We have to learn new behaviors. We need to learn how to have sane, intimate relationships. We need to learn how to date, set boundaries, and have fun. Otherwise, we go from compulsive sex to no sex. Too many of us have answered this thorny problem by becoming clerics, when what we are looking for is intimacy that includes sex.

Luckily, when I needed professional help, I had insurance and could pay for it. But many people with AIDS, ARC, or HIV antibodies don't have adequate insurance. We need to make sure that anyone who wants it is able to find competent professional family-of-origin and abuse therapy. It's a quality of life issue, a prevention issue, a survival issue.

CHAPTER FOUR

Recovery

The stories in Part Two of this book are survival stories. We are doing more than surviving; we are recovering. We are regaining balance and harmony. We are learning how to live normal lives. We are not just clean and dry, we are sober and serene. Our abstinence makes our recovery possible. That's why our first step is to let go of the drink and the drug; from then on, our recovery is about learning to live.

Some people tell us that if they had HIV or were diagnosed with AIDS, they wouldn't be able to stay sober. Certainly, some of us started using again after we were diagnosed or after we received a positive antibody test result. And, of those people who started using again, many found their way back to recovery. And, gratefully, many of us have not found it necessary to drink or drug because of AIDS.

The point is, the stories in this book are not really about the amazing ability of people with AIDS to either get sober or stay sober. They are the stories of the amazing miracle that sobriety is for *any* alcoholic or drug addict. The miracle isn't that people with AIDS are able to recover; the miracle is that addicts do recover. AIDS or HIV is just another aspect of our lives — it's how it is for us. Even if you don't have AIDS, how it is for you makes your miracle just as amazing.

If you are a person living with AIDS or ARC, or someone who has tested positive for HIV, and you are still abusing alcohol and other drugs — including the mood-altering and addictive pharmaceuticals that your doctor prescribes — please know that there is hope. All you need is to be willing to ask for help.

Recovering Lost Self

I believe that every time we stuff a feeling we lose part of ourselves. Some essential part of ourselves stays frozen in the experience while the rest of us moves on. Alcoholics and addicts know what it's like to avoid a feeling. We'd rather smoke, drink, take a pill, shoot up, have sex, cruise, eat, or otherwise run away, rather than have what may be painful feelings. Every time we did that, or if we are still doing that, a little part of ourselves disappeared. Recovery is about going back and recovering ourselves, collecting our lost parts. It's the process of becoming whole.

When I first got sober I was working in a stock photo agency. One day, a woman was in the shop selecting photos for a series of sobriety posters. She let me know that she was recovering, too, and she talked about feelings. I don't remember what she said, but at the end of the day, when everyone else was gone, I asked her how one would recognize a feeling. To her credit, she took me seriously, smiled, thought a moment, and said that usually with a feeling your body changes. I didn't know that; it was new, wonderful, useful information.

For me, the process of recovery involves learning how to express my feelings as I am having them, and allowing myself to have some of the feelings I stuffed when I was growing up. As I do, I become a bigger, more substantial person. I fill out, become whole.

In recovery we discover we are much bigger than we thought we were. We discover our powerful human selfhood, which begins what I believe is the heart of recovery: stepping out of the trap of victim thinking.

Stepping Out of Victim Consciousness

The irony of the Twelve Step recovery program is that after we surrender and give up trying to control the world — especially our drinking and drugging — we are asked to take responsibility for our lives. First we admit *power*lessness over the chemicals we are addicted to; then we begin a process of em*power*ment.

When we were using, most of us alcoholics and drug addicts knew what the problem was — *them*. If it weren't for the way *they* behaved, for what *they* did to us, for the way *they* were, we'd be fine. The world happened to us; we were its victims. And deep down, our shame told us we deserved it. If they really knew what we were like, they'd run us out of town. Alcoholics and addicts are great victims.

In the program, we are taught to get honest. We begin to see that we are not helpless recipients of life's bad luck: we are involved in what happens; we have something to do with our lives. We begin to see ourselves as actors — subjects, not objects.

Obviously, some things did happen. We weren't born with low self-esteem. But in order to deal with what happened, in order to change our behavior and beliefs, we must take responsibility for our lives now, today. No matter what happened to us, no matter where we learned our behaviors and beliefs, at a certain point, they became *ours*.

For many of us, responsibility is a scary word. It implies that we have to do everything ourselves. God knows many of us tried that. By the time we reach recovery, most of us are tired of trying to hold it all together, make it work, fix it.

The wonderful thing about responsibility in recovery is that outcomes aren't our job. We're only responsible for our effort; outcomes we leave to a Higher Power. We let the universe take care of those. We put in the effort, which starts with being honest, and then we become willing to let change happen.

The result is, we stop blaming *them* or relying on *them* to save us. We become active agents in our own lives.

Recovering from What Happened

Many of us run into some pretty painful realizations when we get honest. Most of my life, I glibly told people that my childhood was normal and happy. Once I got sober and started to be honest, it hit me that I hadn't been happy; I had been lonely and miserable.

We medicated our pain, anxiety, and depression with alcohol and drugs. Once the alcohol and drugs are gone, we're left with anxiety, depression, and with what happened. The point is, we adopt victim-thinking because *something happened* that taught us the world wasn't safe and that we weren't good enough.

Sobriety gives us a chance to go back and find out what happened and what beliefs we internalized as a result of what happened. Not everyone was abused, but what seems small to an adult may have been huge to a little boy or girl. Regardless of the incidents or situations, the message is often the same: that we ought to die or disappear; we don't deserve to be happy.

Recovery gives us a chance, a day at a time, to go back and replace those old beliefs and death messages with life affirmations. AIDS demands that we do.

Recovery and AIDS

My experience has been that complete healing occurs only when the underlying emotional, psychological, and spiritual stresses are treated as equal contributing elements to disease. With AIDS, these stresses relate directly to victim consciousness. The healing of AIDS requires the healing of victim consciousness. Treatment of the physical body alone will not heal this disease.
— CAROLINE M. MYSS, M.A.
in *AIDS: Passageway to Transformation*[1]

Just as the Twelve Step program of AA and NA, which is used to treat the disease of alcoholism and drug addiction, looks at the whole person — body, mind, and spirit — so I think we need to look at the whole person when treating the disease AIDS.

We need to recover all the lost parts of ourselves. We need to take responsibility for our lives. We need to find all the death messages and replace them with life affirmations. We need to do for AIDS what we do for alcoholism and addiction. AIDS is not just something that happened to our body. Our whole self is involved. And we must involve our whole self in our recovery.

Successfully battling alcoholism requires we do more than put a cork in the bottle; we have to deal with our emotions, our thinking, our spirit selves. Why would AIDS be any different?

Blaming the Victim

A lot of people argue that holistic theories of illness "blame the victim." I disagree. First, the argument identifies people with AIDS as victims, something the National Association of People with AIDS has been fighting for many years. Second, it's rooted in the concept of blame, which is the flip side of guilt. Blame and guilt are about judgment.

When we let go of the need to make a judgment about our experiences, we have an opportunity to lay aside blame and guilt. If we let go of judgment, AIDS stops being a terrible thing that happens to someone for which blame or guilt must be assigned. Instead, AIDS becomes an experience, part of our journey.

When we refuse to think of ourselves as victims, and stop playing the game of blame and guilt, we are open to learning what our experiences have to teach us; we open to change.

Recovering alcoholics don't blame themselves for being alcoholics. Taking responsibility for your illness isn't about blame or guilt; it's about recovery and change. When we take responsibility for our lives, we're saying there is something we can do about our situations — whatever they are. We put in the effort and leave the outcome to a Higher Power.

Twelve Step Programs

The Twelve Step programs of Alcoholics Anonymous, Narcotics Anonymous, Al-Anon, Co-Dependents Anonymous, and Cocaine Anonymous can help relieve us from the psychological, emotional, spiritual, and physical stresses of chemical dependency. They can also help us with the stress of AIDS, ARC, or a positive HIV antibody test.

There are also many Twelve Step organizations around the country designed for people with AIDS, ARC, or HIV antibodies. These groups help people who are recovering from addictions deal with the insanity that often accompanies AIDS. The Twelve Step program is a spiritual program for living, it makes living easier and provides a path out of victim thinking.

Therapy

But a Twelve Step program is not designed to do everything. To replace death messages with life messages, most of us need the help of professional therapists and counselors. We need to find people who are not afraid of our anger and who are trained in helping those who have survived abuse.

Our AIDS service organizations need to make these people available so that those of us without insurance or cash can get the help we need. Our organizations need to place a priority on treatment for the whole person. Compared to the cost of medicine and hospital intervention, therapy is cheap.

Recovery as Prevention

The most important first step anyone can take to prevent infection by agents that may contribute to the development of

AIDS — or, if we are already diagnosed, to prevent illness or further illness — is to stop using chemicals and start a program of recovery. We need to take ourselves out of the category of people who are susceptible.

Anyone who is sexually active, particularly gay men, must live in anxiety about the virus or about becoming ill. One frustration is wondering what to do to improve health, improve your chances. The most obvious first choice is to abstain from drugs and use alcohol lightly or not at all.

If you are made uncomfortable by the suggestion that you may want to eliminate alcohol and drugs, that can be an early warning indicator that you may have a problem. Now's a good time to find out and take steps to treat the problem.

For those of you who test positive or who are diagnosed and who are eager to do everything you can to stay alive and be as healthy as possible, an easy first choice is to eliminate tobacco, alcohol, and other drugs. Again, if those choices are difficult to consider or carry out, then you need to go to someone who understands and can help.

All life is a choice, and in this case, the choice you make can directly affect your life — whether you're going to live or die, how you're going to die, and possibly when. Remember, you don't have to be an alcoholic to have an alcohol problem.

— GEORGE MARCELLE
National Council on Alcoholism
(personal interview)

On a personal level, each of us needs to make those kinds of decisions. On a community level, it's time to recognize that treating alcoholism, other drug addictions, and childhood abuse is part of AIDS prevention work too.

CHAPTER FIVE

Living with AIDS

Some physicians don't give a damn, and they'll let their AIDS clients have anything they want. They'll give them all the psychoactive medication that they possibly can handle. They do it for two reasons. First, they're so busy that they don't know what the hell's happening. County, I think, has like 700 cases; you don't see the same doctor twice; the guy doesn't have time to read your whole chart. If you come to the clinic, he is just trying to keep you alive, so you end up with four or five medications and a drug problem. Nobody's monitoring what you're getting. Or the second, you get the physician who figures, Well, they're dying, what the hell, we'll give them whatever they want.

— RICK DAVIS
Addictive Behavior Specialist
for AIDS Project Los Angeles
(personal interview)

As we confront and dispel our own internal death messages, we must also be aware of the messages coming at us from others. One of the most subtle is the message that because a person "has AIDS," it doesn't matter whether he or she is sober or not.

Basically, if you have an AIDS or an ARC diagnosis, you can get prescriptions for any kind of drug you want. The medicine cabinets of many people with AIDS are filled with assortments of mood-altering, addictive, psychoactive drugs. "Scripts" are written by doctors willy-nilly, without considering the results, without a plan for detoxification, without offering alternative non-pharmaceutical methods for relieving pain and anxiety. The instructions "take as needed" on a bottle of psychoactive drugs is confusing enough for non-addicts; for addicts, it can be mind bending. Nevertheless, often those are the instructions.

> I think there is a pervasive attitude that "this person's going to die. Why should we bother? Why get into that at all?" When they do recognize that, okay, you've got to stop smoking and drinking, they say, "Here, take this Ativan." Most of that comes from a lack of knowledge about addiction in your average health care provider.
> — RON VACHON
> (personal interview)

We're faced with three problems: First, most medical providers don't understand addiction. Second, people affected by AIDS often face discrimination. And third, there is general denial in the entire AIDS community about the impact of alcoholism and other drug addictions.

The first problem, incompetence in relation to addictions on the part of medical people, is not something only people affected by AIDS face. Every addict may face this at one time or another.

The second problem, discrimination, is a different story. AIDS is a disease that qualifies one for a disability. If you are diagnosed with AIDS, you qualify for social security. People who are disabled have a right to the same quality of life options as anyone else. It's a civil rights issue.

Certainly, homophobia and racism contribute to discrimination, but I think that when society takes AIDS out of its "special" category, and thinks of it as "just a disease," we will be in a much better position to fight the discrimination that goes along with AIDS. Right now, there are all the other diseases, and in a separate category, there is *AIDS* — the "universally fatal disease." Because it is "different," all sorts of rights violations are excused.

The third problem, denial, may be the hardest to deal with. Denial is the handmaiden of alcoholism and addiction. Those of us who used to drink and drug know that denial kept us going long past when it was time to stop. "Problem? What problem?" The problem is, society as a whole is in denial about alcoholism and addiction. Certainly, society is in denial about alcoholism. In the war on drugs, I don't hear anyone talking about booze. But that's only part of the denial.

In America, the addiction to prescribed legal prescription drugs is astronomical. Nobody looks at that figure; they only look at the heroin, at the illegal substances. We've denied the existence of a major drug problem in the United States. I'm not talking about the sale of drugs; I'm talking about the reason why so many people are addicted. There's something wrong and nobody looks at that. The question that needs to be answered is, "Why do people want to get high?"

Professionals, when they have a person with AIDS in front of them who has a history of drug use, forget the drug problem. They go right into what they've got to do to deal with AIDS. But the minute they hit the streets, they're probably going to go back to using drugs. You've got to deal with the drug problem first, before you have any chance to deal with the problem of having AIDS. The drug addiction, the chemical dependency, is still the person's first disease.

— ALAN RICE, CSW
Social Work Supervisor,
Beth Israel Medical Center
HIV program
Manhattan
(personal interview)

The Consequences of Ignorance, Discrimination, and Denial

The consequences of this lack of understanding, discrimination, and denial are that a lot of people with AIDS, ARC, or AIDS-related illness stay trapped in the isolation and helplessness of victim thinking.

Victims may be easier to deal with in a medical or service setting — they don't create a fuss by standing up for themselves. But when you're mired in victim thinking, and you're using drugs and alcohol to numb your pain, it's impossible to come up with a positive plan for recovery from AIDS or from any one of the many illnesses that are associated with a weakened immune system.

If you are a doctor or an AIDS service provider and you fail to understand or if you ignore or deny the issue of alcoholism and drug addiction when treating a recovering person with AIDS, you can contribute to that person's relapse — you can do harm.

If you are a recovering person with AIDS and you ignore your own disease of addiction in all the fear and busyness of AIDS, you run the risk of relapse. Ultimately, it's your responsibility. You can't expect your doctors to be addiction experts. Maybe they ought to be; the reality is, most doctors aren't. Ten minutes after you explained that you are chemically dependent, they're likely to prescribe an addictive sedative for your anxiety. Drugs are, after all, what they know. They want to help, so they write a script. We can be frustrated with them, we can be angry, but we cannot use them as an excuse to relapse.

How to Be Sober: Addiction Versus Abuse

It's up to us to be in charge of our treatment. It's also up to us to find physicians who will respect our desire to be clean and sober. It's also up to us to empower our support team. Sponsors, friends, family, and others should not be intimidated by HIV or AIDS. AIDS is not an exceptional disease; it does not qualify us, as recovering people, for exceptional treatment. The sobriety guidelines for substance use and pain medication management apply to all people in recovery, whether we are cancer patients, having a wisdom tooth extracted, or living with AIDS.

The flip side of prescribing all kinds of drugs to a person living with AIDS is the tendency to refuse needed pain medication to someone who is chemically dependent because they might become addicted to it. No one should be refused necessary medication because of a history of drug or alcohol abuse — that's another form of discrimination.

There may be times when any one of us will need to go through a necessary period of addiction. Addiction just means our body is used to something and will react if we don't supply it. Three days on percassettes every three hours, and we'll probably be addicted. That doesn't mean we're abusing chemicals. It doesn't mean we've blown our sobriety. Abuse is when you take more than you need, when you use it compulsively. Abuse is when you take the drug to get high, to numb out, to avoid your feelings. Abuse usually is a secret.

The point is, what we all learned about getting sober and staying sober applies to AIDS or to any illness that may require pain medication: you can't do it alone. So ask for help. Get a sponsor (someone in AA, NA, or Al-Anon who agrees to be your official advisor, confidant, or friend). Enlist someone who understands chemical dependency. Don't wait until you're alone, in pain, and facing your doctor in a hospital room.

It's possible to be addicted and retain your sobriety. It's not possible to be addicted and sober in secret. When I was interviewing Linda, she was in great pain. A doctor was on his way with a narcotic to help relieve some of the pain. But Linda stayed connected spiritually through prayer and meditation, and she stayed connected to her friends in AA and NA. They took her to meetings when she was able and brought meetings to her apartment when she wasn't. Because of the narcotics Linda was taking for the extreme pain she experienced, Linda was addicted. Because she stayed connected, and because she took responsibility for her life, she was sober.

Relapse

I once heard someone explain that there are two kinds of people who come into recovery. The first kind are the ones who sit down in a meeting and stay clean and sober from then on. "The second kind," he said, "are those of us who are more patient about our recovery."

A lot of us relapse because of AIDS. We get a positive antibody test and drink. We get an ARC diagnosis and go back to shooting dope. Our Kaposi's sarcoma gets worse and we have a slip.

A lot of drug addicts and alcoholics relapse too. We get laid off and we use. A parent or a spouse dies and we go back to using. It's five o'clock and we pick up a drink. We get in a relationship and get scared. We break up and fall apart.

And then, if we are lucky, after a slip or a relapse or a period of using, we call someone, we go back to meetings, and we continue our sobriety a day at a time. Sometimes, we end up in treatment. We do what we need.

The Right to Die Sober

I think that one of the ways people with AIDS are discriminated against happens in the dying process. In too many hospitals and nursing homes, large doses of morphine are given to people who are leaving the planet, regardless of that person's wishes or his or her pain situation.

Next to our birth, death is the most important event of our lives. At least that's the way it seems to those of us who haven't yet experienced it. Maybe we'll find out later that it isn't such a big deal. Still, I want to be present when it happens. I want to go with my eyes open. I don't want to miss a thing.

Now, that may not be possible, and certainly I may sing a different tune if I'm in terrible pain. Nevertheless, as much as possible, I want to be there for the show. I've worked hard to live sober; I want to die that way.

We all have that right; we need to make sure our rights and wishes are followed.

A Community Response

Clearly the problem is being glossed over. If someone's reason to connect to the medical system is around HIV or AIDS, the people who are providing that care are glossing over the addiction issues. And they always have. It's not just the medical people. The gay community has never been good at facing those addiction issues; I don't think it's any better now. There's lots of training that has to happen and lots of work that has to go on. People who are providing services to people with AIDS and HIV related illnesses must know more about addiction and how to handle it.

— RON VACHON
(personal interview)

What AIDS projects need to do, what we all need to do if we're going to look at this AIDS business, is get our heads out of the sand and start treating alcoholism and other drug addictions, start treating childhood abuse. We need to support people in being sober, and we need to support people in dealing with their childhood abuse.

— RICK DAVIS
(personal interview)

When I started working on this book, I asked a local nun, who was involved in AIDS work for the Catholic church, what she thought about these issues. She said that she didn't think there was a problem, and besides, issues of drugs and alcohol were the purview of social workers and doctors; we should leave it to them.

I think it's time all of us who are involved with AIDS, in one way or another, to stop denying the issue of addiction. It's time to stop kidding ourselves and admit that this is a big problem. And it's not the doctors' problem; it's not the hospitals' problem or the social workers' problem; it's our problem.

It's time to address the issues of alcoholism, addiction, childhood abuse, and AIDS and develop systems that solve some of the problems faced by people with AIDS, our doctors, our families, friends, caregivers, and our service organizations. It's time to pull our heads out of the sand of denial and admit that it's not enough to tell people to have safe sex and use bleach, and then call that AIDS prevention education.

In most cities in this country we have the resources to deal with the problems associated with AIDS and addiction. It's time to pull those resources together. It's time to act.

Surviving

Recovery from alcoholism and other drug addictions requires total commitment — a one hundred percent willingness to go to any lengths and to do what it takes to stay sober. We change our friends; we change our lifestyles; we pray and meditate; we examine our lives; we humble ourselves and admit our mistakes. We go to therapy; we go to meetings; we reach out and help others; we read and study; we call people and ask them to help us. We get honest and real and humble and spiritual, and we start liking ourselves.

We do a lot of amazing things for the chance to stay clean and sober one day at a time. And we do these things week after week, month after month, year after year. Why? Because we want to live, and we know that our disease will kill us if we don't arrest it's progression, and because, somewhere deep inside, we have a desire to live well and be happy.

So we do all these amazing things that are so unlike us.

Basically, we accept our disease and change. And change and change and change, until we are transformed.

I think that recovery from AIDS is also a day at a time proposition that requires one hundred percent total commitment and willingness to change — completely. A lot of the things we have to do are the same. We have to change our attitudes, our lifestyles — everything. That is the challenge of AIDS. That may also be the gift.

CHAPTER SIX

Living with Alcoholism

Intensive psychoimmunologic studies are being done at the University of California at San Francisco on specific immune functions and psychosocial variables.... The factor most highly correlated with positive immune function is the ability not to do an unwanted favor, to say no, reflecting assertiveness, and the ability to take care of self.
— GEORGE F. SOLOMON, M.D.
in *Keeping Hope Alive*[1]

The ability to say no is a major survival skill. For people who grow up in alcoholic or otherwise dysfunctional families, one of the hardest things to do is say no. Survivors are people who, when they don't want to do something, say no.

If I'm asked to do something, I almost immediately think I "should." I worry that people won't like me if I don't do what they want me to do. Saying no and taking time from the pressures of volunteer-type work is the part of my recovery that comes the hardest. As a child and adolescent, I got validated through my good works. At the top of my list of things to do was what my father thought I should do. Next was what I thought was expected of me. That took up most of the page. It never occurred to me to say no to requests for my time and energy. It never occurred to me that what I wanted to do was important enough to be on the list.

Dealing with Family Issues

The family disease of alcoholism teaches us to lose ourselves in the busyness and craziness of someone else's drinking or someone else's crisis or someone else's idea of a good time. All of a sudden, *we're* gone, disappeared. We end up not taking care of ourselves; we become personally neglectful and self-hurting.

The consequences of not treating this family illness can be just as devastating as the consequences of abusive drinking and drugging. Thankfully, there is recovery for people who are affected by alcoholism but don't drink or don't drink anymore. Many people use Twelve Step programs such as Al-Anon, Adult Children of Alcoholics, and Co-Dependents Anonymous to find the support they need to bring the focus back to their lives. They learn that they can say no or yes according to what is best for them. They use the Twelve Steps, the support of people who have similar problems, and the help of professionals to stop thinking and acting like a victim.

Caretakers, Martyrs, and the Medical System

The difference between codependence and service is the difference between living with your fists clenched and your palms opened. What we're finding is that if the doctor, nurse — whoever — are really there to take care of the patient, when the patient is healed, they're thrilled. If they're really there to take care of their own needs, when the patient becomes responsible, stops acting like a victim, they're devastated. It's like you took their job away.

— SALLY FISHER
Founder and director of the AIDS Mastery,
Northern Lights Alternatives
(personal interview)

During the fall of 1988, I wrote a wide-ranging article for *PWAlive*, a Minneapolis-based regional newsletter by, for, and about people with AIDS. In it, I was critical of the medical establishment and called for more community-based AIDS research. Shortly after the article appeared, I was having my blood tested at the regional AIDS Clinical Trials Unit (ACTU).

After drawing my blood and telling me that I had Hairy Leukoplakia, the nurse went after me. She was outraged that I had criticized the medical establishment. She took it as a personal affront to her dedication and to the dedication of the entire ACTU staff.

There was nothing wrong with the nurse disagreeing with me. What was wrong was she used her power and authority to attack me in an inappropriate place, at an inappropriate time. I was having my blood drawn. It wasn't fair.

And by writing this article, what had I done? I stood up and said, "I don't like what's going on and I want it to change." I was not acting like a complacent, grateful victim; that was my crime. I'm afraid that as long as we are compliant, uncritical, appreciative, quiet — as long as we turn over all our power at the door of the clinic, hospital, or service organization — the caretakers and martyrs will love us to death. They are long-suffering, self-sacrificing, and dedicated as all get out.

The minute we hang on to our power and say, "This is what I want," we are seen as ungrateful and not appreciative of their dedication. We also risk losing their services.

I had the temerity to criticize the medical establishment. Imagine that. Luckily, the ACTU was not an important part of my recovery team. Many people with AIDS aren't that lucky. They must rely on caretakers and martyrs for medical care.

When we do what we must do to survive — stand in our own power — we threaten those service people who feel the need to always be in control, who are validated by sacrifice. When we start living our lives for ourselves, we threaten people who think they have to sacrifice their lives for us. We change the rules, and they become resentful. Resentful, because they know that they are not taking very good care of themselves, and they know they have no one to blame but themselves. That, however, isn't an option. So, instead of taking responsibility for their own lives, they get mad at us.

Anyone familiar with the dynamics of an alcoholic family recognizes the scene. One spouse, the long-suffering codependent, gets rageful when the other spouse finally gets sober. All of a sudden, the non-drinker is face-to-face with his or her own reality. He or she has to live his or her own life. There's no excuse anymore. Damn it.

Standing up to a raging doctor, or nurse, or social worker, or whoever, may be more than most of us want to do. Especially alone. Especially if they remind us of our parents or some other childhood authority figure. That's why it's important we get support from people who understand how necessary it is for us to be powerful people with AIDS, people who don't cave in to pressure to be a "good patient."

In his wonderful book, *Beyond AIDS*, George Melton describes how his lover, Wil Garcia, after his diagnosis, went looking for characteristics of AIDS survivors.

> Lastly, the patient who had a certain reputation for stubbornness and was cited by the doctors and nurses as a difficult patient, tended to be among those that survived. These were patients who refused to blindly accept treatment or medication. Instead they wanted to know both the benefits and the drawbacks involved in any therapies they were to be given. They insisted on participating with their doctors in their own treatment. They refused to turn themselves over totally to the doctor to be fixed. Instead they questioned and researched the doctor's proposals and in the end would accept no treatment that went against their own inner guidance. They had a great deal of trust in themselves.
> — GEORGE MELTON
> in *Beyond AIDS: A Journey into Healing*[2]

The Pain of Caregiving

Of course, not all medical people or AIDS service people are caretakers and martyrs. There are many caregivers who know that in order to help others, they must first take good care of themselves. And there are many people who, through the crucible of AIDS, are learning that they need to be healed too.

An AIDS doctor recently described to me the pain and frustration he felt working with active addicts and alcoholics. He knew how inadequately prepared he was; he knew he needed help. He didn't feel shameful because he wasn't perfect. The disease of alcoholism and addiction affects everyone who comes in contact with it. None of us can escape it; we have to deal with it.

Caregivers, including doctors and nurses, need and deserve support groups too.

Circle of Hope

On a community level, this is an advocacy book. We must change the way we approach AIDS; we must include the issues of addiction and childhood abuse. On a personal level, this is a recovery book. Here's how people affected by AIDS were able to get clean and sober. You can too.

On another level, this is a book about healing for everyone. It's about healing our childhoods, our shame, our damaged sense of self. It's about learning that our issues are the same, that AIDS is not about *them*; it's about *us* and *our* planet.

Hopefully, you will find in the pages that follow the information and inspiration you need to continue your healing, your recovery.

ENDNOTES

Chapter One: AIDS and Addiction

1. Larry Siegel, M.D., "Is AIDS Always Fatal? Siegel Says No," *Alcoholism & Addiction* (May - June 1988): 15.

2. Larry Siegel, M.D., "AIDS: Relationship to Alcohol and Other Drugs," *Journal of Substance Abuse and Treatment*: 3:2710274 (1986): 271.

3. Herman Friedman, et al.,"Drugs of Abuse and Virus Susceptibility," in *Psychological, Neuropsychiatric, and Substance Abuse Aspects of AIDS*, T. Peter Bridge, et al., eds. (New York: Raven Press, 1988): 125.

4. Max Schneider, M.D., in *Keeping Hope Alive*, Milan Korcok, ed. (Providence: Manisses Communications Group, Inc., 1988): 58.

5. Margo Adair, "Conscious Recovery," in *Psychoimmunity and the Healing Process: A Holistic Approach to Immunity and AIDS*, Jason Serinus, ed. (Berkeley, Calif.: Celestial Arts, 1986): 168-169.

Chapter Two: Voodoo Hexes and Other Death Messages

1. Sanford I. Cohen, "Voodoo Death, The Stress Response, and AIDS," in *Psychological, Neuropsychiatric, and Substance Abuse Aspects of AIDS*, T. Peter Bridge, et al., eds. (New York: Raven Press, 1988): 95-96.

2. Ibid.

Chapter Three: Sexually Compulsive Behavior

1. Eli Coleman, *Chemical Dependency and Intimacy Dysfunction* (Binghamton, N.Y.: Haworth Press, 1988): 189-190.

Chapter Four: Recovery

1. Caroline M. Myss, *AIDS: Passageway to Transformation* (Walpole, Mass.: Stillpoint Press, 1988): 65.

Chapter Six: Living with Alcoholism

1. George F. Solomon, M.D., *Keeping Hope Alive*, Milan Korcok, ed. (Providence, R.I.: Manisses Communications Group, Inc., 1988): 17.

2. George Melton, in collaboration with Wil Garcia, *Beyond AIDS: A Journey into Healing* (Beverly Hills, Calif.: Brotherhood Press, 1988): 40.

PART TWO

THE STORIES

EDITOR'S NOTE

In writing these stories, the author has made every effort to preserve the speakers' voices. Consequently, some of the stories contain graphic language that may be offensive to some readers.

In the case of each story, pseudonyms have been used and circumstances have been changed to protect the speakers' anonymity.

CHAPTER SEVEN

Jails and Prisons

VINNIE

Last year, I was at the world convention of Narcotics Anonymous and I met a girl there. She was beautiful, she was like the girl of my dreams, and she was attracted to me. I started goin' out with her and we didn't have intercourse. . . and I'd say to myself, I gotta tell her; I gotta tell her. . . .

I am forty-two years old. I was born in Queens, New York. My mother and father separated when I was three years old, and I spent a lot of time with my grandmother. When I was about ten years old, my mother remarried and took me and my younger sister to live with her. My sister just brought this up the other day: for some reason, I forgot about the beatings I used to get. I was always getting beat up by my stepfather.

I was chubby and I didn't feel good about that, so I used to hang out with the kids who got in trouble. I was accepted, I was a leader with them, and that's how I got my self-worth. As a result, I got suspended a lot. I got arrested in 1959, when I was thirteen years old, for shooting another kid with a BB gun and got put on probation for three years. Through my teens I had periodic run-ins with the police.

I started smoking pot and drinking alcohol when I was twelve years old. All through my teens my drug use progressed; I was always willing to try anything. I went from pot and pills to amphetamines, barbiturates, and hallucinogens. When I was seventeen, I used heroin for the first time.

He Was a Better Fighter

When I was seventeen, things were really bad between my stepfather and me. I was trying to fight back, but I was still losin' 'cause he was a better fighter. I resented him, but I was scared of him. There was so much conflict in the house that I moved out. I got a room right behind the poolroom. I spent all my time in the poolroom and I stopped going to high school. My mother somehow arranged for me to take my final exams. I passed them, so they graduated me.

At this time, I was selling pot, I was taking ups, and just hanging out with guys. I was seventeen; most of my friends were anywhere from twenty-one to twenty-five. I felt good about that. I never had much of a role model growing up. My value system was all about finding the easy way, what's in it for me, and don't do anything for anyone else. I've come to find out, finally, after all these years, that that's not what life's about. Life's about being of service to other people, and I feel really good about that now. I heard some people share at a meeting a couple of weeks ago how they were taught as kids to be of service to other people. No one ever told me that; you know, I just didn't have those values.

My real father was like a bullshit racketeer. He was a bookmaker and a gambler, and he always had a lot a money — big rolls of money, flashy diamond rings, cars, and pretty women. But he didn't work. So that's what I thought life was about: that I had somethin' comin' to me, and I didn't have to work for anything.

When I was seventeen, livin' in the poolroom, I met this woman. She was twenty-four years old, had two children, her own place, and she was good lookin'. That's all I identified with: she was good lookin', and I'd have my own place. So I got into a relationship with her — I didn't even like her. She came from a welfare family and she was on welfare. I got involved in a very sick relationship with her. She was like a surrogate mom to me; she would take care of me. I would fuck up and it would always be okay to come home. I would spend all the money or go out with other women, and I'd come home for a week or two and she'd yell and we'd fight, but I'd hang my head down and she'd always take me back. She was the one that was responsible for the bills, and she wasn't very responsible. I just didn't know how to do that; I didn't know how to go to work and pay bills. I couldn't do it. We always had the welfare there for stuff like that.

On the Run from the Army

When I was nineteen, I got drafted into the army. That was in 1966. I didn't want to go to Vietnam; I was scared. Besides, I didn't believe it was right. When I went into the army, I brought a supply of drugs with me. After three days they were all gone, and I was very uncomfortable having to interact with all these other people from all over the country. A friend of mine from New York was at boot camp there and we decided we would go on back to New York. The army wasn't the place for us, so we just took off.

It was during this time, while I was on the run from the army, that I got addicted to heroin. About that time, LSD was in the vogue and I started using it heavily, about two or three times a week. I also started doing heroin more and more. I didn't know what I was gonna do; I knew I was gonna have to face the army sooner or later, but I didn't know when. I was split up from my girlfriend, I was livin' with friends on the run, and I was depressed, really depressed. I was livin' in a motel where there were pot heads, acid heads, and junkies. Lesbians lived in this other part of the motel. It was like we were all outcasts from society, and so I felt pretty good in any group there.

I thought I might as well be a junkie. I felt like, at nineteen,

I had seen everything, that life had nothing to offer me. What had happened was, I got strung out and I tried the suicide trip. I didn't really wanna kill myself — I wanted sympathy; I wanted help. My family rallied behind me and they took me back to the army. The army gave me a summary court martial, which is the lowest form of court martial you could get, and the most time they could give me was thirty days in the stockade. I went to the stockade and felt like I belonged there, with the other fuck-ups. It was easier for me to be in the stockade than it was to be in the army. I didn't like it, but I felt like I fit in.

I got out of the army and proceeded to use heroin. By this time, I liked it; I liked the way it made me feel. I was runnin' with my friends and doin' burglaries, robberies, and dealing heroin. I had a double life.

At that time, I married the woman I had been living with on and off since I was seventeen. She got pregnant and I thought that maybe, just maybe, it would make things okay in my life by gettin' married. Naturally, it didn't work. For my honeymoon, I went into the hospital with hepatitis. I stayed in the hospital a month. The doctors told me if I used again, I'd probably die. I didn't believe them. I didn't believe that anything could kill me. I didn't believe drugs would kill me; I believed I was indestructible. I continued to use drugs, but my mother and my wife believed the doctors, and they tried to get me arrested to stop me from usin'. They wanted to have me put in a hospital. When the police came to arrest me, they found drugs and paraphernalia on me. There were real charges then; you know, they weren't trumped-up anymore.

So, in 1967, I ended up in Rikers Island. I walked into a cell block and there were like 600 guys there, most of them addicts. I'd say 90 percent of them were Puerto Rican or black, and I was scared to death. I was twenty years old and I didn't know what to do. I watched what the other white guys did, the guys that were older than me who had been in and out of prison. I saw how they handled themselves and I used them as role models. I became a convict. When I came out, I was a New York City street addict.

I Knew What to Expect in Prison

About 1968, I tried a recovery house, only we called it a therapeutic community. But I left. I just couldn't do it; it was too hard for me. I couldn't let other people know who I was. In 1969, I was in the recovery house one more time. My parole officer had put me in there. This time, I was on ten years' probation for a robbery. It was real hard for me to interact with other people. My only option if I left there was to go to prison. I thought I'd rather be in prison; I knew what to expect in prison. I knew if I just did my time, I'd get out and I wouldn't have to do anything that was hard — like letting people know who I was, being Vinnie without the con stuff. In prison, I had an image.

I left the recovery house and ended up in Gracie Square Hospital in a methadone program. Eventually, they said that enough is enough, and I had to go out now and do it on my own. For a couple of months, I didn't use heroin, but I didn't do anything to change me. Okay, so the need for heroin was taken away, but I was stuck with these feelings. I didn't know just what I was feelin'; I just knew that I was scared of life and scared of responsibility. I used to try and act like I wasn't. I'd get a job and be with the wife and the kids, but I'd be totally miserable. It would build up and build up, and I'd just go off, empty out the bank account, and go on the road. Usually, I'd end up in jail or broke, then I'd go back home. My wife would verbally abuse me, I'd hang my head, and she'd accept me back. Then I'd do okay for awhile, but eventually, I'd go on another binge.

On one of these binges I did a robbery with someone. I didn't even have a gun; I had a broomstick to make it look like a gun. I was so loaded — I was taking methadone, goof balls, and heroin — I forgot to get rid of the stolen car. I was drivin' around

65

in a stolen car that I used in the robbery, so the police started chasin' me. I smacked the car up, I got out, and I started to run. And the cop shot me. He didn't fire a warning shot; he didn't say halt; he just shot me. The report said that I was armed and dangerous, and I guess he wasn't takin' any chances. I was real resentful about that for a lot of years. Now, I can understand his position; he was coverin' his own ass. I remember layin' on the ground — there was snow on the ground — and everything was magnified. The cop walked over to me and I heard crunchin'. I remember comin' to the realization, Oh my God, he shot me; this mother fucker shot me. Why'd he shoot me? I'm not a bad guy. I'm just a nice guy from a nice family. I wouldn't shoot him; why'd he shoot me?

Anyway, I got shot in my back, through my lung and out my chest. They sent a police ambulance rather than a regular ambulance and took a roundabout way to the hospital, so I was almost drained of blood by the time I got there. The doctor at the hospital said it was a miracle that I'm alive, walkin' around today. By all rights, I should have been dead. I got four years in state prison behind this. Once again, I felt like I was fucked. I got shot in the back and they gave me four years on top of it. They commended and promoted the cop.

While I was in prison this time, I didn't get loaded very often because there were no drugs where they sent me. It was all the way up by Canada. When I was in Sing-Sing, I got loaded whenever I could. Up there, there just wasn't any way to get loaded. In the prison population, I'm at the top level as far as intelligence. I'm confident and I'm responsible in a prison. If they gave me a job with responsibility, I would do it. This time they put me in a warden's house. It was the best job in the prison, 'cause I got to be out of the prison most of the time. Before that, I ran the phone program, which was a new program for the state of New York. I set it all up and I ran the thing. I had little perks and I was able to do favors for friends. Everybody knew me in the prison; I was everybody's friend.

I Looked Like A Hippopotamus

This time in prison I got real fat. All I did was eat. I couldn't see how fat I was; I knew I had to keep changing pants, you know, that I was gettin' bigger and bigger and bigger. When I went to the warden's house, I saw myself in a full-length mirror and I almost died. I looked like a hippopotamus: a little head and a big fat body. I thought, Oh my God, this is unacceptable; I'm gonna be goin' home soon. I went on a crash diet: one meal a day, vegetables, no potatoes, no bread, nothin'. And I lost fifty pounds in three months. I felt pretty good about that. I thought, Hey, if I could do this, I could stop shootin' dope and I could stop smokin'. I could do anything I wanted to, if I could do this. Anyway, I went on a furlough and I didn't shoot any heroin, which was a real accomplishment for me. I didn't see my wife, which was also a real accomplishment. I wanted to end our relationship.

But what I did do was smoke pot and smoke hash, and when I went back to prison, I brought a couple ounces of hash with me, and one more time, I was like the big guy on the block. I got paroled from there in '71 or '73, and after a couple of months, I started using. I tried goin' to work, I tried bein' responsible, and life would get boring. It'd be boring to get up every day, go to work, make the salary. I wanted excitement in my life. So, I would hang out with other addicts, and the next thing I know, I'm strung out on heroin again, and my PO's threatenin' to put me in prison again. I'd go on methadone, stay on methadone for a while, and then start with the binges and go back to prison. This happened over and over and over; for over twenty years of my life, this was my pattern. I got so I didn't mind goin' to prison.

In 1981, I got released from prison, and I was scared because I looked at the last bit I just did and I did better in there than I did on the street. I was able to send money home; I was able to deal drugs and have heroin — better drugs than were on the street. I ran a poker game every night for two years and so I had plenty of everything. I kept asking myself, Why can't I do this on the street? In prison, I felt better than the rest of the people; on the street, I felt like a piece of shit, like I was just a sleazy addict who couldn't take care of himself. I was nobody. So I told myself, Okay, it's time to stop goin' to prison.

But I still thought I could find a way to use drugs. I still thought there was that way, that easy way. I thought that if I had money, I could find a way to make it work. My sister was a big drug dealer, a smuggler, and she had plenty of drugs and plenty of money, and that was my idea of a successful addict. I felt bad about myself 'cause I couldn't do that. You know, I just couldn't manage the drugs and the money.

For the next five years, I stayed out of prison. I was still on methadone, living in a furnished room in Queens, shooting cocaine, taking pills, selling pills. Every once in awhile I dealt a little heroin, and I was miserable. My day consisted of gettin' up in the morning at six, going to the methadone program, buying my Valium — how ever many Valium I wanted that day — buying some pot, getting some cocaine if I had the money, and goin' home to watch TV, read books, and stay in that little slimy room. I totally isolated myself from the rest of the world. I was tryin' to tell myself, I don't need anybody, I'm making it, I'm staying out of jail, but I was miserable.

I'd Still Share Needles

About this time, they were startin' to advertise AIDS in New York, about the consequences of it, and how addicts need to be careful. I had heard about it before, but I thought it was strictly a homosexual disease. It was one of those things I didn't believe that I could get. I felt it was just somethin' they were tryin' to use to make me stop shootin' dope. Then I read an article in one of the New York papers that said they had tested one of the methadone programs in New York City and 80 percent of the addicts that tested came up positive. Somethin' clicked in my head: Hey, I'm on the methadone program and

I've been shootin' dope with all these people; I've shot dope in shootin' galleries. But it didn't stop me. I'd still share needles with other people, not knowin' their HIV status. I'm sure a lot of them were HIV positive.

I didn't feel as good physically anymore. It was harder for me to keep up; I was always draggin'. Then one day I was chasin' the city bus and I was loaded. I fell under the bus and got my legs crushed, so I couldn't even take care of myself anymore. I couldn't even get to the methadone program. And one more time, I had to move back to mom's place. I felt really worthless. I was thirty-nine years old and I couldn't even take care of myself. My counselor on the methadone program was a good guy, and I tried not to bullshit him; I let him see part of me. He suggested I go on with the treatment program. He must have seen something in me that I didn't see myself.

During this time, I conned my mother into stealing a couple ounces of pure heroin from my other family member, under the pretext that I just wanted to make a couple thousand dollars and get an apartment and get on my feet, 'cause my leg was bad and I needed some help. And she went for it. In two months, I used two ounces of pure heroin — china white — which is a lot of heroin. I sold a minimal amount. I got to that point where I didn't bother lookin' for a vein anymore, I would just skin pop it. Every hour I'd take a spoon of pure heroin and skin pop it. And I wasn't gettin' high. I was just usin' it 'cause it's somethin' I'd always wanted to have — a lot of heroin to solve my problems. I guess I had reached that bottom, that point where the drugs just don't work anymore.

I talked to my counselor and he got me into rehab. When I went in, I was real beat up. My leg was messed up, I was on methadone, I was on Valium, and I just felt real, real shitty. I wasn't bouncing back like I'd always done in my life. I always bounced back in a couple of weeks and I just wasn't doin' that this time, and I remembered that article in the paper. So I started thinking that maybe I should go for a test. Maybe I could find a reason not to recover. That's the only thing I could think of good enough not to recover: having AIDS and dying. Why bother to recover? Why bother to do things that I hate doing? I'll just kill myself. So I went for the AIDS antibody test.

When I went for the test results and they told me that I was positive, I got real emotional. When I walked out of the room, I just started thinking, I'm gonna die. My head was runnin' with this information. I remember sittin' on a curb outside the health center with another resident from the program. I sobbed my heart out and said, "You know, I'm gonna leave the program and I'm gonna go shoot dope; I'm gonna kill myself. I don't wanna go through this." He meant well, but he told me that he would probably do the same thing.

When I went back to the house to tell everyone good-bye, my counselor, who is a friend of mine, took me into the office. He and another guy, both Italian guys, sat down with me and just listened. I sobbed and I told them all the reasons why I was leaving, what I had to do, and why I was gonna go shoot dope. It sounded stupid comin' out of my mouth at the time, you know; I could hear myself sayin' it. I guess it was God that kept me there, 'cause up to this point in my life, I had always run away from things. I never did anything that was really hard. The only thing that gave me the strength to go through with it had to be God, but I didn't know that at the time. I didn't have any concept of a Higher Power. This wasn't a Twelve Step program; it was a therapeutic model.

I didn't wanna talk about it to anyone else in the house. I didn't want anyone else to know. I felt dirty and contaminated. I was afraid other people would just go, "Yuck, stay away from me; I'm scared of you; I don't wanna catch it." So I didn't talk about it.

Now, another friend that was in the house too, God bless him, was fallin' asleep all the time and he was havin' trouble walking. It turns out that he had AIDS. So, now, I had someone to identify with. I started lookin' around for support groups. I knew I needed to talk about it, but I just didn't know how to talk about it in the house, in the groups there. I found an

AIDS support group through the Long Island AIDS Project. I was afraid to go to this group because I figured it'd be all homosexuals. I was scared that other people would think I was a homosexual. But, by goin' with Bob, I had some support.

We went to this group and I would say maybe 20 or 30 percent were other addicts like myself, and the gay guys were just people. All my fears were groundless. Now, while I was in this support group, one of the guys was sharing, and he said he was a member of a fellowship of recovering addicts. He said, "You know, I'm five years clean and I'm married and I'm HIV positive. I work at Rikers Island as a counselor and I'm goin' back to school for my master's." He had all these things that I wanted. And somethin' popped into my head, Hey, here's a guy just like me — Italian, from Brooklyn — and he's doin' all the shit that I wanna do; he's livin'. Maybe there's a chance for me in whatever he's talking about here, this fellowship.

I went over and talked to him after the group. I said, "You know, what is this? What are you talkin' about, a secret society?" And he told me about Narcotics Anonymous. I had heard about it before, but I figured it was like AA. I'd been to AA meetings and didn't like them. I always went for the wrong reasons. I didn't hear anything; I wanted some magical cure. I thought people went and got loaded after meetings, or went there to meet different connections. And even if it did work for them, fine, it couldn't work for me, not for the type of addict I was. But now I saw something: this guy was the type of addict I was and he was clean, doin' all these positive things with his life — in spite of bein' HIV positive. And I started participating in Narcotics Anonymous. Eventually, I started talking about it at the house. You know, I just put it out there.

And I Trusted Him

I stayed in this place nine months. I remember leaving the program, hitchhiking to my mother's house, one more time, with no money. I didn't know where I was gonna live, and the only thing I do in situations like this, is go use. And I didn't wanna do that this time. I thought, I've learned somethin' this nine months in this treatment program. I can do things that are hard. I never knew I had the backbone to be able to do certain things, and I learned I can do them. I went and called my friend, and he said, "Let's go to a meeting tonight. I'll come pick you up. I think we need to go to a meeting." And I trusted him.

I went to the meeting and I felt sorta like I felt in prison, because there were other addicts there. I had twenty-five years of usin'; I knew about addicts; I knew about addiction. And I started to hear things like, "You don't use no matter what and one day at a time, that's all you have to do, is just one day at a time." And I thought, I could do that; I can do it one day at a time.

At this time, I decided to go to California. My brother said, "Come on out here; maybe you'll get a job in recovery." That's somethin' I wanted to do; so, I came out here. Another reason I came out here is I wanted to run from being HIV positive. I figured I didn't have to tell anybody; I could just start my life off out here. I could get in a relationship and not have to tell her. That's one thing that I felt when I was in New York: I felt that I'd never get in a relationship with someone new.

I came out here and I didn't tell anyone. I got very involved in Narcotics Anonymous and I had a lot of commitments, but I felt like I had a secret. You know how they say, "Secrets will kill us?" I did have a secret: You think that I'm serene and have a good attitude and help people, but if you really knew me, you wouldn't wanna be near me.

What I did was, I told one girl who was from New York, and it didn't make any difference. So then I told a couple more close friends and I didn't get rejection. But I didn't take care of myself. I wanted to be an addict, just like everyone else. I didn't wanna be special. I didn't want people to say, "That's Vinnie. He has AIDS." I didn't want to admit that I couldn't do what other people do, that I had to make certain concessions to the disease. I didn't wanna admit that.

I slept and ate irregularly. I was always going, and I ran myself down. I started gettin' fevers, constant fevers. I ended up in a hospital for bronchial pneumonia. The doctors told me my T-cells were 160, very low, and I had to get on AZT right away. It was right before my second anniversary in recovery. I remember sittin' downstairs at USC, thinking, Oh, well, you're right down in East LA, go shoot dope; go kill yourself. I got in my car and started crying. I felt hopeless. Then I thought, Let me just get home; let me get out of this neighborhood; let me not make a decision right now, because I'm too emotionally fucked up. I got home, called my sponsor, and I talked to him. I took a nap, and that night, I went to a meeting. I got through that day.

You know, we never know how we're gonna react to a certain situation. When I tested positive, I thought I knew how I was gonna react, but I didn't react that way. I didn't get loaded. When I found out that the disease had progressed, I didn't get loaded. Now, I've come to accept that AIDS is part of me. I don't want it, but it's there, so it's part of me. If you know me, you know all about me now. I started sharin' about it at meetings, and of course, I've shared about it at work. I haven't seen anyone back away from me. No one's rejected me; no one's thrown me away. I'm still me. I came to find out that people accept me for me, as I am. And I started talkin' about it, I started speakin' out of town, and I started encouraging other people to talk about it, to disclose.

The Girl of My Dreams

Last year, I was at the world convention of Narcotics Anonymous and I met a girl there. She was beautiful, she was like the girl of my dreams, and she was attracted to me. I started goin' out with her and we didn't have intercourse, but we would make out and pet. I always stopped before that point, and I'd say to myself, I gotta tell her; I gotta tell her before we have intercourse; I gotta tell her. But I couldn't find the words to tell her. I was in a support group over in West Hollywood, and I'd talk about it. Every week my group would ask, "Did you tell her?" And I'd say, "No, not yet." I was gonna tell her a hundred times.

Finally, after about two months, we were laying in bed and I said, "Don't you think it's kinda weird that we always stop right before intercourse?" And she said, "No." Then she said, "Yeah, you know, I've thought about it, but I figured you'd tell me what's goin' on whenever you're ready." And so I just told her, and she didn't reject me. I'm still with her today. We're gonna get married next year.

What I do today is, I participate in life. I try and live life to the fullest. It's real important for me to be of service to other people, because all my life, I've never done anything but for me. I have a soft spot in my heart for other addicts in the same situation as me, addicts who are dealing with AIDS. They're afraid of it, afraid of dying. They think, I can never have a relationship, never really participate in life. But that's not true. I felt like that because I didn't have anyone to show me. I have a client here who just tested positive on his birthday. I was able to take him home with me that day to see the interaction between me and my girlfriend, to show him that it's possible to live, that *I'm* living. And if I'm living, you can live too.

It's real important that there are people around that can talk about this, that are role models. My friend Bob has AIDS and he just got married three months ago; he danced at his wedding. He works in AIDS education. Another friend, Al, is gettin' married in July. It's possible to live a healthy, fulfilling life.

I'm on AZT, but now I control my own dose. I'm on 400 milligrams a day and I haven't needed a transfusion in six months. I'm also taking Bactrim™. My T-cells are nine. People have full-blown AIDS and have a couple hundred T-cells, but I haven't been sick in about eight months. I haven't even had a cold. I remember when they told me about the T-cells,

I was really depressed: When am I gonna get it? Tomorrow? Next week? I'm still fine. I'm frightened of getting sick, but I don't drown in it. Deep down, I know that I'll get taken care of, that God will be there for me. But you know, I'm still scared of it.

I've had to make myself a priority, to take care of my needs. I've had to learn how to say no. It all interrelates; my recovery and AIDS work on one another — positively and negatively. When the physical elements of AIDS kick up, and I'm real exhausted and don't feel good, my addiction kicks in. And vice versa. If I don't get to my meetings, if I'm not active in my recovery, my thinking gets all screwed up and I don't feel good physically. So they're all interrelated.

Once I accepted the AIDS virus as being part of me and learned how to live with it — to coexist with it, not fight it, not give in to it — a burden was lifted off my shoulders. There was anger, denial, then finally acceptance. And I don't dwell on it all the time. Most of the time I have a positive attitude. I really do, and I feel that I'm very lucky to have lived the past three years. Before that, I didn't live life — I just existed. These past three years, I've experienced life and I've had good feelings. I've been in love; I've been sad. I've had friends die, and it hurts, but I've been able to participate in all of this. That's real important to me. I feel I'm blessed, and I like who I am today.

If you're in Narcotics Anonymous, AIDS is going to affect your fellowship. It's our common problem, our common welfare. And that is important to me, because I don't have to do anything alone; I have support from other addicts; I have a sponsor who's real loving. I don't have to carry that burden anymore.

MARILYN

I went to the county jail for a felony. . . . There was a man there from the University of Southern California who was doing a study on the incidence of HIV in women, IV users, and prostitutes. . . . He asked if I would take this test for AIDS, that it would be an anonymous test, and I asked, "What's in it for me?" And he said, "I'll give you a pack of cigarettes." So he gave me a pack of cigarettes, and I gave him a tube of blood.

We lived in a town outside of Boston, a suburban kind of town. If you wanted to categorize it, it was a middle-class town, a middle-class family. I was always looking for more exciting things to do than what was there. At eleven years old, when I started drinking, life became kind of fun. Up until that point, it wasn't. I was always home and my parents fought a lot when my father was there, but he wasn't there a lot; he worked a lot. My dad used to break things. He was violent, but he didn't batter my mother. I think I was just neglected. My mother's a little bit cold as far as physical contact.

For me, life began when I started drinking. Around sixteen years old, I knew deep inside that I had a craving for alcohol. I didn't know about being an alcoholic, because my stereotype of an alcoholic was someone older, on Skid Row. My parents drank and their friends drank. I'm Italian and drinking was always there. I didn't see it as a problem; I saw it as a grown-up thing to do. But when I was fifteen or sixteen, somewhere around there, I remember having the inability to go anywhere without drinking. When I didn't drink, I felt like I had nothing to offer, nothing to say, that I wasn't funny. I wasn't voluptuous and all that, so I believed that I had to be funny or I had to be outrageous, because my looks wouldn't get me attention. I was real concerned with being popular. So anyway, I drank and started to smoke a little pot too.

It Made Me Feel So Good

I went to a big party college. I wasn't very serious about my academics. I had already tried a lot of drugs by the time I got there, and I was hanging out with people that weren't serious about anything except using. And so, one day I was introduced to heroin. It wasn't like, Oh my God, that's awful. It was like, Well, I'll try it, sure. I mean, I was so easy and so matter-of-fact. I think I grew up a little jaded or something because nothing was shocking to me. I didn't equate heroin use with the ghetto or AIDS or all of the things that were to come from it. I had no clue. When I tried it, the feeling I got was definitely euphoria. I didn't worry about the pimples on my face or the boys that didn't like me or my small breasts. It made me feel so good. I put it on the back burner though, because I did know that it was something to be reckoned with; it was something that could cause problems. I knew that an addict — a drug addict, a junkie — was bad. So I didn't jump right into it; I kept it at arm's length for a long time And I went to school and I kept drinking. I always drank. I drank a lot and I got a lot of drunk driving charges. I never went to Alcoholics Anonymous, but I went to counseling; I went to psychiatrists. The court would tell me I needed to go to counseling, so I did.

During the summer, I got a job at a radio station and I really liked it. It was a very small station in Massachusetts, so I transferred schools, and I worked and went to school down there. It's a tourist's type of place and during the winter the locals drink up a storm, so I drank a lot.

Twenty-One Years Old and Making a Lot of Money

Then I got a job at a real station, a large station in New York, and I was in a whole different league. There was a lot of socializing with people who were older than me, more sophisticated, and I tried to drink socially. I could do it to some extent, but a lot of times I couldn't. I worked at that particular station for about a year and was offered a network job. I was twenty-one years old, and I started making a lot of money.

Then cocaine came along. The first line I did was on the turntable of the station. It was glamorous, it was fun, it was social, and it was exciting. And pretty soon I started shooting it, and it wasn't fun, it wasn't social; it was anti-social. I went back to using heroin, and I began to use it alone. I used that way for a few more years, and then eventually, I lost that job. I reached a bottom, so I stopped using drugs. I still didn't know about a program; I still didn't know about AA. I didn't know about any of that; I just stopped.

I Had No Defense Against Drugs

A lot of the people I had worked with in the radio business had moved to Los Angeles. So I came here and decided to stay because Los Angeles had always been a very clean place for me. I hadn't used drugs here. I had been real lucky and had only seen a real good side of town. When I moved back here, it stayed that way for a while until, one day, I was out in front of the house and this man was there. He had his little briefcase with his bag of cocaine in it, and it began again. I had been off it almost two years, but I had been drinking. Of course I did the cocaine; I never had any resistance to drugs.

The whole cycle started again: losing jobs, cleaning up. Finally, I went to an AA meeting. I had to move out of the Valley, where the man I was living with had decided that I was out of control and he couldn't help me. So, I moved into Hollywood and I went to AA, and I stayed sober for about thirty days. I got another job, stopped going to AA, and started drinking in more of a controlled way.

I was down on Santa Monica Boulevard one afternoon getting a hot dog, and this guy came up and he had some stuff for sale, some heroin, and it just seemed like the thing to do, so I bought some. He took me to a different neighborhood. You know, LA's a big town, and I thought if I could stay in sections of the city where there weren't any street drugs, I'd be fine. Well, he showed me a whole part of LA that I didn't even know existed: east of Highland, between Hollywood and downtown. They were selling balloons of heroin for $8 and $10. Back East when I used, it was extremely expensive. So he took me down there and I scored, and then I started to do it myself. This was about five or six years ago. I started using heroin again, and heroin became the most important thing for me.

I managed, for a while, to work and use, because heroin doesn't make you go on those binges like cocaine does, where you can't function, you hide out, and snort and freebase and all that. With heroin, you can do a little, and you can sit down and have a conversation. I was showing up is what I'm saying. I was showing up for work and I wasn't drinking. Now, I was a functioning heroin addict, and as a functioning heroin addict, I was not in the best company. I was sharing a lot of needles. I wasn't in shooting galleries, but I did use with different people. I wasn't on the street; I wasn't a prostitute. What I knew about AIDS was that it was a gay disease, and I thought, It's awful that it's devastating my brothers, but it's not really applying to me.

The County Jail and a Study About HIV and Women

I began to get arrested again. I hadn't been arrested in over ten years. In '87, I went to the county jail for a felony, and I came down with hepatitis and was housed in the infirmary. There was a man there from the University of Southern California who was doing a study on the incidence of HIV in women, IV users, and prostitutes. He asked me if I was an IV user and I said, "Yes." I had the marks and I had hepatitis; it was pretty obvious I was a user. He asked if I would take this test for AIDS, that it would be an anonymous test, and I asked, "What's in it for me?" And he said, "I'll give you a pack of cigarettes." So he gave me a pack of cigarettes, and I gave him a tube of blood.

Three weeks later, the hepatitis had been clearing up and they moved me to a different side of the jail. It was an isolation unit. They put me in a cell about six feet by six feet. When I laid down, my head would touch one wall and my feet would touch the other wall. It was all cement walls and the door was sealed. It had a small window they could look in, and a little trap door they would serve the food through. That's where I was. But I wasn't sick. It was used to isolate extremely sick people and people for discipline reasons; I wasn't either of those. I hadn't even thought about the blood test that I had taken. Finally, after a couple of days, I caught on that something was up. The man doing the study finally came back and said, "Well, your test is positive." And I said, "Well, I thought it was anonymous. What happened to *anonymous test*, asshole?" He said that it was out of his control because the county hadn't decided what they were going to do with people who were HIV positive. They didn't have a policy at that time. This was in the very early part of 1987. The county hadn't decided on what the policy was going to be. And I said that they had better get a policy because I'm not sick and I am going real crazy in this small cell and I'm holding you responsible.

Four and a Half Months in Isolation

I'd been in there a month without any privileges except showers and occasional phone calls, and I didn't tell anybody on the outside what was going on because I didn't trust anybody. I didn't know how to deal with it. I started to read what information they would give me on the AIDS virus. I started to get a little bit educated, and I was going to court and fighting this case. I eventually ended up spending four and a half months in that cell. To this day, when I'm in a group — I'm in the treatment program now — and there's somebody right next to me, I have to set my chair back. I don't know if it's from that, or what, but I was never that way before. It was really painful being in that small room.

They put a sign outside the cell that said "AIDS." It was a twenty-four-hour monitoring cell which meant that on the hour, every hour around-the-clock, someone came through and wrote on paper what you were doing. They observed you. They would come through and write, sitting, sleeping, reading, throwing food, whatever was the case. When they'd leave the little door open, I'd reach up, grab the sign, pull it in my cell, and cross off the word AIDS, because I didn't have AIDS. I had tested positive for HTVL-3, the HIV virus. I was not physically sick. So I would grab the sign and I'd cross it off. When they'd serve my food, they'd have these ridiculous gloves on. The whole thing was funny because, as I became more educated, I realized that it was me who needed to be protected against getting an infection, not them.

There were times when I would just go off. I had a lot of anger in there, a lot of anger. If I acted the anger out, then I wouldn't get a shower, so I had to just stuff all that in.

When I got out four and a half months later, I knew that I shouldn't use drugs. I lasted two weeks. I went to meetings, but I did not share that I had the virus. I didn't share that I had been in this situation in jail. I was embarrassed; I felt like I was infected. I just didn't feel good at all, about anything, and so I started using again. When I used, if I used with anyone else, I would tell them, "You know, I have a very good friend that has AIDS, so you'd better use bleach." I tried to do what I knew I should do as far as protecting other people, being considerate of other people as far as spreading this thing. The truth was that most people didn't care. "Oh, so what if your friend does; you're not sick. You don't look sick." And so I kept using.

The First Disease will Bring on the Second

In May of 1988 I began to get really weak and then I started having night sweats. When I finally went to USC for follow-up, they diagnosed me with ARC. They pretty much told me that the most important thing was that I stay clean. My T-cells weren't low enough to have AZT — there was no miracle cure — and if I continued to use, I would go into full-blown AIDS. That's when I started to really realize the seriousness of this disease, the second disease. The first disease, addiction, will bring on the second one, AIDS. And you know, both of them could kill me. So, it made me feel really backed into a corner.

I'm very slow in doing things, I guess. I started to go to the doctor a little bit; I started to at least read in the paper about support groups. I mean, I just didn't jump into this thing at all. I didn't jump into my recovery; I didn't jump into dealing with AIDS, or with the virus, or anything. I just couldn't. I was incapable of it. Even though I knew a lot in my head, I just couldn't talk about it. Now, I'm five months clean and sober, and I'm in a treatment program that is probably the best in Los Angeles as far as dealing with the AIDS issue. We have AIDS support groups, we go to outside meetings that deal with AIDS, and I have a regular meeting outside of here that I go to every week that is about living with AIDS.

When I Used, It Did Not Make It Go Away

My Living with AIDS meeting is made up of people with sobriety and AIDS, sobriety and ARC, and sobriety and HIV who are living through and living with this disease. It gives me a lot of hope. It also is the first place that I've actually said, "Yes, I do have this, I am living with it, and my sobriety is the most important thing in my recovery." I try not to lose the focus of that. The focus of my energy, my willingness, is to stay clean. I have experienced using with this virus, and my health went down faster than it has ever gone down. Also, using is a no-win situation. When I used, it did not alleviate anything; it did not make me feel good; it did not make it go away.

I get support from the AIDS department here. They make sure that I get to certain meetings and go to the doctor. They take care of a lot of it, so I let them handle that end of the stuff.

And you know, I finally feel — the AIDS issue aside — like I have a center. My life has a center. I finally believe that I want to be clean and sober more than anything else. The virus is not making it harder to stay clean this time; if anything, it's making it easier. It's not making me want to use and it doesn't make me feel hopeless. This is the truth. I'm not just saying this to give you a pep talk. I'm thirty-four years old and I've used drugs since I was sixteen — and I used them heavily. So, for me, finally wanting to be clean and sober is a big deal. Whether it's with AIDS or without AIDS, being clean and sober is the main thing in my life.

When I first read or heard about AIDS, it was a gay men's disease. I wasn't a prostitute; I wasn't even having sex. I knew I used needles, but I didn't think any of the people I used them with had AIDS. So AIDS was not something that I thought I was going to be dealing with; I really thought I was going to slide through it.

I'm in the Light with AIDS

AA and NA are my strength and hope right now. Seeing other people sober is what encourages me and gives me hope for those people who are like me, who have had problems for a long time with alcohol and drugs. So, I go to meetings, but not as much as I'd like to. I am in a program now called The Family, which is a behavior modification program. Recently, we've been paying a little more attention to the Twelve Steps. We're not a Twelve Step program, but we go to meetings, we have to have a sponsor, and we have to work the Steps.

I was focused on death the first year and a half after being diagnosed HIV positive and, eventually, being diagnosed ARC. It was hopeless. It was fatal. My focus was the darkness of it all. Today, the focus for me is that I'm in the light with my addiction; I'm in the light with AIDS. I'm in recovery, I'm in hope, and I'm very much alive. I don't even like to use the term ARC. I feel that my spirit is healthy, and my body is healthy too.

I have to be careful about being in denial. Your T-cells are something that you need to check. Mine went down 200 points, and so I have to be careful that I don't deny that there is a certain amount of stuff that I do need to be careful about. In the drug program, they have us busy from early in the morning until late at night, so I have to take time to rest. I have to take a little time to be centered.

Living with AIDS in the AA program and living with AIDS outside the program is like night and day. In the program, it's a lot better, a lot safer. It's still very difficult to stay off drugs or alcohol, but it gets easier; it gets easier to live clean. And I feel better because I feel I'm being responsible. I'm being responsible for my health, for my well-being.

When I was using — knowing I was HIV positive, knowing I had ARC — my world was real dark and gloomy. I was very pessimistic. I just couldn't see any good. It's not that way now. I mean, I'm not a grinning idiot, but for the most part, I have to say that I feel good about being alive. I'm finally in touch with the fact that I want to live. I've stuck it out this long. Being sober is the way to be. I'm among the living, so I might as well be sober. Otherwise, I don't have a chance. I really believe I will get very sick, very fast, if I use. I believe that because I've experienced it. I get overwhelmed and scared sometimes, but for the most part, I'm doing what I know I need to do, and the rest will follow.

JESUS

My son was born in 1983. He was born addicted. I remember him going through withdrawal. I remember how he cried and how he used to shake. It hurt me, but it didn't stop me from using.

When I was six, seven years old, my father found him a new woman and left. So it was just me, my sister, and my mom. We were still living at the projects, and I was hurt. My mom is an epileptic and seein' her shaking — it was rough on me. That's when I started my bad habits.

We were poor and I was ashamed. I had to get shoes from my cousin, and I didn't have nice clothes like some of the other kids. We'd want candy, and I didn't have money for candy, so I'd go in the store and steal it. In grammar school, we broke into the school and took a bunch of stuff. I got in trouble 'cause I found one of the teacher's rings in a drawer and I took it. I had this little girlfriend, so I gave her the ring. So the teachers saw her with the ring, and I got in a bunch of trouble.

Then my father came back. I was about ten, eleven years old. He came back in the house, and he looked familiar to me, but I was afraid. My mother told me, "Go to him, that's your father." He took us to Jersey.

My mom and dad were back together, and I was kinda glad about that, but the one thing that I remember clearly is that my father always had a preference toward my sister. Anything that my sister wanted, she could have. He wasn't payin' me that much attention. I needed clothes; he didn't care. My sister wanted something, no problem. Every year she'd get a new bedroom set. I'd have to sleep on a cot in the livin' room. I kinda felt left out. I knew my parents loved me, but they didn't love me the way they loved my sister. I was jealous of that. So, I'd go out in the street with my friends, and if I needed clothes, I'd go in the store and steal them.

When I was about fifteen, I started runnin' away from home. The truant officer took me to court. They told my father that he'd have to put me in a school for boys where I could get discipline. My father said no. So the judge sent me to the state home for boys instead. He gave me an indeterminate sentence. Basically, I went to jail because my father didn't wanna send me to a school.

She Came Up Pregnant
That's When I Started Shooting Dope

I did nine months there, and I didn't have to go to school anymore. I was sixteen, and I was runnin' around in the streets with my friends. I had this girlfriend then, and she come up pregnant, man. Oh God, and I didn't know what to do. That's when I started shootin' dope. Some of my friends were shooting dope and they were telling me how good this was, and I had all this pain and this misery inside, so I said, "Let me try this." When I tried it, I thought, Man, I've found it. I mean, I got sick, I threw up, but after that, I didn't have a care in the world. It solved all my problems. I started shooting dope every day.

Then they took me to court for this girl I got pregnant. They charged me with contributing to the delinquency of a minor. But I was a minor too. The judge said that I would have to pay support. How was I gonna pay support? I was usin' drugs. All the money I was gettin' was goin' to get high. So I never did. I just continued running the street and shootin' dope.

One day, I woke up and I wasn't feelin' too hot. My stomach was queasy and I had a hard time gettin' up out of bed. I finally dragged myself down to where everybody hangs out, and a friend of mine said, "You've got you a habit." I got high; then I felt better. As long as I got high, I didn't have a care in the world. Then I started dealing.

My dad found out that I was shootin' dope and he got on my case. And he told me, "Here, smoke some reefer; leave that shit alone." How's he gonna tell me to leave this shit alone? It's what I needed. It was takin' away all my problems. I kept using, and I got to doin' burglaries, stealing from everybody.

When I was seventeen, I used to see the airplanes go by and I'd wanna be on an airplane so bad, goin' anywhere. One day I packed up and came here to Chicago. When I turned eighteen, I started roamin' the country. I figured if I'd go somewhere else, I wouldn't have no problems. All I gotta do is go somewhere else.

I was hitchhiking through Nebraska, and I saw a truck parked on the side of the road. I looked in it and it's got the keys in it. So I got in, started it up, and took off down the highway. All of a sudden, here comes all of these police cars. I just kept going. They're tellin' me to pull over. I wasn't gonna pull over. Then they had a roadblock. So I pulled over and locked the doors, and I'm watchin' all these cops through the windows, with their guns drawn, and I thought it was funny. They're tryin' to open the door and I'm just lookin' at 'em.

The Lifer Wouldn't Even Talk to Me

They took me to court in Grand Island, Nebraska. The judge sentenced me to a year at the Nebraska State Penitentiary doing hard labor. This was in 1968. First they sent me to the reformatory because I was eighteen, but then they said because I was from out of state they couldn't leave me in the reformatory, so they sent me behind the walls.

When I got there, they put me in a cell with these other two guys. One of them was doing twenty to sixty, and the other was a lifer. I had seen his story in a magazine; he had killed his wife. I'm sittin' there, and the guy doin' twenty years asked me how much time I got. I said, "I got a year." He said, "Oh." I was eighteen; a year's a long time. The lifer wouldn't even talk to me.

They knew that I was an addict because I was gettin' these pills so I could withdraw, but they were just keepin' me loaded. I'd keep complaining that I wasn't feelin' good, to get more pills, and they'd keep givin' them to me. As long as they gave them to me, I'd keep complaining.

They finally let me out and I went to Omaha, and then I went down to Denver. From Denver, I went down to Albuquerque, and then I finally made it to Los Angeles. I started dealin' acid and got busted. I stayed at the county jail for about a month. I started shootin' dope again. I went to San Francisco, back to Chicago, and then I went back to Jersey. In Jersey, I ran into this guy. He said, "Man, I just came back from Miami. Man, it's nice down there. You can make a killing. There's drugs galore."

Miami: The Weather Was Fine and Drugs Were Everywhere

I took off to Miami. The weather was fine and drugs were everywhere, man. Nice women everywhere. I couldn't believe it. I thought, This is it, I found it man; I found paradise here. Solution to all my problems. I was still gettin' high and doin' cocaine, stealin' like crazy, and doin' all the wrong things, but I was enjoyin' it. I was havin' such a good time.

And then I met this nice Puerto Rican girl. I started layin' a rap on her, and she wouldn't go out with me for nothin' in the world, man. She kept tellin' me no, no, no. And so I thought, I'm gonna get this girl if it's the last thing I do. I kept on and kept on.

She was nice. She didn't get high, she didn't drink, and she didn't smoke. I thought, This is the kinda woman that I need — a woman with a good job. I was out in the street, you know, stealin' and carryin' on. Finally, we started a relationship.

She was goin' to Puerto Rico to see her family. My family had moved to Puerto Rico some years back. My mom and dad got tired of Jersey, got tired of the cold, and went to Puerto Rico. So, she and I went to Puerto Rico to see her family and my mom and dad. And sure enough, there's drugs there. I started burglarizing, and I got caught and ended up in jail.

After they let me out, I went back to Miami and my girlfriend and I got back together. She got pregnant. I started usin' every day. She had the baby, and I got real, real crazy. I got outrageous. I didn't care who I was stealin' from. She knew somethin' was wrong, 'cause I was kinda alienated. Sometimes I wouldn't come home. And I didn't care; I just wanted to stay high. Then I got busted again.

When they let me out, I came to Chicago. I was running. I caught some more cases up here, couple of burglaries, and then I couldn't run no more. I couldn't go to California, 'cause I was on probation there. I couldn't go to Jersey, 'cause they had a non-support warrant for me in Jersey. I couldn't go to Puerto Rico; I had cases in Chicago. I had cases in Miami. Where could I go? There's nowhere I could go; there's nowhere I could run anymore. I knew I was goin' to the penitentiary.

I ended up in prison for two years. December 28, 1978, I got out. I didn't wanna be in Chicago, I didn't like the cold weather, but I had no choice.

My Son Was Born Addicted

In 1981, I met this other girl who became the mother of my little children, my young children. She liked to get high too. We got together and we were gettin' high and carryin' on, and she got pregnant.

My son was born in 1983. He was born addicted. I remember him going through withdrawal. I remember how he cried and how he used to shake. It hurt me, but it didn't stop me from using. And then she got pregnant again. I was tired of runnin' the streets. After all these years, I was tired. And so I got on the methadone program. I figured, I'll get on the methadone program. I thought, I can slow down a little bit, get healthy. But I was still getting high.

On the methadone program they were talking to us about AIDS. This was in '84, '85. I used to see this stuff on TV, but I thought, That's a gay disease I don't have to worry about it; I'm not gay. It wasn't my problem. I was just a dope fiend. Anyway, they made everybody who was on the program go get a physical. The doctor comes and checks me: he feels my

89

neck, he feels under my arms, and he feels my groin, and he tells me to get dressed and sit down. He said, "I got some bad news for you. You've been infected with AIDS." And I said, "I'm gonna die. I'm gonna die and there's nothin' I can do about it." As I said it I thought, If I'm gonna die, I'm gonna stay high until my time comes.

At that time, I was gettin' sick with endocarditis. I had had endocarditis about two or three times before I found out I was HIV. After I found out I was HIV, I kept shootin' dope. My daughter was born, and she was HIV positive, and I felt bad about that. Then I caught endocarditis again. I went in the hospital and the doctors were tellin' me I had to stop shootin' this dope or I was gonna die. And I said, "I'm gonna die anyway. I've got this virus. Why should I stop shootin' dope?" I left the hospital and went right back to shootin' dope. A couple of months later, I'm back in the hospital again — another case of endocarditis, with pneumonia. They told me, "You have ARC." I had the night sweats and my lymph nodes were always swollen up. In my groin area, one of them got so big; it was painful.

And I said, "Well, now it's just a matter of time, but I'm gonna stay high until I die. Me and the old lady weren't gettin' along, so I packed up and I left. I was runnin' the streets, sleepin' wherever.

And then I got busted. I was sittin' in the cell, and I thought, I got these cases, I'm gonna go to the penitentiary, and I'm gonna fuckin' die in the joint. And I thought, Well, fuck this, man; I'm not gonna die in the joint. I'm gonna take it upon my own hands when I'm gonna die. So I took off my clothes and I hung myself. At the jail, at Belmont and Western. And I fucked that up too.

I woke up a couple of weeks later in the jail's hospital. By then, my head was kinda clearing up, and I started thinking, Do I wanna die a dope fiend? And I thought, No, I don't wanna die a dope fiend. Let me at least, before I die, get my act together.

They had this drug program at the jail, and I saw the social worker and told her I wanted to go there. And I got on my knees and started praying.

So, I got involved in treatment at the drug unit in Cook County Jail. I got four years' probation, and they mandated me to Gateway. I stayed at the drug unit, learning about me, who I was. I started accepting myself a little bit. Rumors were goin' around, so I said, "Hey, yeah, I have ARC. So what?" I found that some people stayed away from me; other people said, "Hey, it's okay, we can still be friends." And I enjoyed those people. They were the kind of people that I needed to be around. I found that I could be open. I was learning to love myself bein' HIV. I had accepted me bein' HIV. If the other people didn't wanna deal with it, it was okay. I could accept it; I could handle it.

While in treatment, I learned that as long as I can get up out of bed and do the things that I need to do, I'm okay. A lot of people don't wanna go to groups; they'll get sick, conveniently sick. I never did that. I thought, I've been sick enough. I don't need to be sick, and I'm not gonna pretend I'm sick. If I'm feelin' okay, I'm gonna go and do what I have to do. I learned the best way to handle something is to meet it head on. Deal with it and go through it. I'm grateful, man. I'm grateful. From the time that I went to jail, I stopped gettin' sick. Before, I was gettin' sick all the time. By the time I got out of treatment, I was feelin' healthy. And I was startin' to enjoy life without using.

I Got High Again

One day, I was comin' home on the bus and I met some people, and I heard about some other people who had died from AIDS. These were people who I used with, but we also had a lot of fun together too. I felt bad that these people were dying. Anyway, I made a terrible mistake. I went with these people, and sure enough, next thing I know there's the drugs and there's the outfits, and I got all this hurt inside, and we're gonna get high here. And sure enough, I got high.

After I got high, I thought, What the fuck am I doin', man? So I left. And then it got bad. I didn't wanna go to meetings; I didn't wanna go nowhere. Then it got cold out. That was a good excuse for me not goin' anywhere: it's cold out and I don't wanna leave the house. I stayed in the house and watched cable TV.

In March, it started gettin' warm, and I said to myself, It's gonna get warm out; I can't stay in the house when it's warm. If I don't get my ass back to the meetings, I'm in trouble. My T-cell count had fallen like from 500 to 225 from that drug relapse. I knew I had to get back to meetings, 'cause I didn't wanna go back to using.

So, I did it. I started going back to NA meetings and going back to HIVIES, which is a Twelve Step program for people with HIV. And I got a sponsor who has AIDS. Who better can relate to me than somebody who's been through it, who is recovering? Now I go to meetings every day. I have to go to meetings. I know how easy it is for me to fall back into that addiction. Sometimes I'm on the bus and I see people who I used to run around with, and I think, Damn, we can go get high. But I can't do that. I have to remember the consequences: being in and out of the hospitals, going to jail. I don't wanna put myself through that anymore.

Today, I'm okay. I go to my meetings and I can talk about whatever I need to. I go to NA, and in NA I deal with my disease of addiction. And I go to HIVIES, and I deal with my disease of HIV. I don't go to NA and talk about my HIV. I don't think it's appropriate. We're there to deal with addiction. If somebody else wants to deal with it there, I don't have a problem with that. As far as me, I have what I need. I have my meetings that I go to, to deal with whatever issue I have. And I do it that way. If somebody else decides they wanna deal with their HIV at NA, that's okay too. I do what I have to do for me, and I try not to be judgmental.

I still feel bad sometimes, but I don't have to use behind it. Today, I can go and talk about it. I can go to a meeting and leave that problem there. That's what works for me.

I Used to Have a Problem with Gays

I can accept people, today, for who they are. I used to have a problem with gays; I couldn't deal with gay people. The first clinic they sent me to, there's all these gay people around. I didn't wanna be around all these gay people, so I left. Today, it doesn't matter who you are; I try to look at the similarities instead of the differences. We're all individuals, and I try to respect people as such. I demand respect, too, just the way I give it. But if you don't wanna respect me, fine. It's not my problem; it's your problem. I've had enough problems of my own; I don't need to take on somebody else's. Why should I worry because you won't accept me? I can't change you. I'm powerless. So I do what I have to do for me. And that's it. And it works.

Today, I feel good, and my life has gotten a lot better. I don't have to take nothing from anybody. If I need something, I can ask somebody for it, and usually somebody is here. I don't get sick as much. I no longer get the sweats; I haven't had the sweats in over two years now. I am not having a lot of the problems that I used to have.

"Dad, You Could Stop. How Come Mom Can't Stop?"

I'm goin' on four years now with HIV. My son is six and a half, and he's okay. My daughter is three and a half; she's HIV. She's okay too. Oh yeah, she's chubby; she's okay.

I take them with me on weekends and spend time with them. Now, when I go by their house, they come running up to me. Before, they didn't. They probably thought, Here's this asshole again, and then they'd go in the other room and play. Today, I can spend time with them, play with them, take them to the park, and do things with them. I enjoy that. I'm having such a good time being with them. I worry about my daughter; I worry more about her than I do myself. But I can't dwell on it, because if I start dwelling on that, I'm in trouble.

My son said, "Dad, you could stop. How come Mom can't stop?" She doesn't wanna stop. She's got it in her head that she doesn't have to worry about it; she's not gonna die, so it's okay for her to go and use. That's how she justifies it to herself. There's nothin' I can do about what she does. When she gets ready, she'll stop. I hope it's not too late. The thing is, you don't have to be gettin' sick. You could be okay and all of a sudden, boom, one day you got pneumocystis. Especially if you're using.

Hey God, I Don't Know How to Handle This. You Take It.

I've had doctors tell me that they don't see how I'm still alive. They tell me, "Five cases of endocarditis should've killed you, and the fact that you're HIV. What is keepin' you alive?" I tell them, "It's my Higher Power; He wants me here. And until He says it's time, I'm gonna be here." The medical community, I go to them when I'm sick, but they don't have all the answers; they don't know everything. They're human, and humans can make mistakes. So, I don't depend on them for everything. When something becomes more than I can deal with, I can say, "Hey, God, I don't know how to handle this. I don't know how to deal with this. I don't know what to do. You take this; You show me. You give me the strength." And He does. My God works. I feel better, and I don't have to tackle everything. I do what I can and that's all I can do. I try to do the best I can, and when it becomes too much for me, I turn it over.

Like right now at HIVIES. I'm glad these people are there, but I think, There's so many people that are HIV who need this, who need Twelve Step support around their HIV. And then I think, Well, it's a program for people who want it, not for people who need it.

If Not for This Disease, I Wouldn't Have Stopped Shooting Dope

When I was in Cook County jail, I was in the cell, and I had all this misery and guilt, and I didn't know what to do — no drugs were around. It was terrible. So I got down on my knees and I prayed. When I had prayed to God before, I would say, "Hey, look, help me get out of jail." But this time, I didn't ask Him to get me out of jail. I prayed and asked Him to help me with these feelings that I had. I was feelin' so bad. I wanted Him to help relieve me of this. And, you know, I went to sleep that night. I didn't toss and turn; I slept. And I woke up in the morning and I felt better. And I said, "Thanks Lord, thanks."

It worked; all of a sudden I didn't have all this turmoil inside. I felt better. I started attending church, and then things started happenin' for me. I got to the drug unit. A lot of prisoners were trying to get into the drug unit, but I got there with no problem. There's not that many slots for it, and I got there. I went to court and they offered me the program. This was God working in my life. Before that, everything was all messed up, all wrong. All of a sudden, things were startin' to get better. It's not because of anything I did; it's because I turned to God and I asked Him to help me. And He's helped me ever since. He's helped me a great deal.

I hear somebody talking, and they have the disease, and they say, "Well, I'm gonna die," and I say, "Hey man, you woke up this morning. A lot of people died last night — didn't have diseases, didn't have nothin' — they died. I woke up. I'm grateful, man." And that's just it. People get stabbed; people get shot; people get in car accidents — people die.

A lot of times I say I'm grateful that I have this disease, and a lot of people look at me and say, "How can you be grateful?" Well, because if not for this disease, I wouldn't have stopped shootin' dope. If not for this disease, I'd still be out there in that lunacy. If not for this disease, I wouldn't be able to appreciate the trees, the flowers, the grass, the people. My life is better today, even with this disease, than it ever was before I had this disease.

I can't do anything about the way my life has gone. I can only do somethin' about today, about right now. I try to do the best I can. I wake up in the mornin' and say, "God, help me get through today without using." Just as long as I don't use, I'm okay. And I thank Him at the end of every day.

I try to listen. When my stomach starts tellin' me it's hungry, it's time for me to go get somethin' to eat, instead of not payin' attention to it. I listen to my body. When it starts tellin' me it's tired, I know it's time for me to go take a rest. A couple of months ago, I got home and I got this little pain in my chest; somehow it wasn't a normal pain. So I shot out over to the emergency room and told them what was happening. They took X-rays, and sure enough, pneumonia was startin' to form. They gave me medication, cleared it up. We caught it in time because I listened when that little pain came.

Today, I can be aware of my body. Usually your body will tell you when somethin' is wrong; it'll tell you through pain. It knows we obey pain. I'm grateful that, today, I don't have to put garbage in my system that's not gonna allow me to feel. If I would've been gettin' high, I wouldn't have felt that little pain, or I wouldn't have paid attention to it. I would have ended up with pneumonia.

I'm Not Waiting to Die

When I first got in treatment and I heard that I'd have to be going to meetings for the rest of my life, I said, "Are you crazy? I'm not gonna go to meetings for the rest of my life, no way." But then I learned; I deal with it one day at a time; I don't have to worry about the future. I know what I have to do today, and today I have to get to a meeting. And it's not so hard at all; it's not so overwhelming. When you start dealin' with the rest of your life, you get overwhelmed. I'm not worried about the rest of my life; I'm worried about today. It's all I have; it's all I have to deal with. I'm not promised tomorrow. Nobody is, so it's okay. I'm no different from anybody else.

CHAPTER EIGHT

Vietnam

ART

Now this warrant officer said, "I heard you're a fucking queer." I said, "Yes I am." He said, "Why did you come to Vietnam if you're a fucking queer?" I said, "I came to Vietnam to save up enough money to buy myself a good mink coat." I had had it up to here. They threw me down on the floor, handcuffed me, and dragged me into Da Nang to investigate me again. Now they were going to fix me, so they sent me to this officer of naval intelligence. He liked me

Recently I was on a panel that was part of the Catholic church's AIDS ministry work. Before the panel started, I went into the rest room, and there, scribbled on the wall, was "death to all fags." I went out and said to myself, This is really disgusting. They invite me here and what they don't realize is right outside their door is the message that I'm supposed to be dead.

One of the questions from the audience was about how to stop high-risk behavior among gays. I pointed out that in the rest room, right outside the door, was the slogan "death to all fags" scribbled on the wall. This is what we see from the time we're small kids. We learn that we're supposed to be dead. As long as people are oppressed, whether it's women, Blacks, Hispanics, American Indians, gays — any group that feels of no worth to themselves, that feels that they are disposable —

they are going to do high-risk stuff. They start to believe these messages the public tells them.

The gospel they opened up with was a very nice gospel of Christ. It said that we are all part of the body of Christ: the hand is as important as the foot, and so on. But it ended up saying that we who are more honorable must sometimes take care of those who are less honorable. Once again, I'm brought to this group that is supposed to be Christian and loving and what I realize is, I'm only there to help them in their own quest for salvation — to be used as a tool.

The whole thing opened my eyes. You can talk to them and talk to them and they say, "What right do you have to bring up gay issues; we're not talking gay issues; we're talking AIDS here." It's not a gay issue; it's the issue of oppression. They didn't want to talk about it.

It's the same as the war on drugs. As long as a person feels the need to take drugs to survive, they're going to take drugs. But society doesn't want to deal with why these people are in so much pain. They want to deal with everything else. How society looks at it is it's "them" and it's "us." We're the good ones; they're the bad ones. They deserve to die; they are expendable.

If a person is HIV positive, they have heard these things. They've been told there's no hope. So they think, I have it. I'm going to die. I'm supposed to die. I'll do what society wants — I'll die. A lot of times they help themselves along. Some people feel that just to fight this thing is to go against society. They feel they deserve this. They've been told all these lies from such an early age and they believe them.

Anyway, at this conference they took me aside and said, "Arthur, you can't be so radical. Things have to change slowly. You have to work within the system of the church." Well I don't think anyone has time to work that slowly.

"I'd Rather Put a Gun to My Head than Have One of My Children Be Queer."

I grew up in a large Catholic family of eight kids: five boys, three girls. I was the oldest boy. My parents were extremely good, but their background was very homophobic. They had no contact with anyone. From early on, my dad was aware that I was gay. He didn't know how to cope with it and so I think he put a wall up between us.

Childhood was traumatic. I could feel how I responded to boys compared to how other boys responded to each other. I was naive. I did not know about sexuality, but I knew I was not the same, that I didn't fit. I quickly realized that if anyone thought I was gay, even though I didn't know what it was, I was going to get beat up. I had to find some kind of front to play off of. I got through it by being humorous. I used humor to be popular.

By the time I was in high school, I figured it out. Around 1961 or 1963, *Life* magazine did an article on homosexuality in the United States. I remember I wanted to get ahold of that magazine so bad. When it arrived, I took it and ran and hid it. My dad was looking for it too. He wanted to burn it. He didn't want anyone to read about this horrible sin you could not discuss. I read it over and over. I said to myself, This is who I am. It finally became clear to me. But it was such a negative, terrible article. I thought, This isn't who I want to be though; this isn't going to work.

About that time there was a new shopping place in our city. It was an artsy attractive place. My father was on the police force and he had heard there were two homosexual men who ran a shop in this mall who were seducing boys. He heard that I went there a lot and was sure that I was involved in this whole scandal. Really, by this time I still didn't know what gay sex was about; I had no comprehension whatsoever. My father took my sister and me down the basement and he was very quiet. All he said was, "I'd rather put a gun to my head than have one of my children be queer."

I thought, Oh my God, now he's going to put a gun to his head. It's my fault he's going to kill himself. I respected my dad very much. I thought he was a wonderful human being. But he could not believe I wasn't involved in this. He said, "I know you're involved." I didn't know what he was talking about. If a person had told me about oral or anal sex, I wouldn't have believed it. Sexually, I was attracted to the same sex, but I didn't know what anybody did. I didn't know how it worked. Being raised in a Catholic school, I didn't masturbate or anything. I didn't even touch myself.

They had a class on homosexuality once. What I remember is they said something like, homosexuals are perverts who burn in hell and are stepped on by society. I was sitting in the classroom and probably no one was looking at me, but it felt like I had a sign tattooed on my forehead. I was getting redder and redder. I just knew that I was the *one* out of the whole school. I guess I was about fifteen at the time.

There were people in school who were obviously gay and they were getting beat up. I wasn't part of it, but I would go along with it just to protect myself. That was really a crime, but as a child you don't know what you're supposed to do. I never cared for childhood.

At Sea, Men Don't Wear Uniforms; They Wear Shorts and Swim Trunks

I graduated from high school when I was seventeen and decided to go into the navy. Anything to get me out of that environment I was in. I went in as a kiddy cruiser, which meant I would be out by my twenty-first birthday. Once again, I saw that the more effeminate you were the more you were picked on and beat on and stepped on. But I could always play games; I could always hide who I was. My self-esteem kept going down because I thought that if I ever let anyone know who I was or how I felt, they would lock me up or shoot me. I had heard these stories that in most states gay people were locked up. I remember as a child thinking, I can't move to Maine, and so on. These thoughts would go through my mind all night long: I can't live here. I can't do this.

When I got through boot camp they said my scores were so high in all the tests that I should be in submarines. Well, I thought if I went to that submarine school I would have three more months to fool around. I had no intention of going to sea; I just went into the service to get out of that house. I thought, Now I'm in here and I don't know what to do. I went to sub school in New England for a month and a half and they told me they had this billet open right away on the USS Swordfish out of Hawaii. It was the oldest sub in commission. Because it was gone from home for so long at one time, the crew was completely single, the only sub in the navy like that, so I said, "Great!"

Basically the crew was either gay, bi, or asexual. And I would say 95 percent were alcoholics; the other 5 percent were on their way. Most of these guys had been on this boat for ten years. They were confused about their own sexuality and masking it with alcohol. And of course I said, "Well, this must be the way to live." So I immediately tried to drink right along with them. At first I couldn't drink like that, but my tolerance built up.

At sea, men don't wear uniforms; they wear shorts and swim trunks — it's just too hot. One day I saw these two legs come out of the conning tower. His name was Mickey Darvis and I knew this was love. I was crazy about him and he was very confused. I was eighteen and he was twenty-three. He was trying to deny everything and I didn't know anything. In Honolulu he introduced me to some officers he knew who were quite well-off. He kind of lived with them. Mickey and I had great fights. Once, he tried to throw me off a twenty-third floor balcony in the Queen Anne apartments. That was when I thought, This really isn't what I had in mind for my life. So I decided to leave the sub.

At the time, every ship in the service had to send a certain number of people to Vietnam. They decided that as long as I'm going to get off, they'll send me to Vietnam. In the meantime, this air force officer I met through Mickey was investigated because he picked up a guy in the armed service's YMCA men's room and was turned in. I'd been to the officer's club with him and my name was turned in too. So they put me in the locked psych ward of the navy hospital in Hawaii and sent me to a psychiatrist. The office of investigation kept telling me all these things about dirty homosexuals, that I was one of them, and that I had to fess up — like I had murdered somebody. I was very confused by this whole thing, but I didn't admit anything.

Then they said they'd send me to counter intelligence school. The armed forces don't always make sense. Anyway, I'm off to Corinado Island in San Diego for four weeks.

There was a gay bar there called Sherman's that I went into by mistake. It was across from the Plaza and I thought, Well, doesn't this look like a friendly place? I was in there three times and never knew it was gay. I thought, These people are really nice here. It was very mixed, very hustler. Owned by a person named Al. I started to meet people there. I think you had to be twenty, twenty-one to drink then, so I wasn't even drinking. Finally, I figured it out.

At Sherman's, I met this person named Roger Ford. He ran church bingos, a nurse's school; he was about as corrupt as could be. He didn't have any scruples or values and usually had a house full of young men. But from my point of view, all these people were light and fun. They'd camp a lot. On a sub no one camped; they were "men." Well, these were "queens." I thought, This is more fun. Then Roger was investigated and because I was living at his house I was in another big investigation.

At the same time, as part of counter intelligence school, I went on a trip to the middle of Washington state where you are left alone in the wilderness for a week with a knife, and you're supposed to eat clams or something. The last three days you're captured by the enemies — marines dressed up like Nazis — and they put you through this hell. It's really very sick. Well I had hepatitis or mono then and I got very ill. But they put me in this cell, this locked box, anyway. It's a disturbing macho game they play with human beings. So I'm sick as a dog and they think I'm lying, just to get out of it. I finally ended up in Balboa Hospital for three months. Meanwhile, they investigated Roger and a guy named Shirtsleeves who turned me in.

This time they said they had me and were going to throw me out of the navy. They sent me to a psychiatrist who happened to be a friend of Roger's, and who I had just met two weeks before at a party. I walked into his office and he said that I was fine, no problem, and I was sent to Vietnam.

How I Got Through Vietnam

I no sooner got to Vietnam and they investigated me again. I said, "I won't admit to anything." By this time, I was very sexually active and drinking. Their thinking was, If we can't get rid of him, we can give him the worst jobs in Vietnam and that will kill him off. So they sent me down to Saigon and put me on these boats, these riverboats that went up the Mekong Delta. People only lasted three or four weeks; the Vietcong would just blow them out of the water. Well, I didn't want to die so I went to the PX and got all the makeup I could get. I smeared my face with it — lipstick and eye shadow and everything — and went on this boat. The whole boat signed a chit saying they would not go up river with me; they would not serve with this dirty faggot. I thought, You can call me names, but I've just got to get off of here. So they threw me off, sent me back to Da Nang to off-load ships. Two weeks later, that whole boat — they're all dead. They blew them out of the water.

In Da Nang I started to meet all these people on the base. There was this corpsman, Joe. Joe was from Detroit and he was in love with the guy in the bunk across from him. Joe was short, fat, very quiet, and very closeted. One night he got drunk at the EM club and went crazy and jumped on this guy in bed. He couldn't stand it anymore. He immediately got investigated and thrown out — but he turned me in first.

Now this warrant officer said, "I heard you're a fucking queer." I said, "Yes I am." He said, "Why did you come to Vietnam if you're a fucking queer?" I said, "I came to Vietnam to save up enough money to buy myself a good mink coat." I had had it up to here. They threw me down on the floor, handcuffed me, and dragged me into Da Nang to investigate me again. Now they were going to fix me, so they sent me to this officer of naval intelligence. He liked me.

It was just a lucky break that he liked me — or maybe not. Maybe I should have gotten thrown out; I'd have been much happier. He said, "Why don't you go to Bangkok on R-and-R? I'll see to it." He went along and we partied the whole time. So I got through Vietnam like that. If I had been 300 pounds with pimples on my face, they would have killed me because I was gay. But because I could be used by someone else, someone in power at the time, I was saved. What if I wouldn't have played a certain game? Basically, you almost had to be a prostitute just to get through. I was just being used. If he wouldn't have been attracted to me, who knows?

I had a lot of other bad experiences after that. I was there during the Tet offensive and I think they thought, We'll fix him. After the offensive, the bodies of all the dead were piled up. There were GIs mixed in with Vietnamese. By this time, the worms were coming out of them. They pulled me specifically — I wasn't working in that area at the time — to separate all the bodies. By the time I left Vietnam, I had no respect for myself. I couldn't talk; I stammered real bad; I was on the verge of being a chronic alcoholic; I had no self-esteem at all. I really didn't care if I lived or died.

"Daiquiri, Daiquiri. I Can Say 'Daiquiri.'"

When I got out of the navy, I moved to San Francisco to go to the San Francisco School of Fine Arts. While going to school, I'd get these jobs in restaurants as a waiter, but I couldn't talk. I'd walk to work saying, "Daiquiri, daiquiri. I can say 'daiquiri.'" Then someone would order one and I couldn't say it. I'd run crying out the door and go to the next place. After awhile, I took the money I saved from Vietnam and opened a three-two joint called the Plush Poodle Bar. Me, Neal from Vietnam, and Big Al opened it together. That didn't last very long. The police closed it down because we didn't have a dance license.

I came back to the Midwest and started school at the university. I was twenty years old. Right away, I got fired from this fancy restaurant. I was a busboy there and a waiter came by and kissed me on the cheek. One of the cooks was so upset he went and complained. I thought I deserved to be fired. I was allowing myself to be hurt and abused and I was accepting it. That's the terrible thing: the more I would accept it, the more my belief in myself would go down; the more I would drink, the less I could talk. I was in this rut that was getting worse and worse.

Then I ran into this guy who used to call himself Susie. He had just applied at this exclusive club, but he didn't think they'd hire him because he was a little too swishy. He told me to apply. They hired me right away, even though I couldn't talk. That's where I met Helen. She wanted everything her way and she didn't want anyone to talk to her customers anyway; she was perfect for me. I found my spot. She always said, "I never fell in love with you. The first thing I felt for you was pity."

Helen's dad drank a lot; she was used to taking care of someone who had an alcohol problem. She never drank herself. We decided this was great. We made good money and Helen kept building me up: you can do this; you can do that. Slowly I built up my self-esteem. We became very dependent on each other.

After awhile, we moved to Arizona and I began to drink very heavily. I think from this time on, I drank every day. There was not one day I didn't drink; there was not one day I didn't get drunk. Every day, day in and day out. I'd work late and stop in a bar for a drink and come in at four or five in the morning. A few years of that and Helen said, "Enough of this. This isn't healthy for either of us."

So we moved to Chicago where we lived for seven years. That's when I became a real alcoholic. It hit me one day, the only thing I was interested in was that next drink. I had no other interests — that was it. It wasn't that I enjoyed alcohol more; I didn't enjoy anything. And with the alcohol abuse was this terrible sexual abuse. When I got drunk I went to the baths. I didn't care what I did or with who. It didn't matter. I just wanted to check out of life.

While in Chicago, Helen's mom called about this new gay plague she heard about in New York. I got a little scared and cut down a lot on my drinking and sexual activity. Even so, after a couple years I started getting more and more tired and run down. A person I was going out with at the time was real sick. He got diagnosed with AIDS and he died. That's when I went to the hospital for an AIDS test. The doctor didn't know what I was talking about. He gave me a few tests and told me not to worry, that I was fine. I jumped for joy! No more drinking for me. I joined AA and was doing very, very well.

I Walked to the Washington Avenue Bridge. I Was Going to Jump Off.

But I kept getting weaker. I was very smug about it, though. I relied on the doctor who said I didn't have AIDS; yet, I kept getting more tired. In the meantime, Helen and I moved back to her hometown. Finally, I went for an HIV test and was positive. I started drinking again, then stopped, but I didn't go to AA. I thought I could do it myself. Nine months later I got diagnosed with KS — right after Christmas of '86. Then

I really started to drink. I was drinking like I'd never drank before. I didn't know I could drink like that, and I had always been a heavy drinker.

It was suicide. I'm supposed to be dead, I told myself. I had decided that if I ever came down with AIDS, I'd just kill myself. That's what I thought I was supposed to do. So when I got diagnosed, I started to walk toward the Washington Avenue Bridge. I was going to jump off. I wasn't upset; it was the rational thing to do. It was what I was supposed to do to save all these other people from lots of problems. I didn't mean anything. I was completely expendable — even to myself. I thought, I'm not important to anyone; if I jump off this bridge, it'll be better for everyone.

Well, then I had another thought. Maybe I'd better go see a lawyer; maybe I can get disability. After all, my employer was very happy with my work. I was a workaholic. I had no self-worth. I thought you had to do the job of two human beings. If they ever found out you were gay, you'd better be worth two human beings. If they were getting two for the price of one, they may not fire you.

I talked to a lawyer and then bought a bottle of vodka and drank it. I just stood by the sink and drank. I couldn't even get to the chair and sit down. Helen said, "If you're going to kill yourself, kill yourself, but don't let me be part of it."

I drank for two weeks, then God or a Higher Power came to me and said, "Art, if you're so afraid to die, why are you killing yourself?" It happened in the middle of the night and I woke Helen, and in my drunken, slurry speech said, "I'm never going to drink again." And she said, "Oh yeah? That's a good one. Drunk talk. I love your drunk talk." The next day I made some calls. This time I knew I really needed help. I knew I couldn't do this by myself.

I went to a very good group at the gay AA center. It was real down to earth, real plain, real healing. After being drunk for so many years and being so depressed by AIDS, all of a sudden life was kind of alive and sweet. Then I'd say to myself,

Well this is easy; I don't need this meeting. And I'd slip. More and more it was coming to me — I am an alcoholic. I really, really, really am an alcoholic. It's such an amazing thing. I always thought that was the one thing I understood about myself, but I didn't understand what the disease was. I thought I was just an old lush.

If People Don't Like Me, That's Not My Problem

Sobriety has helped me become very happy with myself. I can be myself. If people don't like me, that's not my problem. I thought people had to like me, so I'd become the person I thought they wanted me to be. That was true for all my relationships — at work, my parents, my friends, people I was having sex with. I thought, Well, I'll find out what you want, I'll be like that, and you'll like me, because I really don't like myself.

I see this pattern in so many human beings. But when you're in the middle of it, you don't know you're there, you don't know what's wrong, and you don't know how to fix it. You just think it's supposed to be this way. People shouldn't have to go through that. There's no reason. If I had been told from a very young age, It's okay to be gay; it's wonderful; it's beautiful; it's a part of who you are," I know I would have made some mistakes in my life, but I also know I would not have gone through this massive amount of pain. There was no reason. It was a total waste of time and a total waste of a life.

That's my regret. What I'm thankful for is that I've been able to have this time to dig my way out of it. Some people don't have that chance: they are in it; they stay in it; and they die in it. They don't ever feel beautiful in themselves.

It took me seven months in AA to figure out that I'm here to take care of me. I'm an alcoholic; that's why I'm here. I'm not here for people to like me. I don't have to please anyone. I've got a problem: I've got to stay alive. I use the Twelve Steps because I've got to heal myself. I think you can use the Twelve Steps with any illness.

If a person worries about what's going to happen four years from now or even next week, well, a person could go crazy. But if you say it's one day at a time, I'm here now, and there are things I can do for myself today, life is much easier. It also helps to get involved in helping other people. When I started helping others, I realized that I'm not alone, that there are people worse off than I am. I stopped feeling sorry for myself. I think it's easy to go through life feeling sorry for yourself and liking it. It gives you a safe feeling. I'll just sit here and pull the shades down and feel sorry for myself.

It's important to avoid self-pity and even more important to get in touch with exactly how you do feel, and then, to really stand up for how you feel. I think a person who is gay needs to fight for the right to be gay, especially if he has AIDS. Unless a person comes out and can be proud that he's gay, he's going to come back to this death thing. That image that we are supposed to be dead is ingrained in us. When I see how many people who are diagnosed still smoke, I believe that somewhere within them they do not want to live. They're still listening to those old tapes: I'm supposed to be dead; I do not deserve to be alive; it's all right if I die, I'm of no worth to anyone; I'm of no worth to myself.

It Is an Illness of the Oppressed

That's what I was trying to explain to this Christian crowd. We're bombarded with it wherever we go. We are the only group left that from the pulpit of churches it's okay to say we should be dead.

AIDS has become a way to fulfill society's expectations. If people are really interested in stopping AIDS, then they have to realize it is an illness of the oppressed. It has nothing to do with a virus.

I'm still very upset about some of the church groups who want to get involved. As nice as they are, I still believe in my heart that many of them have this double standard. They look at people with AIDS, or gays, or IV drug users as lepers. Christ went among the lepers, but they *were* lepers. "The more honorable take care of the less honorable." That gospel message really was a stab in my heart.

I believe AIDS is an outward manifestation of what we were taught from the time we were children — that we are not good enough. Well, that's a lie.

I have been given the chance to find out who I am and to live my life. When I do, I know I'm feeling better. I'm healing myself spiritually, and I believe that helps heal me physically too. I believe it extends my life; I don't know by what extent, but if I should die in a state where I'm happy with myself, that would be wonderful. To live, even till I'm ninety years old, and hate myself — that's not living.

People say you can't cure AIDS. That may or may not be true, but the point is, people can heal themselves, and some people can heal more than others. It's all based on learning to love and accept yourself and going out there and learning to fight for what you believe. I know I started to heal myself when I could walk up to anyone who asked me and say, "I have AIDS." I have a much clearer attitude now about what I want and who I am, and that I deserve to live. I think that's the big statement: *I deserve to live.* I have a right to live. It's my right as much as anyone else's.

CHAPTER NINE

Gay Junkies

SAM

I was very lonely, very confused, and very frightened about the future because my mother had gotten so much worse; I feared for her life. She was killing herself with alcohol. She wasn't able to walk. She was on the couch urinating on herself. I was cleaning the house, cooking, shopping, working full time, promising myself I would finish my education at night. And my drinking was really getting going. I think I almost had a choice at that point; I never stopped long enough to realize it.

I was born in 1945. I'm a quadruple Aries with an Aquarius moon. My father abandoned me before I was born and I was raised by my stepfather who I didn't find out was my stepfather until I was fourteen. There wasn't a lot of honesty in my family. My stepfather was a bartender in the South Bronx. He never graduated from the eighth grade. My mother had attended a private college; she was an English major. She was also a frustrated writer and pianist.

My stepfather was a very heavy smoker and died of lung cancer when he was fifty-eight. That was in 1955; I was nine. At his funeral, I was told that I was the man of the family now and that I should look after my mother. Well, my mother started drinking. She always drank socially, but when my stepfather died, she started drinking alcoholically, getting into cough medicines, painkillers, other addictions, and eventually men.

Anyway, my mother became very dependent on me. I slept with my mother until I was twelve years old. I didn't know there was anything wrong with it; I didn't read Cosmo, you know. To me that was how my mother told me she loved me. I didn't know it was unhealthy. How would I know? When she started dating, I was really jealous. I told my mother I did not want her to get married again.

I kept hoping my mother would stop drinking. She'd cry, "Please go to the liquor store, please. He'll give you another bottle on credit." I'd swear that I wouldn't do it. But how do you say no to your mother? She said it was like medicine. I understood that, so off I'd go to the liquor store. It was painful, very painful. My mother was always sick, hung over, or drunk. I would have my friends over and she'd pass out, throw up, fall down, and have who knows who with her. She was not Jane Wyatt, and Robert Young flew the coop years before. It was not festive. Just getting our next meal was really an effort. It really was.

As her drinking increased, my mother deteriorated physically. When I was fourteen I started to drink. The first time I drank I had three quarts of beer. I finished all three quarts. I did not get sick; I did not have a headache; I did not throw up. What I did do was realize that alcohol worked. Even though I had no control over what I did or what I said, and even though I went into a blackout, it worked.

I started drinking on weekends. It was heavy and it was continuous. I drank as much as I could afford with my part-time salary. My grades dropped; my spirit started to break. I was supporting my mother who eventually went on welfare. I quit high school to help her out. She started getting cirrhosis of the liver, and I realized she was sicker than I thought. But with my own alcoholism blooming, I was really in denial. I knew a lot of alcoholics, but I didn't know a lot about alcoholism. I had never heard the two letters AA in my life.

My mother and stepfather were fairly liberal with their attitudes as far as other nationalities and other races go. When the neighborhood changed, we had black friends. My parents were the first ones in the neighborhood to go against the common view and invite whoever they wanted into the house. My mother carried that even further. When my stepfather died, she started bringing men home and they stayed overnight. I was sleeping in the same room. I knew it was very damaging to me psychologically.

Out of a need to be accepted or loved, or maybe out of hatred for her, I tried to seduce one of my mother's boyfriends one night. I was really very lonely, very confused, and very frightened about the future because my mother had gotten so much worse; I feared for her life. She was killing herself with alcohol. She wasn't able to walk. She was on the couch urinating on herself. I was cleaning the house, cooking, shopping, working full time, promising myself I would finish my education at night. And my drinking was really getting going. I think I almost had a choice at that point; I never stopped long enough to realize it.

Our First Job

Things were getting much worse and I knew, I damn well knew, I wasn't going back to school because I was just too physically tired. I was working the mail room at a major book publisher. That was my first job and I loved it. I was there four years. My drinking got me out of there. I sort of left and they sort of asked me to leave. It took four years, but I hooked up with all the alcoholics in the company — and there were a lot of them. There were a lot of parties too. I met the greatest people. James Baldwin, he was my favorite. He had just published *Giovanni's Room*. Just an outrageous, free person.

Anyway, my drinking and drugging picked up; I always experimented with everything. I was the first on my block with the latest drug, and I encouraged other people to take drugs. This was like 1961 through 1966. I was sixteen, Janis Joplin was my idol, and I couldn't wait to take something stronger. That's how I ended up doing heroin, speed, crystal meth — all of that stuff.

I got this publishing job when I was sixteen, got my mother a job there three years later. She was working in the file room and was drinking all of her check. I was drinking all of my check. I had to leave because of my drinking and she left because she was physically too incapacitated to work. We both went on welfare. We wound up drinking together, reminiscing, getting melancholy — typical alcoholism.

On my twenty-first birthday, she took me to a gay bar to celebrate. She was pushing sixty and she told me that she would be dead by the time she was sixty. She did not like the fact that she was getting older. She was a very attractive woman: tall, stately, well-spoken. She didn't deal with the prospect of becoming an old lady very well. She started regressing mentally; she had brain damage. Worst of all, the cirrhosis was getting worse.

One night, I rushed her to the emergency room at a hospital in the Bronx and they told me she had three to six months to live. There was more than 50 percent liver damage. That sort of put me in shock. The only person that I loved in my life was leaving and I couldn't do anything about it. I had not been given many coping tools by my stepfather, who was there the first half of my life, or by my mother, who was not there for me mentally, emotionally, or spiritually for the rest of my life. I learned early on how not to cope. I was a ready-made alcoholic; the disease of alcoholism was so convenient for me. I learned how not to answer the door when bill collectors came around. That was the story of how we did everything.

My mother went into the hospital and started hemorrhaging and losing her mind. I had watched her dying in the apartment: yellow eyes, urinating on herself. Now I watched her liver explode in the hospital. It took three months for her to die; it aged me ten years. On August 5, 1966 she passed away. She was exactly sixty. She was a very willful woman; I believe my mother willed herself to death.

I Had Two Drinks and Told Him My Life Story

After my mother died, I started hanging out in a Manhattan bar where I met my first lover. He was five years older than me and black. I had two drinks and told him my life story — a typical drunk. He felt really sorry for me. I knew that he would; I manipulated him. I went home with him that night, and stayed for six years. I never paid rent. He became my Higher Power. I went from being totally responsible for my mother to being taken care of completely by him. Soon, I felt guilty about that, so I decided to get a job as a waiter.

I worked as a waiter for six or seven years and spent all my money on drinking and drugging. The progression got worse: I started snorting, then skin popping, and then, three years into the relationship, mainlining heroin. Then I got into methadone and detoxified myself. I was also doing other drugs and drinking about a pint to a fifth of booze a day. I weighed 125 pounds. I had sores on my body from cheap wine. I was, at one point, panhandling in the village for booze. I had no self-esteem. I felt that I wasn't worthy of anyone's love, that I was born on the wrong side, on the other side of the invisible line, and that I was destined to die from alcoholism.

I thought the '60s would never end until people started dying, friends and Janis included. We were watching the David Susskind Show and we heard a woman qualify, a speaker from AA. She said that she stopped drinking through the help of AA, and I said, "What the hell is that, AA?" Mark, who was still my lover at the time, called the woman. Being very afraid of admitting and accepting his homosexuality, he called and said his wife had a problem with alcohol, what should he do? She said to have his wife call AA. That's how it works; the person that needs help has to call. So he told me that I should call AA. I got very angry and said, "Why should I do that?" I'm sitting there, smoking, drinking. He said, "Well, you're an alcoholic, fool. You're an alcoholic." Mark was a lovely person. He probably should have gone to Al-Anon, but he never did.

He thought I needed help, but that he was okay.

Finally, Mark packed his things, got another apartment in the next building, and said he was leaving and taking his belongings with him, but I wasn't one of his belongings. So I'm having a temper tantrum on the floor: don't leave me, I love you, and all this. And he said, "If you really love me, you'll stop drinking." I said, "I will, next week. I will really stop drinking. I promise you." He said, "You've said that for years now and you're not going to stop. I love you, and you're gonna die, and I'm not going to watch you kill yourself. So good-bye now, it's been a great six years."

She Told Me I Never Had to Drink Again

So he left. I wound up sleeping here and there. I finally called AA. Mark had moved to the Upper East Side, where he still lives. He said he couldn't see me sleeping all over New York and I could move back with him. He said he would rent me a room in his place or give me space on the couch, but the relationship was definitely over, sex was over, and drinking was not allowed. He knew I needed help, and he was still willing to help me at this point, God bless him.

He had a bottle of vodka in the house. He put the bottle of vodka on the table and he said, "I want you to make a decision." He knew I was dying for a drink. He said, "Here's the bottle, and here I am. You're gonna have to choose which is more important to you." I said to him, "How can you ask me to make that choice? I feel differently about you than I do about the alcohol. I'll take the alcohol first and you know that. This isn't a fair test and I don't think I should be subjected to a test. I'm dying for a drink and I will probably reach for the drink first." And he said, "Then you'll have to leave." So I lied and said no, that I wouldn't drink. I took the bottle and put it in the closet and waited until I thought he was asleep. I pretended to have a coughing fit while I opened the cabinet so he wouldn't hear it, grabbed the bottle and unscrewed the top while I ran some water, and poured myself a huge drink of straight vodka. He was creeping around the corner as I was about to lift the glass to my lips. He said he knew I couldn't do it and told me I had to leave the next day. I didn't drink the drink.

The next day I borrowed ten dollars from him to get a job. Well, that lasted about ten minutes. I went down to the bar and drank it. Then I decided I'd sell my blood, which I'd done once before in Times Square. Well, it took me from one o'clock in the afternoon to four something to walk from East Seventy-Seventh to Times Square. I was pretty drunk, hung over, and weak — I hadn't eaten for a few days. The blood bank was closed. That's when I called AA. That was my first spiritual awakening. I did not see a light; I did not feel a bolt of electricity go through my body. I was hurting, I was going into DTs, I was very sick, and I had no one to call. I mean, I really had no one to call. I was afraid to call anyone because I didn't know what I had done to them or they had done to me.

So I called AA and I walked from Times Square to East Twenty-Second Street. I don't know how I got there; I don't know where I got the energy. It was way past six o'clock when I finally arrived. A woman named Ann was sitting there and she turned around, looked at me, and said, "Sam." She had waited there for me. I couldn't believe it. I thought, Oh, what a stupid woman. She said, "Come in, sit down. My name is Ann and I'm an alcoholic." And I thought, Sure, sure you are. She was well dressed, had nice rings, you know, the whole thing. She was the first one who told me that I had a disease and that if I didn't stop drinking it would kill me. And she said she had a message for me particularly, sort of special. She didn't even know me and she's giving me these messages and I thought, Far out.

She told me that I never had to drink, ever again. That was the most unusual thing I had ever heard in twenty-seven years of my life. She hugged me and she wasn't afraid of me. I had holes in my shoes. I had twenty-seven-year-old teenage acne.

119

I was ugly; my hair was falling out. I had had hepatitis, probably from a dirty needle, and drank through it. I was sleeping on the subway. I had no one left in my life. I didn't know why I was still alive; I was afraid to live. I wanted desperately to die and was afraid to kill myself. I knew God was living somewhere, I thought maybe in New Jersey. I didn't know. I had no one to ask. I had no guides as a child and none as an adult. Of the role models I had, half were dead and the other half were still actively drinking and drugging. I didn't know I had choices; I didn't know that I deserved to be sober.

She introduced me to someone who was gay and he took me to my first meeting. It was straight, intermixed with a few gay people. I was told to keep coming back. I didn't want to even be there, never mind come back. I wanted to know how much the coffee was. They said, "It's free." I said, "Nothing is free." I didn't trust; I didn't love; I didn't like — all I did was hate and mistrust. Yet I was shown the same love that every alcoholic is shown when they walk through the doors of AA. Walking through the doors of AA was my only hope because I certainly did not have $90 for a psychiatrist. Even if I did, I would have drank it. But this was free. My first couple of meetings I used to go in the bathroom during the break and see who was smoking grass. I wanted to know why everyone was so happy. I thought everyone was high and controlling it. I thought that's what sobriety meant.

Well, three months later I decided that I was well. I never got a sponsor, I didn't work the program, and I left AA. And it got worse. That's when I started sleeping with people for a place to stay — if they had liquor in the house. If they didn't, I wouldn't go home with them. I did that as often as I could, but after awhile I just couldn't. So I thought, I'll kill myself.

I walked over to Seventy-Seventh Street and the East River and sat on the edge of the rocks. At that point in my life, I could not swim. I was going to jump in. I had a transistor radio and a quart of vodka. After about two hours of contemplating suicide, I was so nauseous that I couldn't slug the vodka down anymore — it just wouldn't go. I think my pancreas was on the fritz. I called this fella who had been a priest. He came over to where I was. He had a dollar left to his name and with that dollar he bought me an egg salad sandwich for ninety-five cents and hand-fed me. He physically picked me up and put the food in my mouth. I didn't remember the last time I had eaten. Then he got me into a hospital.

I was in intensive care for about six days. Two days after I left the hospital I picked up a drink. I wound up back in another hospital a month later. I don't know how I lived. I went into something like a two-year blackout, thank God, because I don't want to remember it.

Finally, one of the hospitals sent me to Smithers Rehab in Manhattan. I was afraid I would be the only gay person, but as it turned out, seven out of eight in my group were gay. We were strongly encouraged to work the Steps, the first five Steps.

They Found Me a Sponsor, a Three Hundred Pound Lesbian

Then they found me a sponsor, a three hundred pound lesbian who I could not sleep with, fool around with, or lie to. Her name was Elaine. She gave me her phone number, two packs of cigarettes, and told me that if I drank she'd break my legs. She was Italian, and she said the boys from Jersey would do me in. Well, she put the fear of God in me, and I loved her for it because I felt protected. She meant it lovingly and I knew it. She taught me about trust, sharing, giving, caring. She taught me about tough love, which I desperately needed. I did not need Upper East Side sobriety at that point in my life. She bought me a pair of shoes. She helped me get my first temporary job; I was living on $60 a week. She would do anything to help me if I would just not drink. She would buy me dinner once a week as long as after my first paycheck, I would buy someone else dinner once a week. She took me to my first dentist because I had no front teeth. She said that

I would not die if I did not drink and I believed her. I did not believe anyone else. She was a younger version of Mother Teresa — without the garb. She's now an alcoholism counselor and has written a book.

She gave me a lot. She gave me a lot because she loved me and was so up-front that I knew she couldn't lie. After three years of sobriety, she told me that it was time for me to start sponsoring other people. That was fourteen years ago.

After my third year of sobriety, I became involved with someone who was not in the program, which was great because I was starting to believe that life began at a beginner's meeting and ended at the end of a closed discussion. He taught me a lot about Santeria, which is a Spanish religion equivalent to our New Age. I started studying under a spiritualista, a Spanish female spiritualist who would put me under hypnosis. Then I started seeing my aunt who is a channel. I went back to church for about two weeks and that didn't work, so I left. I also became a Buddhist for a week. I was searching spiritually.

Then I decided I should get serious about my life, so I went back to school and got my high school diploma. I got a job in a hospital in the admitting office. That's when I really found out about alcoholism because I saw patients being wheeled into the emergency room around midnight — drunk.

Four Hours to Have My Blood Drawn

A few years later, I got a job at another hospital and I had to take a physical. They found out I had amoebas and wanted to hospitalize me; I had not stopped being promiscuous. They were also asking for gay male volunteers for a study about what they called gay-related immune deficiency. To qualify, you had to test negative for HIV antibodies. I tested positive and I had a reverse T-cell ratio. I asked, "Well, what do I have to do?" The doctor said, "There's nothing we can do, so come back next year." Okay. So I went back the next year. I was working right across the hall; it was certainly easy enough.

At that point, I was not feeling too well. My energy was low. I was working three jobs, so I was really wearing myself thin. I had to give two of them up. I kept my full-time job so I could keep my insurance. I went back to the doctor. He said I was the same and I should come back the following year. That was '86. I did come back and he said my blood tests had gotten a little worse, that they were starting an AZT double blind study, but I wasn't sick enough. So I said, "Am I sick or not? What does sick mean? Is there a new definition? Sick-sick?" He said "You're not well-well, but you're not sick-sick." I said, "Oh, so what does that mean?" He said, "I don't really know. Come back and see me in six months."

That's when I went on the AZT study. I had shared with my present sponsor all along that I was HIV positive. Later, he decided to get tested and he turned out positive. I told him that I was getting really frightened, that I felt physical changes, and I didn't know what was going on. My energy was lessening. Nine months later, I'd had herpes twice, thrush once, and upper respiratory infections twice — all in a couple of months. I was feeling like shit. I had to take off from work a week at a time. Someone told me about a doctor at New York University and I called him and made an appointment. He told me to get off the study, that they were killing me. My T-cells went down to 160, the ratio was disappearing, and my white and red blood cells were going down below normal. I got frightened. I wanted somebody who knew what the hell they were talking about.

I got real angry at the study. I was prevented from taking any prophylactic medication. I wanted to take Bactrim™ and couldn't. They said they would test for it and if I had taken it, they'd throw me off the study. I had a fight with the head of the study. I said, "Not only am I a patient here, I'm an employee. I know better. What about my life? What if the prophylactic works?" He said, "Well it hasn't been proven." I said, "Yeah, but it hasn't been proven that it doesn't. I know people who have taken it and they haven't come down with pneumocystis. I don't want to get pneumocystis. I didn't wake up this morning and say, 'Gee, I really wish I'd get pneumocystis as I haven't had it yet'. And with my tests, I'm a prime candidate." Mentally, I was stressing myself out and lowering my own T-cells just by fear of the unknown. My faith in the medical community was destroyed. This trial turned out to be tortuous. Four hours to have my blood drawn! You know all the horror stories; I was in one of the worst. So I quit the study.

Self-Pity Stinks and Other People's Pity Is Even Worse

I've done everything I can physically as far as HIV infection is concerned. I could exhaust myself by reading eight million more articles, but I don't think there's been anything else that's been discovered lately that's worth reading. If there is, that information will channel itself to me through other people. I keep in constant contact with members in my support group who are also well read, and I work for a physician who is also interested. I surround myself with people I love and I'm open to their love. Self-pity stinks and other people's pity is even worse. I have people in my life that empathize; I have people in my life who have gone through other diseases, including cancer and lupus and other so-called terminal illnesses.

I have more mental energy now than I ever had before because I focus, I meditate, I visualize, and I listen to tapes of readings from this person who is a channel. The tapes remind me that I am a whole person, that I am here because I'm meant to be and because I choose to be. I chose to be born, and I'll know when it's time to cross over and become just energy — become part of the light. I do not fear death. I do not think there is such a thing as death, so I have nothing to fear.

Sammy Davis, Malcolm X, and My Aunt

Three of my favorite words are from Sammy Davis' book. They are, *Yes I Can*. Malcolm X said that to reach out effectively and help others, you must first experience revolution within yourself. That has helped me too. And my aunt, who is a channel, said that there need be no difference between my will and God's will because God is within. Spirituality is not outside of me; it's inside of me coming out. I think that I've been reborn many times. I realize now that everything is all right with everybody; we just don't see it that way at times.

I have felt peace for the last two years; I am accepting who I am. I also realize that I don't have to know everything anymore. I just have to know what's important for me. I think the greatest gift is understanding that the words *I* and *we* are the same. We are a circle; the world is not cubicle or square; it's round and we're all connected. If I had said this ten years ago, I would have committed myself to a mental institution; I really would have. But now it makes me feel good because it feels right. I try to remain open, I try to look forward, because forward is all we have. I'm not on my own; I've never been on my own; I've always been surrounded by love — only now I know it.

RICK

I went off to study art in Spain. The only reason I was able to make such a trip was because I was sober. When in Spain — talk about how insidious alcohol is — I was in a discotheque and the person I was dancing with asked me if I would like a drink, and I said, "I'd like an orange juice." He said, "That's really boring." I said, "You're right, I'll have a screwdriver." It was as if I was never sober. . . . Eventually, I went back to shooting heroin.

I was born in New York City and from a young age I was fascinated with drugs and alcohol. At the age of thirteen I was smoking marijuana daily. At the age of fourteen I was shooting heroin daily.

I grew up in a dysfunctional family. There were no alcoholics in the family; however, there were a lot of secrets. My mother has the attitude that if something is upsetting to her, she prefers not to talk about it and pretends it doesn't exist. My father left when I was two years old. My parents were divorced and I didn't see my dad again till I was seventeen. Instead of dealing with the divorce, my mother decided it was easier to remarry and act like her second husband was my real father. However, I grew up with three sets of grandparents and knew something was really wrong. When I brought it up, everything was minimized. Finally, I was told that yes, your father left, but now this man is your father and be happy about it. I was not very happy about it. I wanted to see my father; I didn't want this imposter. I wanted my father.

My mother is a very narcissistic person who treated me as a love object rather than as a child. I was encouraged to do things that my mother found to be very "ego sympatic" to her. For example, it was very important for me to succeed in school, not so I would learn about anything, but so my mother could brag to all her friends. It was important to do exactly what my mother wanted to do, and if I didn't, I was a bad person. So I grew up very guilty and ashamed.

At eleven or twelve, I wanted to be a writer. I was told by

my mother that that was a very stupid thing to do and I should become a doctor. I had no interest in becoming a doctor. I was told that I was a very cynical person, a very depressed person. My writing had emotional disturbance to it, turbulence that my mother found very upsetting. So instead of being nurtured for my creative talent, I was sent to a psychiatrist.

I was also told that because I was sexually attracted to men, I was very sick. My mother only cared about what other people thought. She felt that people would cut her down for having a son who was sexual with other men. When we talk about nurturing and validating, my mother was none of these things. I remember walking around the natural history museum and there was a couple, two men walking arm-in-arm in front of us, obviously lovers, and my mother said, "Look at them, they're a pretty sick couple." This was when I was about eight years old. It has always stuck in my head. Here were two men who seemed very peaceful, very communicative, and very gentle with each other, and they were denounced just because they were physically attracted to each other.

I know people who are heterosexual who I wouldn't want to emulate and gay people who I wouldn't want to emulate. I also know people who are heterosexual and people who are gay who I learn a great deal from. So I don't think people's sexuality is an indication of who they are. So many of us, myself included, took on a lot of shame and guilt just because of our sexual attraction.

As a young person, marijuana, speed, or heroin offered a great escape from reality. They were the love and the lovers I felt I could never have. They were a refuge, a haven. When I think about heroin and scraping heroin off the mirror and putting it into a syringe, it's a very sexual phenomenon. In a lot of ways, doing drugs kept me from having to be emotionally honest. It kept me from feeling overwhelmed and it kept me from looking at the depth of the dysfunction of my family. It was a coping method that, in the long run, betrayed me — almost killed me.

I Generally Feel that a Problem Shared Is Half a Problem

I always perceived emotion as a defect of character. I've learned in my sobriety that emotion is part of being alive, a very large part. I allow myself to feel feelings today. But what I've learned in AA is, I don't need to feel any of these feelings alone. Beside the fact that I can pray about the feeling to a Higher Power, I have friends in AA who I can call to speak about the sadness I feel about my family. Sometimes I'll be overwhelmed with fear when I do not feel well physically and I perceive that I am dying, and I can call people who will listen. I genuinely feel that a problem shared is half a problem. The greatest part of feeling is to have people to share the feelings with. Even joy, it's much more gratifying to share happiness with another human being than to stay alone with it.

That's how I allow myself, now, to feel a wide range of emotions. None of them are negative. For example, it's okay to be jealous and to share those feelings with other people. Now I say I'm jealous rather than allowing my feelings to run the show.

I Wound Up at an AA Meeting

In 1982 I got sober in New York City. I started going to Alcoholics Anonymous and Narcotics Anonymous. When I first started going, I was without hope. I really felt completely despondent, completely hopeless, completely self-loathing, and suicidal. I thought hope was gone. I really thought that I could never be a happy person, that I could never be a productive member of society. I was completely friendless; I was without any self-esteem, and I thought there was no reason to even try.

Luckily, after going to detox and rehab, I wound up at an AA meeting. I didn't think it could help but I had nothing left to do. I had made a bargaining agreement with my mother: she allowed me to move home if I went to AA. I had no desire to be sober, no belief. Anyway, the first day out of rehab I went to an Alcoholics Anonymous meeting. I was completely blown away by what I found there. I saw people who were smiling; I saw people who genuinely seemed to like each other. And I was invited back by these people. It was the first time I had been invited back to anything in many years.

They say AA is a program of attraction rather than promotion. I was really attracted to what I saw in the rooms: by the quality of friendship, by the fact that there were no rules, just suggestions. I hated rules. One of the things they suggested was, just bring the body, the mind eventually will follow. It really started working for me. For some reason, I took the suggestions. I decided to get a sponsor and I called my sponsor every day. My life was so bad when I first got sober, I thought it couldn't get worse. I was very grateful for the good feelings that started. I was becoming very grateful for being able to sleep at night without narcotics; I was very grateful for waking up in the morning without being strung out; I was very grateful to have my phone ring and have it be an AA member rather than be a dealer who I owed a lot of money to. I was also very grateful to walk down the street and see a police officer and know I wouldn't be arrested. I really enjoyed AA. I looked at AA as a new way of life.

I Went Off to Study Art in Spain

Unfortunately, I suffer from a disease, one of the qualities of which is forgetting where I come from. It's a disease that tells me I do not have a disease. I was a very active member of both AA and NA. I did lots of service work and speaking engagements. Then I went off to study art in Spain. The only reason I was able to make such a trip was because I was sober. When in Spain — talk about how insidious alcohol is — I was in a discotheque and the person I was dancing with asked me if I would like a drink, and I said, "I'd like an orange juice." He said, "That's really boring." I said, "You're right, I'll have a screwdriver." It was as if I was never sober.

When they say this is a progressive disease, it's really true. I didn't believe it could be true. I believed I would never sink to the depth I had sunk before 1982. I believed I could control my use, that I didn't have a disease. And I proceeded to drink as if drinking wasn't a problem. When I got back to New York, I proceeded to use cocaine because I felt that that had never been a problem. The fact was, I was using about $300 a day of cocaine, but I thought that was better than shooting heroin. Eventually, I went back to shooting heroin.

The interesting thing about my relapse is that the self-esteem it took three years to build left the night I got drunk. I became very dishonest again, isolative, and unpredictable. I started going to the same places I was going before 1982.

When I was sober, there was a lot of talk about AIDS. A couple of my friends got sick, and in '84 a couple of them died. As an addict I can only say that there's a universal characteristic that says *it can never happen to me.* The more I told myself that AIDS was something that happened to other people, the less I had to concern myself. In my relapse I did lots of unsafe things. I shared hypodermic needles, I had unsafe sex with people who were known prostitutes, and again, I really believed it could never happen to me.

At the end of 1985, I was desperate again and suicidal, and I decided I was going to kill myself. I bought ten bags of heroin and shot them all up at once. I was found in an abandoned lot with a syringe in my arm. I was brought back to life by the paramedics. My heart had stopped, but for some reason I was found before I could die. I really wanted to die; I believed all hope was gone.

Through a series of events, I made it back to another treatment center, but I was really far gone and that center suggested I go to Minnesota. So, I went to a treatment center in Minnesota. I wasn't feeling well even though I had been sober for five weeks. In 1985, there was not much education about AIDS and chemical dependency. Anyway, I went to my counselor and said I would like to have the AIDS antibody test and my counselor looked at me and told me I was just trying to get attention. I went back to my room not feeling well, with a sneaking suspicion of what was going on.

I completed the treatment, got a job in Minneapolis, and started going to AA. I didn't make a commitment to go for any length. Sobriety was conditional sobriety at this point: As long as reality was pleasant, then I would maintain sobriety. If it became less than pleasant, I would use again.

I Was, in Fact, a Leper — a Modern Day Elephant Man

Two months later I got a positive HIV test. By the end of the day I was at a bar getting drunk. Thinking back to that day, the feelings I felt were tremendous loneliness and tremendous fear. A doctor at the blood bank told me I was positive and I asked him if he would be kind enough to call my stepfather in New York. My stepfather is a physician and I thought it would be helpful for these two physicians to talk about the medical complications.

I was so filled with fear that when I thought of AIDS, I thought of the word *leper*; I thought about being quarantined. This doctor asked me to dial, and when I handed the phone to him, he wiped off the receiver with a rag. I was, in fact, a leper — a modern day Elephant Man. The fear was incredible; the rage was incredible. The hurt and self-loathing. I blamed myself. I thought I had done this to myself. I thought about the other people in New York I had shared needles with, that I had unsafe sex with. I thought about maybe passing this on to them. The amount of self-hatred I felt was incredible, just incredible — beyond description.

AIDS Is Not an Attack on a Lifestyle; AIDS Is Very Much a Part of Life in the '80s

Within a week after testing positive, I was diagnosed with ARC. I knew I was having night sweats, swollen lymph nodes, fevers, diarrhea. I went to see an AIDS doctor and he gave me an immediate ARC diagnosis.

All of a sudden I really found out what fear was about. I believed I was going to die, alone, of AIDS. I remember a phone conversation I had with my mother early on in my diagnosis. I was describing the loneliness and fear, and my mother said, "If you didn't live a certain lifestyle, you wouldn't have to deal with this."

I think what people forget is that AIDS is not an attack on a lifestyle; AIDS is very much a part of life in the '80s. I don't know why, but it's true. AIDS is something that attacks people; AIDS is not something that attacks gay people or heroin addicts. I think it's very important to remember that AIDS is not a representation of who someone is. I am a multi-faceted person and the fact that I presently have a diagnosis of AIDS does not indicate who I am. It says my health isn't as good as it could be; it does not indicate how emotional I am, how intelligent I am, how sensitive I am. It just indicates that I have poor health.

Accepting my diagnosis was a big challenge because, initially, I had a tremendous amount of shame. I felt that if I had not had same-sex partners or if I had not shared syringes, I would not have this diagnosis. The ironic part of the whole thing for me is that when I was having random sex, I really wasn't looking for sex — I was looking for love. And whether I looked in the right places or not is not the point as far as I am concerned. I was lonely and looking for human comfort, and that's the real ironic part of my diagnosis.

The most beautiful thing I can do is to really love another human being — spiritually and emotionally love another human being. And early on in my diagnosis, my greatest fear was that people would not want to be in the same room with me, that people would not want to be sexual with me, and that I was going to lose that part of my humanness. What I have found out since is, that's not the case. I can be very honest about my disease and not be rejected.

In fact, I've been real fortunate in my sobriety. In seeking out support; I've met some of the most loving people I could have ever met. If it was not for my diagnosis, I'm convinced I never would have met the people I have met. That's a real positive side of my diagnosis.

To Love Is to Cure

In Alcoholics Anonymous, they talk about the joy being in the journey, and they talk about living a life you never knew you could live. And AA talks about a Higher Power doing for us what we could never do for ourselves. These things have happened in my life in that last few years of my sobriety. I have met some of the most nurturing and affirming people. I had a woman open her house up to me; she gave me a place to live, food to eat. This was an incredible act of love. To care is to cure, to love is to cure. I think there is a lot of validity to that. AIDS is a problem for all of us. We cannot pretend it doesn't exist. My least favorite topic is AIDS. It's scary for me. It's a lot of pain and a lot of death, yet we cannot turn our back on it and pretend it does not exist. We are all responsible.

I think the real thing I learned from AA is that I alone can do it and I cannot do it alone. That carries over to the AIDS epidemic too. A group can do what no individual can do. In Gestalt therapy they talk about the whole being greater than the sum of its parts. That's really true. As a people, we can do together what none of us can do alone. I think that the AIDS epidemic and alcoholism indicate what can happen when people come together. We can take a crisis and cause great spiritual growth to occur. We can maximize our lives.

In *The Origins of Nonviolence,* a book about Gandhi and Tolstoy, it says it's impossible to heal spiritually without suffering. In a lot of ways, I have grown spiritually. My level of acceptance is much greater. I have more empathy toward other human beings. These results are in direct correlation to my own trials and tribulations, my own struggles.

I Saw a Man Park an Expensive Jaguar

Anyway, after my diagnosis I relapsed and continued to use for a couple of months. I had this plan: I was going to kill myself. I had no money and my addiction had taken me places I had never been before. I was hopeless. I proceeded to go to a bar on Hennepin Avenue, downtown Minneapolis, with this plan. I was going to prostitute myself to get enough money to buy a gun so I could shoot myself. I waited in front of this bar, and being a streetwise person from New York, I saw a man park an expensive Jaguar and I followed him into the bar. He asked if I was willing to go home with him and spend the night and be sexual. I said I was more than willing to do that; however, it was going to cost several hundred dollars. For $300 I'd stay. He could do whatever he wanted to do sexually. When we got back to his apartment, I broke down and started to cry. I told him I was an addict in relapse, I had a diagnosis of ARC, and I needed help and didn't know where to go.

This fellow told me there was a new treatment center that just opened for gays and lesbians, and part of their treatment was dealing with AIDS, ARC, and positive HIV test results. But I had no money for this treatment, I had no money for insurance, and I just really believed I should kill myself.

Talk about a Higher Power, this man said he was a very wealthy person. Money was not a problem; he was a multimillionaire. He told me he wanted nothing from me, no friendship, no sex, and maybe one day I would be in a position to help someone else. I have never spoken to this man since. Now I am in a position to help other people and it's because he helped me. He helped me when I didn't believe in myself.

AA talks about allowing people to really care about us until we are able to care about ourselves. I made it to this center and for the first time I really felt accepted; I felt comfortable. I would sit in the cafeteria and talk about my sexuality and my HIV status. I talked about how I wasn't feeling well physically because of my ARC, how I was fatigued a lot, and no one put me down. People encouraged me to talk about it. There were wonderful lectures on safe sex, acceptance, grief, and loss. Really, I was grieving the loss of my health, which is an ambiguous thing to grieve. Some days I felt great and some days I felt eighty years old and dying.

When I was in treatment, I started feeling hope — something I hadn't felt in a long time. I was able to talk about my health and no one told me I was a leper. I thought, though, that I would only find this acceptance in this treatment center; the rest of the world wouldn't be so accepting. But spending sixty years in this treatment center was unfeasible. Still, I was scared to go back to society.

You Surrender and Actually Win Something

This center put me in touch with the AIDS Project and with Cheryl, who took me in. Her only rule was, I needed to maintain sobriety. I didn't mind; I always really liked AA. It's interesting and paradoxical how it works. It's the only time you surrender to something, and by doing so, you actually win something. You win a great deal of personal freedom and integrity. I needed to keep in mind why I got sober. I didn't get sober for my health. I got sober for the sole reason that I could not live the way I was living as an active alcoholic and addict. I needed to accept life on life's terms. A lot of people, even in AA, said to me, "If I had a diagnosis like yours, I would not be sober." And all I can think of is, That's them, not me. My sobriety is unconditionally based and it's the most important thing to me.

The reality is, I should've been dead a long time ago. I really look at what I have today as extended play; it's a bonus round. A lot of people did a lot less heroin and alcohol than I did and are dead, but for some reason I am alive. I don't exactly know why, but I choose to get the most out of my life now.

I genuinely feel hope, even though at times I feel incredible sadness about my diagnosis. I recall going to the Names Project Quilt and looking at the panels of people who died of AIDS. Initially, I was overwhelmed with sadness — all those people denied life — then it dawned on me how lucky some of those people were. They had panels made by people who loved them.

I believe I can live with AIDS. I do not have to die today from AIDS. I can live a productive life with AIDS. I have no control over whether I'll get physically sicker, but I do have control over what I choose to do today. The reality is, I feel physically well enough today to live a quality life today. AA talks about one day at a time. AA talks about a twenty-four hour reprieve from alcoholism. And AA talks about the promises, how we will deal with situations that used to baffle us. When I was initially diagnosed, I was completely baffled by how I could accept such a scary reality. And a day at a time, I've learned to accept. Acceptance means I don't fight the situation, which is not to say I wouldn't rather it be the other way, but I no longer fight it. I have tremendous love in my life and friendship in my life, and it all stems from the recovering community of Alcoholics Anonymous.

There are only two times I need to go to AA: when I want to and when I don't want to. And I also believe there is never a bad meeting. I've never left a meeting feeling worse than when I got there, and I have left several bars feeling worse. So that's a point to remember. As an addict, one of my addictions is excitement, and sobriety can be very routine sometimes. It's important to remember that my life was so exciting, I went to primary treatment nine times.

I work at a treatment center where 40 to 50 percent of the male population has been exposed to HIV. A lot of them stopped living because of it, stopped being sexual, even with long-time lovers. I can show them that a person can live with a diagnosis, can be sexually active.

Addiction Is a Cofactor

I think addiction is a cofactor in the development of AIDS, absolutely. I feel it is impossible for anyone who is presently drinking a great deal or taking a great deal of drugs to feel very good about him- or herself. I feel there is direct correlation between self-esteem and the progression of physical demise. There is a direct relation between how we treat our bodies and minds, and how we feel. The book *I'm Looking for Mr. Right, but I'll Settle for Mr. Right Away* talks about the correlation between self-esteem and the progression of AIDS. I think there is a direct relationship between actively abusing chemicals or alcohol and the progression of AIDS. It's impossible to stay physically well when we're abusing our bodies with drugs and alcohol.

To change, people have to be tired of how they're living and at least be willing to try another way of life. A person also can't expect to do this on his or her own. If someone does not drink or use for ninety days and goes to AA every day for ninety days, at the end of ninety days that person will feel a lot better. I believe it's a foolproof way of change. If a person surrenders, AA works in mysterious ways.

The only difference between me and the alcoholic who is still out there using is that I have a head start on my recovery.

All I can tell you is that, for me, this is the best I have felt in my life. I attribute it to being an active AA member. My favorite part of AA is that there are no musts and no rules. There are some suggestions, like get a sponsor, call your sponsor, go to a lot of meetings, come early to the meetings, and be a part of the meetings. I really feel a comradery I never felt before. I always felt like an outsider looking in. I felt I was truly a deviant, and since I've become a member of AA, I feel a part of something greater than myself. It's very rejuvenating and spiritually cleansing.

Substitute *AIDS* for the Word *Alcohol*

The Steps that help me the most are the first two. The First Step states that "we admitted we were powerless over alcohol — that our lives had become unmanageable." That Step really works for me. At the time, I didn't realize how unmanageable my life was. When I stopped using chemicals, it stopped being so unmanageable.

Step Two states that we "came to believe that a Power greater than ourselves could restore us to sanity." It's a helpful Step. The Power greater than ourselves does not have to be God. I break down that word God to stand for, Group Of Drunks or Good Orderly Direction. As an addict, I was very willful and self-reliant; I believed that *I* knew best. By listening to AA or a sponsor, I learned that a Power greater than myself could help me be sane, could help me become a much better and more productive person. I do not have to dictate or pave the road anymore. I can allow people who have journeyed down the road further than I have to help me. That's really a great part of AA.

The word *AIDS* has such scary connotations. Fear has a way of causing people to quit. AIDS has a way of causing people to feel tremendous self-pity and unmanageability. The Twelve Steps work for AIDS, too, especially Step One. Substitute *AIDS* for *alcohol:* We are powerless over our AIDS diagnosis. AIDS causes tremendous unmanageability. It has caused people to lose jobs; it has caused people to lose living situations. It creates chaos in personal relationships; it has caused people to lose love relationships, and it has caused people to feel very isolated and very alone. Having people to talk to about all of this can help make it manageable and restore sanity in crazy situations.

Steps Three, Four, and Five have also helped me a great deal. Step Three states that we "made a decision to turn our will and our lives over to the care of God *as we understood Him.''* For me, Step Three means just trying to do the right thing — the right thing spiritually — and not necessarily the thing that *I* want to do. A lot of times we know what is spiritually correct and what is a willful, compulsive decision. I believe that the will of God for me is good orderly direction. And that works for me. Plus, I get a tremendous amount of guidance and power from the group, from allowing other people to care about me, and from taking risks and letting other people know what I'm feeling.

Steps Four and Five state that we "made a searching and fearless moral inventory of ourselves" and "admitted to God, to ourselves, and to another human being the exact nature of our wrongs." When we take a searching and fearless moral inventory, we look at things like fear. We also look at things like egocentricity and dishonesty. If someone asks, "How are you feeling today?" and if I'm feeling afraid that I'm going to die of AIDS and I answer, "I'm okay, thanks," then I'm not maximizing my life. When I take a personal inventory, I look at those interactions. I look at my own fear, my own faith, and I maximize myself. I use Steps Four and Five as avenues of change.

I think that Steps Four and Five can really help put shame and guilt in perspective. By doing a Fifth Step with someone who is nurturing and validating, we see that we didn't bring AIDS upon ourselves, so we don't need to feel ashamed or guilty about an AIDS diagnosis. If left to our own devices, we'll never learn. That's why Step Five is helpful. You share your inventory with someone else. Just don't do it with someone who judges.

I think it's important to look at what sobriety really is. To me, sobriety is a state of mind and a lifestyle; it's not a physical condition. It's important not to confuse abstinence with sobriety. The Twelve Steps are really a way to live life, not just be chemically free. It's a spiritual way to live life, whether we're dealing with AIDS or chemical dependency. I believe every single person who is alive can benefit greatly from the Twelve Steps of Alcoholics Anonymous, which is why so many Twelve Step self-help groups have started. Almost everyone fits into one of those groups. Whoever we are, whatever our situation, we can all grow more; we can all evolve into greater spiritual beings.

I think my diagnosis has helped me with acceptance toward other issues in my life, but I choose not to read into it too much. I try to accept life on life's terms. To me, that's one of AA's most wonderful principles: to really accept life on life's terms and not have to live a certain way. Let the river flow; you don't have to push the river. So I look at AIDS as being part of my life. I don't know why it's part of my life, but I do feel it has helped me spiritually.

AIDS and Chemical Dependency Can Bring Us Together

AIDS, chemical dependency, and alcoholism are things we all need to deal with. As a society, we can all benefit from doing a Step Four, a searching and fearless moral inventory of ourselves. Most families are dysfunctional, there's a huge divorce rate — something is very wrong with how we are in our personal relationships. As a society, it's much easier to blame people; it's much easier to be racist or prejudiced than it is to look at ourselves. I think we all had better start looking at ourselves.

Narcotics Anonymous talks about the things that bring us together being stronger than the things that tear us apart. I think that AIDS and chemical dependency can bring us together or tear us apart, and it's our choice as individuals what we allow to happen. None of us brought on AIDS or addiction, but once we have AIDS or we are chemically dependent, what we do with that is our choice. We don't have to allow AIDS or chemical dependency to be our demise. We can recover, we can change, and we can grow spiritually.

CHAPTER TEN

Lovers and Friends

RALPH

I'm fascinated by rattlesnakes. I like to watch those nature documentaries. These fellas pick the snakes up by the tails, open their mouths, and look at their fangs. They have a way of coexisting with these animals that never occurred to me.... Maybe we should learn a way to pick up that HIV virus by the tail and look directly at the fangs and say, "Let's cooperate with each other."

I'm from Los Angeles. I recently returned from a trip to Paris. We went to some AA meetings in Paris and a Frenchman in the program invited us to dinner. As always happens in a foreign country, they think you want to meet more Americans. So, we went to dinner and ended up in a room with six guests, all of whom were from LA. Within ten minutes we were talking HIV positive, supplements, T-counts — down the line. I turned to the Frenchman at the end of the evening and said, "You have just heard a typical evening in Los Angeles." This is also true of San Francisco. AIDS seems to be the only topic there is. I have the feeling, now, that we're like in the Warsaw ghetto, in a kitchen where we're all sharing as much information as quickly as we can. We want to know how far away are the Nazis, how many blocks are still standing, and if anybody has weapons to fight back with. Like I imagine those kitchens were at that time; there's a great deal of gallows humor going on, a great deal of matter-of-factness.

I remember the very first time I heard of AIDS; I guess this was six, maybe seven years ago. A guy was painting my apartment. He was a guy in the program, and he said, "I have to go to the doctor. I have this funny purple spot in my hairline." He was dead within four or five months. I remember him sitting there in the meetings and — to the eternal credit of Alcoholics Anonymous — there was a woman in the meeting, a regular straight woman, with her arms around this man and his head was on her shoulder. He was almost a cadaver then, and I was very proud of AA because, at that time, there were several reports in the newspaper of nurses refusing to treat people with AIDS. At a large university hospital, there was a brief period at the very beginning when gay men suspected of having AIDS had to wait in the parking lot rather than the waiting room. The doctors would interview you wearing masks.

Anyway, a wonderful thing about being in Paris this last month was that we went a month with only one evening spent in the obsessive re-creation of the plague. I think it's very healthy to get out of it for a while.

At the same time, I read somewhere that there were four common characteristics of long-term AIDS survivors. One was a will to live. The second was some sort of spiritual practice. The third was an ability to work with others or a desire to do work for others. And the fourth was an association with peers who had similar conditions, in order to share information. This is very interesting, because those are four characteristics of the AA program also.

If Not Now, When?

Richard, my lover, is twenty-nine years old and very successful. He owns his own business and is, if not obsessed, then dominated by his work. Because of his AIDS diagnosis, he had this idea that, rather than work himself to death and literally keel over on his desk one day, he should go out and do some things that he's wanted to do, such as going to Paris. So we went to Paris and rented an apartment, and we intend to go there often. It's not a lavishly expensive apartment, but it's a place we can go to. You have to ask yourself, if you believe the program of Alcoholics Anonymous, which tells you to live a day at a time, to live in the present, and to realize your potential fully today, then why don't people do it without being given death sentences? I mean, how many people have you and I heard of who have said the same thing over and over again: I really didn't come to life until I was diagnosed with AIDS?

Richard no longer gives seventy hours a week to his work. He works in shorter periods of time now, and he just came back from four weeks in Paris. He has discovered, to his astonishment, that the business is still running, not running as efficiently as when he is there, but it is still running. And guess what? He actually enjoyed himself. If it hadn't been for the AIDS diagnosis, when would he have finally decided to live. At forty?

EBV, CMV, What Is This?

Richard and I started going together five years ago. At that time, he had night sweats and swollen glands, but didn't know why. The doctor told him that it looked like Epstein-Barr or something called CMV. I didn't know what that was. After awhile, my glands swelled up and I went to be checked for this CMV business and the doctor said that I had a non-active case of CMV. It just wasn't that common to read about AIDS in the paper then, and this doctor wasn't very hip to what was going on. But I got concerned and started reading about AIDS.

When I became concerned about what these swollen glands meant, what these news reports meant, I followed my instincts and I turned to the program. I called nine people with various lengths of sobriety and asked them to come over. They did and I told them the story and asked, "What does anybody know? What is this stuff? What are my glands swelling up for?" One guy said his lover just died. Another guy, who was an old friend, used this as an occasion to tell us that he had been diagnosed. It became a liberating experience for him.

From that meeting, I discovered Louise Hay's group in Santa Monica and started attending. I found the meetings wonderfully comforting. My experiences have come to parallel the concepts in a wonderful book I read about Tibetan medicine. The Tibetan doctor says that his practice in Taoist medicine is to put a person in harmony with those forces that will heal him, unless it's time for him to die, in which case he puts him in harmony with those forces. And that seemed to be going on in Louise Hay's living room.

A Child of God with 300 T-Cells

Then I went to this doctor, an AIDS doctor, and I asked him to check my immune system. I told him not to tell me the numbers because I had so many friends who were obsessively dealing with those numbers. I said, "If there's any remedial action to be taken because the numbers are off, let me know. I'll do whatever you ask. But I'd like you to keep score, because I feel it's not beneficial for me to define myself in any way except as a child of God. I don't need to say, I'm a child of God with 300 T-cells and who, next week, might have 250 or 280." He said that's fair.

The doctor called me later and he said, "They're off, not so far off that we should do anything at this point, but let's keep aware of it." And we agreed that I would come back every four months. I asked if I should get the HIV test. And he said I could if I wanted to. And I asked, "What would you do differently if I tested positive?" He said, "At the moment, nothing." I said, "Well then there's no reason for me to do that. If you tell me there's a reason that will affect my medical treatment, I will immediately take the test. If there is none, I don't need further definition."

Four months later, I went back a second time, had my blood drawn again, and he told me it was better. He said he assumed that I was HIV positive and would treat me on that assumption.

I said, "Wonderful. That's a good agreement. You treat me as though I'm HIV positive and you assume from looking at my T-cell action that I am, so I don't need to get a further test because I don't need that information."

After a year or so, I asked my AIDS doctor to send my medical records to my other doctor who I've had for years. The nurse misunderstood and sent the records directly to me, so out of curiosity I looked. I discovered that when I first saw him I was about 400 T-cells and over a period of time I'd gone up. At that point I was 700 and I went to 900, and now I'm about 800, with the good ratios.

I had been doing everything at that point. I started taking egg lecithin, which required some footwork and research to find out how to get it. It was being mailed to me by UPS from a group up in Santa Cruz. And I had been taking large vitamin doses and a mixture of Chinese herbs. I also started doing guided meditations after reading a book called *Healing from Within*, by Dennis Jaffee. I'd been doing some of that over the years in AA anyway.

The Tao of Living

When I first got into the program, my Higher Power became sort of Taoist. Over the years I have collected translations of the Tao. I've been learning Chinese calligraphy so I can start reading the Tao in the original. It just fascinates me so much; I must have about twelve different translations now of the Tao.

So many people feel that the Tao and Buddhism, specifically Tao which is the predecessor of Buddhism, is fatalistic: you surrender yourself to whatever happens. I don't find that at all. It says, as my AA program also says, that there is some sort of ecstatic release to the notion that you are putting yourself in harmony with powers that will surprise you by their working within you. What AA has done for me is to make of me the sort of person for whom the most marvelous accidents can happen. And I think Tao does the same thing.

I once read a book called *Children of the Universe* by, I believe, a Dutch astronomer. It explains that we are not separated by space, but joined by space. The dust that settles on me comes from distant stars. Alan Watts says in his yoga books that this layer of skin that I have is not what separates me from my surroundings, it attaches me to my surroundings. There's this constant exchange of molecules between my skin and the air and who you are and who I am. The Tao makes me feel included in something; I feel like an appropriate part of an appropriate universe. How wonderful that feeling is.

Making Peace with Your Rattlesnakes

I had read a newspaper interview with Wil Garcia and George Melton, who wrote *Beyond AIDS*. They were talking about loving the virus and telling it to go to sleep. What I loved about that, as shocking as it may be, is that it allows you to take the principle of love and apply it to all areas of your life. If love is infinitely healing, then it should be healing to something you consider dangerous, like the virus. You take the fear out and replace it with love.

As hideously awful as it may sound, the virus is also one of God's creatures. It's like rattlesnakes. I'm fascinated by rattlesnakes. I like to watch those nature documentaries. These fellas pick the snakes up by the tails, open their mouths, and look at their fangs. They have a way of coexisting with these animals that never occurred to me. Now I'm not about to go out and pick them up by the tail, but I imagine that there's a way to live in harmony with rattlesnakes if you find yourself surrounded by them. These people do. I don't think these people are hating their rattlesnakes; they're not out chopping their heads off. They pick them up by the tail. Maybe we should learn a way to pick up that HIV virus by the tail and look directly at the fangs and say, "Let's cooperate with each other."

God bless them. I Xeroxed the Wil Garcia and George Melton interview, and I must have sent thirty copies of it to friends.

The Shame of It All

I went to the memorial service recently of a successful guy in the film business. He died of AIDS, but none of us knew he had been diagnosed. He went into the hospital and within a month or so he died. He lived a very guarded life. At the memorial service, a lot of people from the industry got up and spoke, but no one ever mentioned AIDS. No one mentioned homosexuality. And since he had no lover, no one stood up and said, "I will miss him." I got very upset. Shame is harmful to the process of healing, and I felt that this was a perpetuation of shame. Somebody said to me, "Don't be an idiot. If he had died of cancer, would people stand up and talk about cancer?" Maybe. They might have said, "I am gonna support the American Cancer Society in memory of my friend."

Self-Forgiveness Is Like a Large, Warm Bath

I think shame is very harmful to us. I feel that self-loathing is absolutely defeating the process of sobriety. The most difficult process that we all face when we work with newcomers to the program is helping them with the process of self-forgiving and the forgiving of others. We turn to Hazelden books and other materials for the formats for the Fourth Step. We're told very clearly that what we're looking for in our inventories are the parts of us that are keeping us from functioning well. And resentments bring us back to a point where we must forgive. It's there very clearly. One of the first steps to forgiving others is self-forgiveness. Self-forgiveness is like a large, warm bath. We lower ourselves into that bath and it spills over on everyone. Everyone benefits from the release of our self-loathing.

I think that shame can cause cancer; it can eat holes in us. I think it deeply, deeply compromises our immune system. For example, my friend Abe. I've been very close to Abe for many years. When he was diagnosed, he went up to the top of the hill to his house, closed the doors, and wanted no one to see him. I didn't see him for the last nine months of his life. And here was a man who could pick up the phone and get through to the most influential people in the country. He could have been enormously important to the community. God knows what *I'll* do when the chips are down, so it's very difficult to make these judgments, but when the chips were down for him, he retreated in shame. He could have been very helpful to others by saying, "I am not dying of homosexuality. I'm dying of a virus."

Self-Hatred in the Gay Community

One aspect of shame in the gay community that makes me want to scream is the number of my homosexual brothers who hate effeminacy. It drives me insane. If, in order to realize my sexual identity, I had to put on high heels and a dress and walk down Hollywood Boulevard, God bless me, I'd do it. And if I'm a young guy and I have a limp wrist and an effeminate way of speaking, why should I turn off a large segment of the only society that I'm accepted in? I hate that.

Our self-hatred gets expressed in other ways too, like sadism and masochism. We're so afraid of being effeminate, we put on these butch acts and hurt each other. About fourteen years ago, when I was two years sober, a very attractive, big strong guy in the program got "terminal" cancer. They told him he had about three months to live. I remember going to the hospital and feeling such anger at this cancer that I actually put my hands on his chest and something happened. Because of this anger, some sort of spark went between us. My friend was a masochist and had spent long periods of time chained to beds, things like that. When he got sick, he had to make a choice. He had to give up the desire to be punished in order to replace it with a desire to live.

The man is alive today, fourteen years later. He is a writer now and has had some plays done. He is a beautiful man.

I'm a Gay Father

AA has really helped me with self-acceptance. I'm a gay father and AA has given me an open, honest, wonderful relationship with my kids. I'm about to become a grandfather in November, so this grandchild is going to have an AA grandfather. Richard and I traveled in Europe with my ex-wife. She's got thirteen years in the program. All this repairing of the family specifically happened because of AA.

When I had been in the program about a year, the guy that got me into the program asked me, "When are you going to talk to your kids about being gay?" I thought the man was insane. I couldn't believe that he actually said something as horrifying as that to me. I was shocked, but by the time I was two and a half years sober, I found myself happy to talk to my kids. It's the same thing I say to guys like me now, usually after I speak at an AA meeting. They call me and mumble — they sound like they're CIA operatives — "Can we meet for coffee?" We meet in the coffee shop and it always turns out to be the same kind of guy. He's married, he's gay, and he's living a double life. He wants to know what he should do, and should he tell his children? Or else he was arrested in the toilet or whatever the story may be. I always say the same thing: "When you're dealing with children, don't tell them about being gay until it's good news." No child wants to hear bad news about a parent. No child wants to have a father mumble in an ashamed, embarrassed way that he's a cocksucker or a homosexual, or whatever hideous word he may come up with. But when it's good news for you, you can tell your children.

Better than Watching TV

Richard is a young guy. He's very successful; he's used to achieving. Here he is smack up against AIDS. At first, he went into total retreat. They put him on AZT and he just stayed in this retreat for about a year. We barely communicated. He stopped going to AA, stopped talking. He ate take-out food and watched television. After about a year of this, I finally said, "I can't sit around and watch this. I want to be a part of your healing. I can't sit here as an observer and watch you disintegrate." And so we had a few tussles, we started going to this therapist, and things changed. Things absolutely changed. A wonderful new type of honesty developed between us. This has all happened in the last six months. That's when he finally decided not to give himself entirely to work. It was his idea to go to Paris. I noticed in Paris, he liked going to AA meetings.

I also strongly suggested that he get into yoga and he did. It took him a long time to even agree to go visit this teacher, and now he goes twice a week and swears by it. He's into the healing process; now there's a different energy about him.

The Human Immune System

It seems obvious that we have a defense against the AIDS virus. If we didn't we'd all be dead. It's called the human immune system. I firmly believe that the human immune system can eat up that virus like it was candy.

I know that there are ways to cooperate with that immune system, to strengthen it so that it can protect us. There are emotional ways to support it too and I think that part of the problem is spiritual. When we desire to die, we do die. I'm not sure if this is always true, and I'm sure that a lot of people want very much to live who are dying of AIDS, but I do think that. When the Black Plague came across the continent of Europe, what did it take out, about 50 percent of the population of Europe? But significantly, 50 percent survived! It's not just that 50 percent died, 50 percent lived. They all had to have been exposed to the plague. Everybody got exposed, why did so many live? They had a defense against it.

Wear the Program Like a Loose Garment

In the last few years there's been an attitude in AA meetings
that says AIDS is an outside issue and shouldn't be brought
up in the meeting. When people tell me that, I guffaw and laugh
in their faces and say, "If your wife were to die of leukemia or
if your wife were, in fact, diagnosed with leukemia, you would
be *running* to AA. It would be an appropriate thing to bring
up in an AA meeting, and we'd all gather around you." I find
it highly suspicious that people have this objection to talking
about AIDS in AA meetings. I have also heard people say that
they're sick and tired of AA meetings becoming AIDS seminars.
Well, I'm sick and tired of my friends dying, so too bad.

I have a sense, maybe because of my Buddhist Higher Power,
that AA should be all-inclusive. I went to a meeting the other
night and the format of the meeting said we'd do a certain Step
and read certain materials. People who didn't have a year
sobriety couldn't participate because they didn't have enough
experience. I was very offended. I mean, who invented that?
Why do these alcoholics continue to beat on themselves? Why
do they continue to put laws into their recovery that are *exclusive* rather than *inclusive*? You know that little meditation
book that I think comes from Hazelden, the brick colored one?
It's really wonderful; it's been around forever. There is one
meditation that says we should learn to wear the program like
a loose garment. Let's not make someone feel more excluded
with rigid rules.

Alcoholics have always felt like their noses were pressed to
the glass, watching life go on inside. Let's not now give to the
homosexual alcoholic the further burden of feeling like a pariah
in his own family because he has AIDS. What a hideous thing.
And let's not make him feel he has to go over in a corner and
meet with the rest of the lepers. We're all the lepers, darling,
and we're all healing in some manner — leper to leper. I have
a leprous disease called alcoholism. I also have some sort of
virus chomping around in me. Let's all get together and be

inclusive because I think in that inclusiveness is a sense of mutual trust that is very healing.

The God of Surprises

When I first got sober I was very skeptical about anything to do with Buddhism. It was 1972 and there were still all these hippies going around with copies of *Siddhartha* in their backpacks, heading for the Redwoods. Oh, I was so contemptuous. I was in Toronto and I happened to go into a bookstore — I can't tell you why, maybe there is a God — and my hand fell on this book called *The Way of the Zen* by Alan Watts. I started reading it and it suddenly solved the problem I had.

I come from a southern background and I hated the language of the Big Book because it sounded like Southern Baptist language. So I'm reading about Buddhism and Taoism and one thing struck me between the eyes. Watts said, what Zen proposes — and I substituted AA for Zen — is to make of us the sort of people for whom the most marvelous accidents can happen. I have found in AA a new God and He is the God of Surprises. If I truly, truly take at their word the Steps of the program and let go of the results, then the God of Surprises will fill in the blanks. I'm always astonished that God accomplishes for me the things that I never thought I could accomplish for myself.

I have this idea that when I die, I may cross that great divide and come upon these bleachers of all my friends, and they're laughing their asses off because they're already dead and they discovered on the other side that there is no God. And I, like some idiot, have been praying to the air molecules around my ears. Except that I also have the realization that the air molecules around my ears are better equipped at managing my own affairs than I am. That because of my surrender — even if it was to air molecules — I've had a far more successful life than I had while keeping different rules. So suddenly, it's a wonderful experience; it really is.

BILL

I seem to be at peace with myself now, and I was never at peace when I was doing things my way. I was never happy standing around in bookstores or bars or walking around in bathhouses.

I was born on the South Side of Chicago. I have three brothers: one older, two younger. We lived in a house that my grandparents owned; we lived upstairs from them. Most of my upbringing was done by my grandparents. My folks were there, but I don't remember too much as far as learning anything from them, except that I was very sheltered; I remember that. Until I was like ten years old, I wasn't even allowed to go out in the neighborhood. I sat on the front porch or stayed in the house and watched grandma bake or helped her bake and wash clothes, just like a little girl. I was really never in with the guys, the kids in the neighborhood. When I got into grammar school, I had one best friend.

It was a pattern that would continue; I always had just one close person at a time in my life. My mother was at school almost every week sticking up for me 'cause kids were picking on me and beating me. I was a mama's boy. We lived two and a half blocks from school and my mother still walked me to school. She was very protective.

Diving for the Men's Underwear

I had feelings of being gay when I was in grammar school 'cause I can remember getting excited seeing somebody at the beach or even watching TV; if somebody had their shoes off on TV, I'd get excited. My brother was two years older than me and I can remember when I was nine or ten years old, and he was getting pubic hair, I used to coax him into letting me touch him. We never really had sex. He used to raid the garbage can every time my mother threw the catalogues away and he'd cut out the ladies panties and brassiere ads and I'd be diving for the men's underwear. He accepted it and didn't call me a geek; that's what I was interested in and we never discussed it.

We shared a bedroom together and he used to beat off all the time, and I never knew what was going on. All I remember was my mother saying things like, don't touch yourself, don't play with yourself, don't talk to strangers in bathrooms, don't smoke cigarettes, and all this other stuff. So, I started smoking cigarettes in alleys when I was ten years old. When I got to eighth grade — this is like 1959, when I graduated from grammar school — my parents assumed I wanted a radio for graduation. Instead, I asked them for permission to smoke and I got it. They knew I was doing it anyway.

That summer, between grammar school and high school, I even got permission to go to the neighborhood theater which was a block away. It was a real small theater where they changed films three times a week and always had two shows. It was thirty-five cents to get in. I remember I used to go in there and stand in the bathroom and smoke cigarettes, and I'd always notice guys standing by the urinals and would get excited watching them. One day I was in there and this guy, this adult, was standing there and he started getting a hard-on and he motioned me over. I went right over there and I got a hard-on and he reached over and grabbed me. I touched his dick and that was the first time in my life that I remember coming. I didn't know what it was; it felt good, but it was scary. It was something unknown.

I remember going home from the show that day. I had to be home by dinnertime when my daddy got home from work. We all ate together. My grandmother had dinner ready and I wasn't hungry. I was all flustered; I didn't know what was going on. I remember my grandmother making a comment; she said, "No wonder he isn't hungry, God knows what he puts in his mouth at that show over there." She meant junk food. Within a couple of days I was right back over there again.

From then on I started hanging out in theaters.

Science Club Every Night

I turned fourteen and once in awhile some of the guys would get together and we'd have a couple of beers at a science club meeting — once a month, maybe a few beers. Once I tasted it, I wanted it. I had a job at a drugstore and I used to get a waitress who worked across the street from the drugstore to buy me a quart of beer when I'd get off work. I lived on the South Side and I went to school on the North Side, so I'd have to travel through the Loop on the subway. I discovered the bathrooms on the subways. Four nights a week I would tell my folks that I had science club meetings after school. Actually, I'd be spending an hour and a half cruising the bathrooms. Then I discovered department store bathrooms and the movie theaters downtown. I was probably around fifteen, a sophomore, when I started paying bums who panhandled money for drinks. I'd buy them a bottle if they'd buy me a bottle. Then I'd go into theaters and drink it, watch movies, cruise bathrooms, and smoke cigarettes. It was like, I'm really an adult and I really have my freedom.

I Figured One Pill Couldn't Hurt

I was also stealing drugs from the drugstore. Nobody turned me on to drugs. I just started experimenting. The druggist used to have me count the pills and put them in the bottles and go through the cabinets, and if something got low, I'd just call the drug company and reorder it. This was in the early '60s, before they had the federal forms and all that stuff. So every day or every couple of days I would take a different pill home with me and I'd take one. I figured one pill couldn't hurt. Some nights I'd get home, take the pill, and nothing would happen. Some nights I'd get home, take a pill, and I'd be up until three o'clock in the morning doing homework. Sometimes I'd take a pill and I'd get real dizzy or go to sleep right away.

I used to keep track of which pills were which and I'd go

back to the drugstore and steal a couple hundred at a time. We used to have bottles of 500 and I'd dump them in my pocket and keep them at home. Then I started turning the guys on in school with the stuff. That was my way of getting in with these people. I didn't want to go through what I did in grammar school: being an outsider and a troublemaker, for being a mama's boy. I wanted to fit in. So I fit in by drinking and by selling them speed for a dime a piece. That went on straight through high school. I was probably having sex four or five times a week through high school, although I went home with only one or two people. I never had sex with anybody my age; they were all older. I was getting validated by all these people and it made me feel like I was somebody. I was using the drugs, the alcohol, and the sex to become part of life, I guess.

I wanted to become a pharmacist, so I went to the university, but I stayed for only a couple of months. The university bathrooms were quite cruisey; there were glory holes all over the place. I used to spend all my study periods in bathrooms and then it got to the point that I was skipping classes and sitting in bathrooms. I was running from one end of the university to the other just cruising bathrooms. I was also working part time, and when I wasn't working, I wanted to go out and cruise. That was in addition to the time that I cruised during school. Soon, there just wasn't time for school anymore and I dropped out.

Marshall Field's, Martinis, and Black Eyes

I got a job downtown working at Marshall Field's. I wanted to cruise their bathrooms. I had a phony ID and I used to go out and drink at lunchtime and after work. There was a real cruisey movie theater called the Avon Theater, in those days, and there was always some action going on in there. I met some guy there who was probably a good ten years older than me. This relationship went on for three years. He lived at home, I lived at home, and we used to spend maybe three or four nights a week in a hotel downtown. By that time, I was drinking martinis and so I taught him how to drink martinis. It was like adding gas to a fire. I was still out fucking around, you know; I wanted to have my cake and eat it too. He always knew what I was doing 'cause he'd always catch me, and we'd get into these big fights. It would be very physical, a lot of bloodshed: black eyes, bloody nose, bloody mouth, stuff like that. I was always giving some sort of excuse to friends about what was happening to me, like I walked into a door or something.

While I was still working at Marshall Field's, my folks said to me that if I wasn't going to go back to school, I should go get a real job, go to work at General Motors where my dad and grandpa have worked all their lives. At General Motors, I started drinking my lunches. I maintained by doing drugs. I didn't think of myself as having a drug problem 'cause I'd do speed in the morning and sometimes in the afternoon. I did it like people did vitamins — just to get by on. It wasn't to get high or crazy or anything, it was to get by on, to exist. And then I did my Valium or Tuinals so I could get to sleep. Then I'd get up the next morning and take the drugs again, that way I could keep drinking at lunch.

Oh, Sailor!

When I was twenty, it was 1965, Vietnam was there, and I was afraid of being drafted, so I had a long conversation with my dad. It was probably one of the only things I can remember we ever talked about. We decided I would join the navy. So I joined the navy and I went active for two years. I was drunk every night. Plus, I had an open prescription for speed and my grandmother, bless her heart, would go to the drugstore and ask for Billy's vitamins and she'd mail them to me overseas. So I always had my drugs.

I got out of the navy and moved in with my grandparents. I went through a few real sick relationships. The first one, the one I already described, he was taking care of me because I was a teenager. I stuck around because he would pay for trips, booze, dinners, theater tickets, the hotel, and stuff like that. Not that I wasn't in love with the guy; I thought I was, you know. The rest of them, it was more or less like I was there to take care of them. It was never an equal balance.

Then I met some actor who was in Chicago doing a show for a couple of months and we fell in love. He lived in New York and we kept up a romance. Chicago was getting boring, so I gave a six month notice, worked overtime for six months, got all my bills paid, sold my car, and with $400 in my pocket, I went to New York to live with this guy. When I got there, I found out he had just cashed his last unemployment check. I was very resentful. We lasted about a month before the love wore off.

New York brought more new drugs into my life: Quaaludes, mescaline, coke, angel dust. At first I was doing it right, buying from a reputable dealer. This one guy had a cocktail party every Friday at 7:30 P.M. in a real plush Village apartment. You'd go in and there would probably be about twelve or fifteen people, and you'd sit down and have a cocktail while he'd pass around a joint *du jour*. Everybody would sample it, and on the end tables, he had these little cards that listed the pharmaceuticals that were available, what they were, and how much. After about half an hour, he'd come around with a little pad and take your order. Then he'd go in his bedroom and he'd come out with a little bag and hand it to you. I loved them, the tiny little Ziploc bags. "Here Bill, $280." And you'd get your money out and pay him. For the first year, I was doing this. I don't know how I was paying my bills. I don't know how I was doing it, but I was. My life was manageable. I was working. I was buying drugs. I was getting up in the morning and going to work. This was in '77 and I was thirty-two years old.

Then it got to the point where I was buying drugs on the street from anybody. I didn't know what I was buying. If a guy said it would do this or that to you, I'd buy it. I got another lover out there after a couple years: a young guy, twenty-one years old, real cute Italian guy. I was totally obsessed with this man. This went on for a couple of years; there was always a lot of battling. I wanted to be with him all the time; I wanted a commitment out of him. I loved him very much, and even though I wanted a commitment out of him, the times I didn't see him, I was in the bathrooms in the subways of New York. I got mugged a couple of times in the bathrooms in New York, robbed, and strangled once so hard that I almost bit my tongue off.

I wanted to control the relationship and he would not let me. Probably, if I had gotten what I wanted, I would have said, "Thank you very much, fuck you, and good-bye," because that's the way I am. Tell me that you want me and I run. Finally, it was the first week of April 1982, and he said, "Well why don't you move in for a week to see how it would be to live with me." So I moved in on a Sunday and Sunday went real fine. I came in like a perfect wife, made a pork roast, and drank.

He used to do drugs but he'd only do like one pill; he was boring. We'd get our money together and I'd go out and buy the drugs on the street corner. He'd think I was going to buy two hits of speed and I'd buy four: one for him, one for me, and two for me. He didn't smoke grass; he didn't like to drink. I was drunk all the time. I'd go in the kitchen and fix us a drink and I'd say, "Well, I'm going to have a little vodka on the rocks." So I'd take this big tumbler glass, fill it up to the top with vodka, and while I was fixing his cranberry juice and vodka, I'd be chugging this down till there was maybe a shot of booze in the glass.

"We Never Go Out Drinking Together."

Anyway, it was going fine all week and I guess Wednesday night he said, "Well, what do you want to do tomorrow?" I said, "We never go out drinking together, so let's go out for cocktails after work." So we went out for cocktails. We met at this Upper East Side bar and he decided he was going to have a martini straight up, be real grand, and I'm just washing down my vodka, like I always do, on the rocks. We got into an argument and he said, "Well, I'm going to take off. I'll see you in the morning." I said, "What do you mean, in the morning? We're out. Where are you going? We're supposed to be together, go have dinner, go home, and make great love." And he said, "No, I'm going to the St. Mark's baths." I said, "You can't do this. I'm with you."

I was going crazy and we got in a big fight in the bar. He ran out and I ran after him into the street. He got into a cab and I jumped into the cab with him. The cab driver said, "Where to?" and I said, "St. Mark's baths." Mark said, "No, Thirty-fourth and Tenth." So I think, Oh good, we're going to go home. So we get home and we're arguing and he goes to his drawer and comes up with a Quaalude and said, "Take this and chill out. I'm going out; see you tomorrow."

I was furious. I said, "You ain't going anywhere. The only way you're leaving this apartment is fucking bloody." And he said, "Get over yourself." So I ran in the kitchen — I was crazy, I went berserk, I hated him so much — and I grabbed this knife in the kitchen and I went after him with it. I wanted to kill him. I called him every name you can imagine, and I really meant it too. He overpowered me, threw me on the floor, and sat on top of me. Then he put this Quaalude in my mouth, picked me up, pushed me through the living room, the kitchen, out the kitchen door, and then slammed the door on me. I'm out in the hallway and I have a pair of pants on, no shirt, no shoes, and I went crazy. It was a big metal fire door, very heavy. I grabbed the doorknob — I don't know where I got the strength — and I twisted it off the door. Then I pried myself between the door and the hallway, took my feet and pushed the door in through the frame.

By that time, two squad cars pulled up and they came running up the stairs. Mark was scared to death, "Get him out of here; get him out of here. I don't want to see you again in my life. You're sick, you're an alcoholic, and you're a drug addict. Stay away from me."

To make a long story short, I stayed with a friend, went to bed at two o'clock in the morning, and woke up at six o'clock in the morning. I was sitting there on the bed facing the wall, and when I realized that everything that had happened the night before was not a nightmare, I was scared. I felt totally empty; I had nothing in my life anymore. I couldn't believe that I tried to kill somebody. I could see where bending the rules throughout my twenty years of drinking helped me justify taking somebody's life 'cause he didn't agree with me; he didn't do it my way. I guess that that was my bottom.

I didn't know what the hell to do with myself. In the past, I had thought of suicide. I remember once when I had had a fight with Mark, I figured, Well, I'll kill myself. I bought a gun and a bunch of drugs. I wanted to kill myself, but I wanted to be there to watch the results of it too. So I realized then, and now, that I was not going to kill myself; I was too chicken. And Mark didn't care about me anyway. He was the type of person that if I would make a threat or an ultimatum, he'd say, "Have a nice life."

Anyway, it was Good Friday, we only had to work half of that day, and I went to work totally empty; I didn't know what to do. I was sitting at my desk — it must have been around 8:30 a.m. — and I wasn't doing anything, I was just sitting there, and for some reason AA came to my mind. The only thing I knew about AA was from Ann Landers and Dear Abby. I didn't know how it worked, what it was all about, or anything. So I went to a pay phone, called information, and dialed the number for AA. I got a recording, but I left my phone number. Within twenty minutes I got a phone call at work from somebody from the Intergroup office in New York. I told them I had a drinking problem and that I was gay. They told me that they had gay meetings and asked if I wanted to have somebody who was gay and recovering talk to me and I said, "Yeah".

Somebody called me over the noon hour and we set up a place for us to meet and go to a gay meeting. I felt good that I made that move, that decision, but I was scared to death because I didn't know how I was gonna be able to stop drinking. I'd never even tried to control my drinking; I never tried to stop drinking; I didn't want to. I remember having a conversation about a year prior to that with a friend of mine at work. I said I don't know what I would ever do if I came down with cirrhosis of the liver, that they'd have to find a cure for it because I would not quit drinking.

So we went to a meeting. He set me straight on the idea that I couldn't do drugs either. Even though, today, I choose to call myself an alcoholic and a drug addict, then, I didn't. I didn't realize the role that drugs played in my life; I just thought I was a drunk. I really didn't look at the drugs I was using until my first few months in recovery. Then, I craved the feeling of drugs more than the alcohol; I didn't have that instant energy that I had before. The first few months were pretty cloudy.

I had a boss at the time who was very supportive. He offered me the chance to go into treatment if I wanted to. I said, "Oh, let me try AA." He said, "Just make the effort to get yourself up in the morning and go to work." He took a lot of my responsibilities away the first six months. I was too scared to drink and I was like a puppy at obedience school. If someone said, "Go here," I went there. So, I went to meetings. I didn't socialize that much in the beginning. I was very lonely and I chose to be lonely. People asked me to go for coffee after meetings and I would say, "No, I have plans."

In the beginning, my main reason to sober up was to get my lover Mark back, which I did. We went on for another nine months in a sick relationship till God moved my company from New York to Texas and took me with it. I was asking for help in this relationship, but I just couldn't come right out and do it myself. I still think God had a lot to do with moving the company down to Texas. It helped me let go of that situation.

Eventually, I moved back to Chicago. I was going to a lot of meetings down in Texas and I really developed a very good spiritual program. My God was in my life all the time. When I got to Chicago, I didn't want to go through the whole thing of going back to meetings. I figured all I needed in my life was God, so I quit going to meetings for a year. Meanwhile, all this time I'm telling my friends in Chicago — new friends and old friends — that I'm in AA and I don't drink. But I wasn't in AA. I went for a whole year without drinking, but things started happening. God was no longer my friend, He was my enemy: He was doing this to me; He was doing that to me. He took away my job, I got laid off, blah blah blah. I was thinking, Well yeah, I'm going through mid-life crisis, and I blamed it on everything *except* not going to meetings.

What happened was, a friend of mine, who I had brought to AA when I was down in Texas, was celebrating an anniversary. I was between jobs in Chicago and another friend of mine was helping his sister move down to Houston and wanted to know if I wanted to ride along, and I said, "Fine." It was the weekend the Chicago Bears played the Super Bowl and Chicago was colder than...I thought I could go to Texas and be the big cheese who got my friend into the program and make myself look big, you know, that's what I wanted; I wanted the recognition. I had nothing inside myself anymore. I didn't even want to go to the meeting. I was just going to go so he could say, "Yeah, this is Bill over here; he brought me to my first meeting. Isn't he wonderful?"

So I sat there at the meeting waiting for it to get over. The story of my life: You go somewhere and you wait for it to get over so you can go to the next thing. The next thing comes and you wait till that's over so you can get to the next thing. I was sitting there waiting for this meeting to get over and I saw this wall hanging with the promises from the Big Book. I read the promises and I sat there and started shaking and crying. I realized everything I had worked for those first two years in the program were gone and I was really scared. My fears were back. I wasn't working; everything had reversed itself in a year. I talked to the guy who was giving the lead at the meeting and he asked if I wanted to have coffee with him the next day. He gave the lead standing up there on a cane; he was probably in his forties.

I spent a week in Texas talking to the guy and going to meetings. He was the first person I knew who had AIDS. He spent time with me and told me that if I kept going to meetings, my life would change again, that I'd get work and everything would be all right. I went back to Chicago and I started going back to meetings and within two months I had my old job back. They even gave me a raise. The promises were coming true. A lot of fears were gone, especially the fear of economic insecurity.

He Had ARC and I Wanted to Take Care of Him

A year or so later, I met Patrick and we started dating. I heard him share at a meeting that he had ARC. I had been sober for about four years. It was the first good relationship I had since Mark, and I thought, God, this is worth waiting for. I thought it was going to work forever, because he had ARC and I wanted to be there and take care of him, and I knew that he'd be glad to have someone to take care of him. After a few months, he decided he didn't want the relationship anymore and broke it off. That was probably one of the most crushing things that ever happened to me: losing a relationship that I was sure was exactly what God wanted me to have. We went to the same meetings all the time, and after three months, I finally had to let go of it. I thought, Hey Bill, he's not going to change his mind; get on with your life.

So I did. A short time after that Patrick asked me to go out and get something to eat after the meeting. Right away I thought, Okay, he changed his mind; he wants me back. When we got to the restaurant, he made it perfectly clear he did not want to get back together. He said, "You know, I like you,

you have a good sense of humor, you're fun to be with, and I'd like you to be my friend if you can handle it." And I said, "Sure, I'd be glad to." I really did miss him; I liked him a lot too. I figured it would be one of these good friend relationships where we'd go out to dinner once a week and go to a meeting.

What really surprised me was, after the evening was over, he called me at work the next day, then called me that evening, and our relationship just went on and on. We were closer than we ever were. There wasn't a day that we didn't talk to each other. We saw each other probably three to four times a week. We even went on vacations together.

Then, I decided to find out the results of my HIV test. I was almost sure that I was positive, and that's what it was. They had blood samples from 1984, when I started a study, and I had been positive at least since then. Basically, I found out my results in order to make him more comfortable. *I belong and I fit in with this thing; he's sick and I'm sort of sick.* But that's where that was left. I didn't talk about it at meetings.

The following June, Patrick was diagnosed with AIDS and he got real sick. Most of it was a reaction to the pentamidine they gave him for his pneumocystis. He was dehydrated, crawling on his hands and knees, hanging on the toilet trying to throw up. That snapped me out of the denial that I was going through about me being positive. Right away I went from denial into dying.

I didn't give a shit about me at all, but I was doing everything I could for Patrick. I was buying things, taking care of him, taking him to the hospital, sending him flowers. When he got back his strength, anything he wanted to do we'd do. You know, it was everything for everybody else — nothing for me. I needed dental work done, I needed to pay bills, but I just refused to do it. Why bother? I was going to die. Up until this time, my T-cells were averaging 700 to 800. Once I started this negative thinking, my T-cells took a dive. I came down with thrush and shingles; I was getting infections in my stomach, on my legs. That's when the doctor told me I had ARC.

Pushing It into a Hole

Patrick told me to get into therapy and I went. I was one of these people that believed if you work your program, you don't need therapy because it's all there in the Steps — which is a lie. Therapy helped me pull all of this stuff out of this hole that I thought I was turning over so well in the Third Step. All I was doing was pushing it into a hole and burying it. All of this stuff had to be dragged out, weighed out, and sorted out. Then I had to decide what to do with it. Basically, what I did was go through a thorough Fourth Step in therapy with this beautiful woman who I love very much. We dug all this stuff out and we decided we were going to have to start working on some of it.

I was living with Mommy and Daddy who I just realized in therapy were alcoholics. After forty some years, this "Father Knows Best" household that I was raised in all of a sudden turns into a dysfunctional family. There were no feelings ever talked about in my whole childhood; it was always fact reporting. We did this; I did this; we never talked about how we felt.

There were also certain things that I had to do. I had to declare bankruptcy. I was like $25,000 in debt and there was no way I could pay it off. I was really ashamed about that. When Patrick found out about it, he got really mad. He thought I was paying my bills. I felt real bad that I wasn't honest with him about what was going on with me, but I didn't want him to know. I just wanted to take care of him. He forgave me for it, but after that, he wouldn't let me buy him anything anymore. I started taking care of myself instead. I had to start being nice to myself, do things that looked like they were totally out of the picture. Slowly, I was able to get an apartment I could afford. I was able to get my teeth fixed. I was able to do all kinds of things that I never thought I could do before. And I started feeling better about myself. My T-cells started going back up again and I wasn't having any more symptoms. The stress I was creating in my life had been making me sick.

During the last seven months, my T-cells have gone from 296 to 625. I'm giving some of the credit to AZT, but I'm giving most of it to positive thinking, trusting in God, helping other people, and taking care of myself.

Get My Transfer Punched

This sexual addiction I talked about since I was thirteen years old, that did not disappear when I got sober. I didn't fuck around when I was going out with Patrick, but the day he died what did I do? I didn't even get home; I went right into a bookstore. I didn't want to go home and feel this. The sexual addiction was there; it's there right now if I want it to be. When I did the Fourth Step, I talked about it and addressed it, and God is helping me with that right now. My old behavior doesn't work all the time anymore; that's not saying that it doesn't work sometimes, because it does. On the whole, it doesn't work like it used to and I don't miss it. I don't need to go out to a bar or a bookstore or a bathhouse to get my transfer punched, which is what I call being validated.

Before my friend Patrick died, he would get better and he'd be well for a few months, and then he'd get sick and go back in the hospital. It was almost to the point where I didn't think he was going to die. Back in November, he wasn't feeling too well and we had a trip planned to Hawaii. We went to Hawaii and it was fine. We got back around Christmastime and he started slipping again and went into the hospital. They couldn't find anything wrong with him; they did the sputum test, they did a bronchoscopy and they decided they wanted to go in there and find out what was wrong, because he was coughing a lot and had high temperatures. So they cut a hole in his lung and did a biopsy and found out he had pneumocystis, which is what they were treating him for when he came in there in the first place. The surgery knocked a hell of a lot out of him; he never really did regain all his strength.

He went home and I was hoping that we'd go through the

same routine again, where I'd be there and help him, cook dinner for him once in awhile, and get him back on his feet so we could get back out to the meetings again and start doing things. That surgery was a little bit too much for him to handle because he never really got his strength back.

They ended up putting him back in the hospital. Some days I thought he was feeling better, some days I didn't, and still, deep down inside, I was expecting and hoping that he'd come back home again so we could have one more go-around. But I knew I was kidding myself. Every day was like going to a living wake 'cause I knew he wasn't going to come home again. He'd talk; he'd go in and out — they had him drugged up. Sometimes you knew what he was saying and sometimes he'd be talking like he was in a dream. Finally, Friday morning I got a call at work from the hospital. I got there in time to spend his last twenty minutes with him. He couldn't talk; he just laid there with his eyes open, breathing very heavy till he passed on.

I thought it was going to be the end of the world for me. I didn't think I'd ever get through it, but God doesn't give us anything that we can't handle. He put a lot of people in my life — people I love a lot, people who care about me — and they were there for me. I was comforted, I was loved, I was held, and that made it all right. Somebody wrote on Patrick's quilt, "Patrick, Bill will be all right." I wrote on it, "Patrick, I am. Thank you."

So I've got somebody else that I talk to now besides God. I talk to Patrick just like he's here. I've also got five other friends up there who have died of AIDS. Knowing Patrick has really changed my life a lot. He gave me a lot of strength by showing me that we can live with AIDS and we don't have to drink over it.

I know if I was diagnosed seven years ago, before I got into the program, I would not be telling my story today because I'd be dead by now. What more of an excuse could I have wanted to drink? I could be tragic and dramatic and just think,

I might as well drink because I'm going to die. But I want to live now. I figure God's got plans for me, and as long as I make myself available to His plans, not mine, He's gonna keep me until He's through with me. I acted on my plans for thirty-four years. Right now, all I do is make myself available and try to listen to Him.

When they say, "improve our conscious contact with God," it's done through prayer and meditation. The prayer is where I talk to God. But I just can't talk to Him all the time; I need the meditation. I need to listen to His word for me. He doesn't come out and tell me what to do, but He does show me what to do. He puts people in my life that I know I have to do something with. I'm sponsoring a couple guys, something I haven't really done a lot before in my life — helping people. I seem to be at peace with myself now, and I never was at peace when I was doing things my way. I was never happy standing around in bookstores or bars or walking around in bathhouses. I'm comfortable with what I'm doing now, which is going to meetings, getting involved, and just trying to do the next right thing.

CHAPTER ELEVEN

Al-Anon

ADRIAN

After I found that meeting, that was it. I went to meetings. . .every single night. I wanted everything Al-Anon could teach me. . . . They were telling my life story. It was such a shock to listen to these people talk and to finally, in all these years, say there's something real here. This pain that I felt all my life is real. . . . That whole meeting, all I did was cry.

I was an introvert until my senior year when I started break-ing out of that a little bit. By nineteen I was very sexually active. I met guys that were either abusive physically or abusive emo-tionally. Relationships ruled my life. If one relationship would break up, I was in another relationship within a month.

At nineteen I got involved with a guy whose name was Bernie. After two months going out with him, I knew there was something wrong. He did a lot of drinking; I knew that much. If I refused to see him or if I wanted to go home at the end of a night or I didn't want to have sex with him, he would hit me or beat me. At the end, after I would break down and cry, he would tell me he loved me and wait for me to tell him I loved him and then I'd have sex with him. And because I was in the closet — my parents didn't know I was gay — I didn't see any way to get out of it. I stayed in the relationship for eight months. The way I finally got out of the relationship was to run away to school. He didn't have a car, he couldn't get me, and so that's what I did.

He also used to threaten to tell my parents about the two of us, that we were gay. I remember one night, it had been more than I could take. I don't know what the fight was about — anything would set him off. I just wanted to go home. He started in. He started pulling my hair and slapping me across the face and I ran away from him. I was running and running, and at one point I gave up and I fell to the ground. I just laid down on the sidewalk and I cried. I couldn't take it; I had had it. It was like, you can kill me, just get it over with. Then I went home and acted like I was fine in front of my parents. I had this act, this game, but I had been playing this game for so long, it was easy to just shut off every emotion.

I remember being fourteen and thinking that if my parents found out I was gay, I'd kill myself. I would be in my bedroom crying after school, and when my parents came home, I would walk out of my bedroom as if everything was fine. They had no idea how I was suffering. At night, I used to pray to God that when I woke up, I'd like girls.

I thought I was the only person in the world that had these feelings. I was afraid of what my sexual orientation would do to my family, afraid of what they might think. I remember I was still fourteen and my father said, talking about a second cousin of mine who's gay, that if that were his son, he'd get him the best psychiatrist to change him, make him better — whatever it takes. I thought, Jesus Christ, how am I gonna be able to tell him. Plus the relationship I had with my father, we fought like cats and dogs.

Terrible Fights Between My Mother and Father

He'd come home at the end of the day and he'd start drinking his brandy. He and my mother fought. Even as a little kid, two and three years old, I remember terrible fights between my mother and father. By the age of five, things hadn't been going so well for my folks, and my mother took us to Vienna,

Austria. We were going to live in Vienna. My mother took me and my nine-month-old brother there. The first three weeks we were there, we met my grandmother and my aunt, and I knew, even at that age, that I didn't want to go back to my father. It was safe over there and it was nice. What I didn't understand was why, after those three weeks, my mother went back to him. She left us there at the train station and she was gone for two years.

I got beat up a lot as a kid because I was American. There was a lot of resentment toward me for being a foreigner in their country. But, just as I got comfortable there, my parents uprooted me and brought me back. That's when all the changes started. Before, I had friends on the street that I would play with. When I came back from Vienna, that was it; I no longer would associate with other kids. During the school year I had to talk with them, but I didn't socialize. I went home and I watched TV.

I Always Thought Being with a Man Was Beautiful

In high school there was a guy who was a year older than me. Through horseplaying and stuff we started discovering our sexualities together. It's funny, in my head, as a young kid, I always thought that being with a man is beautiful. I would fantasize about it. But this guy changed that real quick, 'cause for him, it was frightening. For about three years we saw each other once a week, and afterwards, he'd always put down what we did as being dirty and disgusting: people would know; people could tell; this isn't right; what we're doing is wrong. It didn't take long until I started feeling that way too.

I Was Called a Jackass and a Stupid Idiot

My father was a periodic drinker. Plus, he liked to have his shots before dinner — have his high before dinner — then eat his dinner, lay on the couch, and sleep. He was also a workaholic. He worked all the time. His favorite line was, "You

173

need anything, you come to me." You needed money, you went to Dad. But, as for being there emotionally for us, he didn't have the time. He worked six days a week. He had one day a week off and he wanted to do his thing. His thing was to get together with people, have a party, and drink.

He could never tell us, my brother or me, that anything we ever did was good enough. I worked during high school and I had a B plus average, but I graduated thinking I was stupid. Years later, I opened up my records, looked at my grades, and thought, You know, you didn't do bad. But I remember I got one D and my father called me a jackass and a stupid idiot.

I remember a relative coming over one weekend and she said to my father, "Clayton, you have to give them support. You gotta tell them they're doing well." My father said, "I don't do that. They have to do better." This is from a man who didn't go further than the sixth grade and was a troublemaker, a bully. His kids had to be perfect. They had to learn and study and be somebody. My father was a tough man. He didn't really have to hit us; we were so afraid of him. We never stepped out of place. We always knew how to behave. We didn't misbehave, that's all there was to it, because if we did we got a beating for it.

He used to give my mother money every week for food, but he never gave her enough. So by the end of the week, she would run out. I used to worry at the dinner table that I was eating too much. Can you believe it? We lived in that type of environment. It was horrible. I remember them fighting over some of the things that she would cook. I remember him going nuts one day and taking a package of cottage cheese and slamming it on the dining room table. It went all over the room.

There was always that insanity in our house. I was always my mother's protector. That's how I grew up: my mother's protector, my mother's confidant, my mother's friend.

My Brother Was Mine

When I was five, my father sent for his father from Romania
to stay with us for a year. My grandfather was an alcoholic.
It was my responsibility to make him hot dogs and eggs. He
would take me to kindergarten because I wasn't supposed to
cross the street, but sometimes he'd forget to pick me up. I'd
wait there and be the last one to be picked up. My father didn't
have much of a relationship with his father.

I have one younger brother. He's five years younger than I
am. When he was a baby, I knew how to change his diapers.
I knew how to warm his bottle and feed him. When I was ten,
after we came back from Vienna, I'd have dinner ready by the
time my parents got home from work. I also had cleaned the
house and vacuumed. When my brother started school, I'd
watch him after school, take care of him. My brother was mine.
He might have belonged to my parents, but he was my little
brother and I was proud of him. I loved him so much. I guess
that came easy, taking care of him. And even to this day, we're
still close. I still think he's great; I love him.

But When He Drank, Then the Emotions Came Out

Affection wasn't shown in my family. At Christmastime, if
my mother bought my father something, she would give him
the present and a kiss, and he responded like, "All right, that's
enough, cut it out." That's my old man; that's just the way he
is. He just can't show emotions. But when he drank, then the
emotions came out: the anger, the frustration, the unhappiness,
and the loneliness. My father came to this country and started
working in the sweatshops; he wanted to become successful.
That's what his life was all about for many years. That's what
he thought was the right thing for him to do. I guess he just
wanted to know that in his lifetime he would have more and
give his kids more than he got, but somewhere along the line
he got his thinking confused.

As I got older, as I became an adult, he was there for me financially. I'm twenty-nine years old now; I got into a relationship when I was about twenty-two. Richard, my lover, and I were together for seven years. That was my first longtime relationship. When I met Richard, I was in college. When I got involved with Richard, we bought a house and my parents put up the money for it. All I ever wanted was a home with a lover; I thought that would be the perfect life. I did a lot of research, constantly looking for foreclosures, something that we could buy cheap, fix up, live in, and call our own. One day, I found it, told my parents about it, and sure enough, without even seeing it, my father put up $20,000 for me to buy the house.

We bought the house and spent the next three years working on it. When we moved in, we had $90 to our name. There was no running water in the house, there were broken windows, and plaster was falling down all over the place — but it was ours. We had all our stuff in one room and we gutted the rest of the house. We'd go to our jobs and come home and work on the house till 12:30 or 1:00 in the morning. As time went on, my life became everything I didn't want it to be. It became like my parents' life: buy houses, fix them up, sell them, and make money on them. Everything I didn't want my life to be and everything I disliked about their life, my life was turning into. At this point, Richard and I had one good thing between us: we worked well together.

But our relationship was insane. At first, it was mainly verbal abuse. Richard was a manipulator, he was a man's man, and he was strong. He had been engaged to be married, he had been involved with the Mafia at one point, he dealt drugs, and he had spent time in prison. He had been arrested for stealing cars and for robbing people's houses. He spent one year in jail for punching out a county cop. The straight guys that he hung out with all looked up to him. I met Richard because I was going to school with his brother. One day he and I went to the mountains to talk, and he told me that he always had an interest in guys. Up until then I thought he was just a nice straight guy. He was only three weeks older than me, but he acted like he was ten years older. As for his jail record and all the trouble he got into, I didn't know about that and he didn't tell me. It wasn't until I got to know his brothers and sisters as the years went on that I found out these things.

At the First Red Light, I Jumped Out of the Car and Ran

I should've known he was trouble from the start, because the first time I met him he was hung over. I should have known then, but I didn't. He came up to school to see me one weekend, but he came with a girl. We went to a bar with some kids from school, and we sat at a table, totally ignoring this girl. As we were sitting there with all these people, he's playing with my leg under the table. So we made an excuse to leave and went back to my room. That was going to be the first night we would spend together, but he passed out on my roommate's bed. All the signs of alcoholism were there and I didn't see them. It wasn't until I did my Fourth Step in Al-Anon that I realized all of it was right there in front of me.

One night I went to a friend's wedding. Richard wasn't invited, so I went by myself. He came to pick me up later. When he got there he was drunk, and as we were leaving, we met somebody I had dated before. I wanted to introduce him to her, but he got extremely nuts and went and got the car. I was afraid to get into the car with him. I kept asking him, "Are you going to be okay?" He said, "Yeah, I'll be okay. Just get in, let's go home." And me, like an idiot, I got in the car and we drove onto the expressway. He was doing ninety to one hundred miles an hour. There were three cars in front of us, one in each lane, and I thought we were going to crash into the back of one of them. At the last minute, he pulled the steering wheel to the right and we went up the side, came down, and spun out in front of these cars. He continued on at that speed until almost Queens. At the first red light in Queens, I jumped out of the car and ran. I spent that night with an ex-lover. I figured this relationship was over. I never wanted to see this man again.

Nothing Was Ever Over Until the Other Person Decided It Was

The next day I had to go back to the apartment to take care of the dogs, and sure enough, there he was with flowers and apologies. So it wasn't over. Nothing was ever over until the other person decided it was. There wasn't anything that I wouldn't take. So we got back together. A few I'm-sorrys-and-take-me-to-bed and everything is okay again. A couple weeks later he found out I had slept with my ex-lover, and it's funny, as the years went on in our relationship, the only thing that ever came up was the fact that I slept with my ex-lover and how much I had hurt him. But what preceded that never came up. It was a great tool to keep me in line. It was always what was wrong with me, never what was wrong with him.

When we would have problems, he would threaten to go to court and take the house away from me. He would also threaten to tell my parents that I was gay, just like Bernie did. That was another thing that made me work on this relationship harder. I had to be whatever he wanted me to be because I didn't want my parents to find out that I was gay. I don't know what would have happened if they would have found out at that time. I'm not sure. I think I could very easily have killed myself. I was so fearful. I was already in a trap; my whole life was in a trap. I was with this man who I could only tolerate by totally ignoring and blocking out all of the bad things. And as far as my parents finding out I was gay, I was so fearful of them not wanting to see me anymore, of them not wanting me to be there.

Swollen Lymph Nodes

Since 1981 I had swollen lymph nodes. In 1983, I went to a doctor and he did a biopsy. At first he said it was low grade malignancy. Then he said it was not malignant, but it could turn malignant at any time. He didn't know what it was. So I went to another doctor, a blood doctor, and I went to her for the next two years, getting checked every three months and getting my blood drawn every six months to check my blood — to see what was going on. In 1986 I still had swollen lymph glands, and at times they were so swollen, I couldn't put my arms down at my sides. Once, I remember I had trouble walking. I didn't know what the hell was going on. Finally, one day my doctor asked me if I was gay. She asked me to have the AIDS test done.

So in April of '86, Richard and I found out we were exposed to the AIDS virus. We both tested positive. We decided we were going to learn how to eat well, take good care of ourselves, and do the best that we could.

That lasted while we were in the clinic. When we got home, Richard said to me, "Don't ever tell anybody. As for going to a support group and talking about this stuff, the answer is no." So the only person I had to talk to about it was Richard. By this point we had already bought our second home, and both homes were in both our names. I felt dependent on him and felt that there wasn't a lot I could do. So I didn't go to any support groups. I had to deal with it on my own. I did eventually talk to two friends of ours and that helped. It kept me sane. I also went to see a good doctor in the city. I did that much for myself.

That HIV Changed Everything

Around that time I was holding down a job and Richard was home working on the houses. Sometimes I'd come home and he hadn't done anything on the houses, or he'd spent half the day at the beach and my dinner wasn't ready, and I'd be a bitch. And we'd argue. But when we found out about the HIV tests, things changed. I didn't care anymore. I started losing my ambition. Up to then, our goal was that by the time we were thirty we'd have a million dollars in assets. And the way we were going, we could've done it. We might not have gotten the million, but we were well on our way. The HIV test changed everything.

I had this virus and I was killing myself on two jobs, besides working with him on weekends. It just started becoming less and less important, and I started giving up. I couldn't talk to Richard; he wouldn't talk about it. Anyway, I didn't want to talk about it. It was too painful to think about. I just started letting go. Besides, taking care of Richard was a job in itself. It was a twenty-four-hour-a-day job and it's what I thought I *had* to do. That's what my mother did with my father. She tried taking care of him in whatever manipulative way she could to get him to do what she wanted. And I did the same thing. I learned from my mother.

I decided to let Richard take care of the bills and money. I thought he'd learn that he can't spend so much money. Ha! It didn't work. Financially, things kept getting worse and we kept going more into debt. As far as the houses, I just stopped having any interest. Before that, I used to come home and Richard used to be happy. He used to work on the houses to make me happy. That's the way he was. He liked to see me happy. Now, I didn't care anymore what he was building, what he was doing.

The next two years, things got progressively worse. We had threesomes from time to time and they turned out to be disasters. In our last year, we got involved with an eighteen-year-old kid who was on cocaine. Up to that time, Richard was only drinking and smoking pot. I dealt with it, thinking it was periodic even though he smoked pot every single day. There was a point when I finally realized that I never knew who I was coming home to. If I came home to a sober Richard, I heard a man who was intelligent, who had good ideas, who I could believe in, who I could really respect, and who I could admire. But if Richard was stoned, he was stupid, and I'd get angry. So I never knew what I was coming home to. I guess that resembled my childhood: I never knew what I was going to get when I got home. Were my parents happy, was everything quiet, or was there going to be a major fight?

Well, we got involved with this kid who was on cocaine, and I tried it for the first time in my life and I thought, Ah, this is not bad. I didn't realize that Richard had had a cocaine problem years ago. He spent a year in jail and that was his way of recovering from the coke. Well, it didn't take long for him to be hooked on it and doing it every single day.

Richard wasn't always physically abusive. He smacked me a few times, and his craziness, his insanity, was enough to scare me. One night at a party he got abusive with our friends and created a big scene. That was the last straw for me. Usually he hid his temper from our friends. I couldn't take it anymore. It was like waking up from a six-year fog. I knew something was changing; I didn't know what it was. That night, I hit my emotional rock bottom. I couldn't hide it anymore. I couldn't live this life anymore.

That Whole Al-Anon Meeting, All I Did Was Cry

The next morning, I went to see Richard's sister who's in AA. She got me in touch with an Al-Anon woman, and that Sunday night I went to my first Al-Anon meeting. You know, I could never see anything bad that Richard did. I could only focus on what I did: How could *I* be so mean; how could *I* not love him; how could *I* not care about him? Look at what nice things he's doing for me. Every week he brought me nice flowers. He always told me he loved me. I didn't always tell him I loved him. I didn't know what I was feeling half the time. I got such a wonderful guy, you know; he works on all the houses, and this and that — so it had to be me. It was always how fucked up *I* am, how screwed up *I* am. Anyway, I went to this Adult Children of Alcoholics Al-Anon meeting and there were fifteen women sitting at this round table. They had this list of characteristics of adult children of alcoholics. I read that and it was like, Oh shit! They were taking turns talking and I was a mess. I was a wreck; tears were coming down my face.

They were telling my life story. It was such a shock to listen to these people talk and to finally, in all these years, say there's something real here. This pain that I felt all my life is real. There's something to say, there is a reason, and there is a cause for all this. What an awakening. That whole meeting, all I did was cry. I sat there without saying a word, just crying. At the end, they asked me if I'd like to share. It was hard, but I told them what had happened.

From that first night, I knew I was in the right place. The few months before this, I thought I was going insane. I really did. Why is it that I'm always so unhappy? Why is it that I'm just walking around like a zombie? What is going on? After I found that meeting, that was it. I went to meetings every night, every single night. I wanted everything Al-Anon could teach me.

I stayed away for four days before I went back to face Richard. I went home with *easy does it* on my mind. Whatever's going to happen is going to happen, so easy does it. I'd been working on putting a formal English garden on the house, and when I pulled up to the house, what do I see? He had bulldozed everything. I walked into the house and I was determined that, easy does it, there wasn't going to be a fight. I talked to him, and again, his emphasis was on what I had done to him. Never mind the fact that the night I left, he kicked me in the stomach and slammed me up against the wall. Never mind what he did to our friends; it's what *I* did. I simply told him I had had an emotional breakdown and I couldn't take it anymore. I told him I left because I needed help and finally realized it. I didn't say anything about the garden out in front; I just let that go. And I kept going to my meetings.

I had been going to Al-Anon for about six weeks, but I stopped. I wasn't going regularly anymore and I knew why. If I kept going, Richard and I wouldn't be together much longer. That much I knew already. So I stopped, and Richard and I continued to use cocaine and alcohol. Then one night he freaked out on me so bad that I was scared for my life, and I got in the van and left. He just went nuts. He told my parents that I was gay, which they already knew by this time. But in my mind, they didn't know anything. He told them about the AIDS virus and he told them that we owned the homes together. I remember the first conversation I had on the phone with my father. I was hiding out at a friend's house and I said to him, "Dad, if you can't accept it, I'll just leave; I'll just pack up my things and leave. You don't have to see me." But my father said, "Son, you're my son, and you're no different from your younger brother. I love you both the same. And whatever trouble you're in, whatever is going on in your life, come home and we'll talk about it. We'll deal with it as a family." It was a big change, you know, from what was going on as a kid.

And I did. I ended up having to hire lawyers to separate the houses. Richard threatened my father's life two times; he verbally abused my mother in letters, and threatened to go to her family and tell them this incredible story. He painted the windows on the house black and ripped out the carpeting 'cause that's where we had sex. It was just so insane. The only thing that kept me going was Al-Anon. I'd go to meetings one after another, every single night. I couldn't even focus on the topic. I didn't know if I was coming or going when I was sitting there. Thank God I would hear something that would keep me going until the next night.

I Dreamt of My Death and Funeral

I finally spoke to my sponsor about AIDS and he put me in touch with David. The first time I called him, I was too scared to talk to him. I said I'd call him back. When he asked if we could meet, I told him no. Three or four weeks went by before I finally called him again. My T-cell count had been dropping, probably from the breakup and everything that was going on. In a six-week period my T-cell count dropped from 192 down to 77. I was terrified. My aunt died and we had the wake and the funeral, and all I saw was the plot right next to her. Maybe I should be buried right next to her. That's all I could see, that I was going to die. So I dreamt of my death and funeral, and that was it. I couldn't get past that point.

Meanwhile, my father developed a heart condition, and he really slowed down on the booze. It changed his life a lot; he really mellowed out. My father went with me to my doctor right before I started the AZT. It's funny, you know, I always thought Richard was going to be with me through all of this. But how could he support me through anything? When I was in the hospital having my second biopsy, he was getting loaded. And he was going to support me through this?

I started the medication and had a bad reaction to the Bactrim™. That went on for a month and a half. The first two weeks were horrible; I was so sick. But I didn't realize it was the Bactrim™. I didn't realize what was happening. I also became anemic from the AZT, and so I went off the medication for three weeks. I am now on half dosage.

On the way to my doctor's office one day, I saw my reflection in the store window and I thought, "You know God, with everything that I've had to deal with — losing Richard, losing my homes, losing people that I loved in Richard's family, and having to deal with AIDS — I thank you for one thing: You gave me my life." That's how it feels. A lot of times I can really hold on to that. Without the program and what I got out of Al-Anon, I don't know where I'd be right now. I'd probably be with Richard.

I'm Learning About Adrian

The program helps me put the focus on myself and finally take control of my life, instead of living my life through somebody else, through someone else's expectations, wants, and desires. I was trying to control Richard. It was a mutual manipulation, a way of controlling each other. We were both codependent. We were both living in this tiny little world we set up for ourselves, this bubble: keeping our heads in the sand, hoping our problems would go away, hoping that maybe tomorrow would be better than this insanity.

I've been in Al-Anon since I left Richard. I go regularly, three or four times a week. For the first six months, it was more like five or six times a week. Whether it's straight meetings or gay meetings, it makes no difference. At straight meetings, they know I'm gay; they know that I'm dealing with AIDS. There's so much support, so many things that I've learned. I guess the best part of this whole thing is that I found myself. I'm learning about Adrian. I'm dealing with Adrian for the first time in my life and for that, I'm really grateful. I'm not just Richard's lover anymore. Through the program, I found myself.

I'm Going to Take an Acting Class

When I first started talking about AIDS, one woman said to me, "Adrian, we're not responsible for the outcome; we're only responsible for the effort." At first it sounded mean. In my case, the outcome could be death if I don't get this virus under control. That's how I felt, at first, when she said it, but then I realized I don't have control. God's got control over this. I'm only responsible for doing the best I can. Being on the medication that I think works, trying to lead a healthy life, trying to be the best person I can be — that's all I can do. I can only put in the effort. The outcome of this is up to God.

Another friend of mine from the program said to me, "You know, Adrian, dying is the easy part. It's living that's the hard part." It's true. It's so true. Al-Anon has helped me with everything. It's given me the Twelve Steps which I also use with AIDS. I think that's the only way to deal with it. First of all, Step One. I say I'm powerless over having this disease. There's a certain point when you just have to give it up to your Higher Power. And as for the Fourth Step inventory, it's changed my life. I look at things differently. I ask myself, What do I want out of my life? I had the choice of going back to work full time at my old company. I've chosen instead to go on social security disability. I'm going to take an acting class and a singing class. I'm going to do the things I've always wanted to do, but didn't do because of work or fears. This is my time and my life. And you know, it's the program that helps me do these things. I don't plan anymore for down the road. My big thing was that by the time I was thirty, I'd have a million dollars in assets. Well, today that just doesn't matter. When thirty comes around, and if I'm here, I'll be happy. I'm really learning to live my life for today.

There are times when I'm really scared; I'm terrified. But I know I'm not alone. I know I can talk to people about it and that's a good feeling. For years I went around thinking that Richard was the strong one and I was the weakling. But now I look at how he's dealing with the AIDS issue, and he's out there doing cocaine, partying, and getting wasted. I'm dealing with it by talking about it, going to the doctor, trying to get help, and trying to understand myself.

CHAPTER TWELVE

Sexual Compulsions

HAROLD

There's something intriguing about danger and sex. It's like this death wish saying, I'm too chicken to kill myself, but there's something satisfying about having someone else do it. Plus, it's walking on the edge. There's a lot of energy, a lot of liberation, on the edge. I'm a people pleaser and I'm so trapped most of the time, but when I walk on the tightrope and everybody — all my enablers, all my perpetrators — stands back in awe, wondering, Will he fall? They have no power over me up there.

I was incested in my mother and father's bed by my oldest brother when I was four years old. He told me it was our secret; I was never to tell anybody. Those words stick out so clear. He also told me, before he incested me, that I had to go through with this act before he would let me go out and play Cowboys and Indians with the other little kids. My brother was four-teen or sixteen years old. This went on every day for two years. For years I've carried around this guilt that I caused him to do this, that it was my fault. I felt that I seduced him. There was a lot of shame around my brother. I couldn't face him because I felt I had done this awful thing to him. When I was six years old I went to elementary school, and as far as I know, the incest with my brother stopped.

My father and my brother's father were best friends. My mother was pregnant with my oldest brother when my father married my mother. Twelve years later he found out that my brother wasn't his child. At that point, his alcoholism progressed very rapidly.

My mother gave my brother all the attention; she was obsessed with my brother. Then I became the obsession. When I was born, my mother wanted a little girl; she had two boys already. She bought me pink clothing and treated me as if I were a girl. She braided my hair; she kept it long. She put me in all the little girl's clothing. I think I would have done anything to please my mother. To win my mother's love, I was willing to do anything, even be that little girl that she wanted. When my mother finally had a girl four years after me, she dropped me into the lap of my brother. She and my father became obsessed with my sister.

At the age of four, five, and six, I didn't play Cowboys and Indians anymore; I would hump on my friend's legs and back, expose my penis, and do all kinds of strange behaviors for a little child. I was emulating what my brother had done, I guess.

It was an alcoholic household, both Dad and Mom. Her disease progressed later, but my father was an active alcoholic when I was a child and my mother certainly was an enabler. So when I came on the scene, the scene was entirely crazy: my mother was carrying this secret about this child not being my father's, and she was a compulsive gambler; my father was a compulsive overeater, and he was an alcoholic.

The Hero, the Scapegoat, and the Little Girl

I also had another brother who lived with my grandmother. He was the hero of the family. He was very smart in school and planned on going into the military. He ended up being a hero. My other brother realized he just couldn't compete with this and he chose the other available role, which was acting out — the scapegoat. Of course everybody was distracted from what was really going on in the house. One brother acting out, saying look at me over here; my other brother getting praise, saying look at me, look how I'm shining. I had a role to slip into too. I was to slip into being something that I wasn't — a little girl.

It got crazier and crazier in the house and I started having sex with cousins who would sleep over. Eventually, I had girlfriends, but they came late in high school. My mother's demands changed. All of a sudden she wanted a normal little boy, someone that wouldn't draw negative attention from the neighbors. So then I started dating this girl, figuring that would change me and heal what had happened. It didn't work.

My brother's father in New York invited me up for a visit. He was like a stepfather. I was twenty, but emotionally, I was a twelve-year-old kid, if not younger. I was there less than two days before he exposed his penis and wanted me to touch it. I freaked out and ran to a friend of the family who I called an aunt. She lived in Brooklyn. I was crying and screaming hysterically, and I told her the story. She didn't tell my mother; everybody was into keeping secrets.

Piccolo in the Air Force

I didn't have my first drink till my first year in a junior college. I got a scholarship to a junior college in my hometown. I went one semester and discovered drinking. I couldn't attend the second semester because I couldn't get it together. And so I joined the air force.

I joined special services. I played flute and piccolo. It was my escape, and I was very good at it. It got me out of the household and away from this woman I was to marry. I realized that that would have been a big mistake. I was very promiscuous in the military and my drinking took off too.

One Christmas, I went to visit this aunt in Brooklyn, and we found her boyfriend dead in his apartment — alcoholism. I discovered the body. It was a traumatic experience and I started to drink heavily and self-destructively. I would drink round-the-clock.

That's when I started going in and out of military mental institutions. I started breaking windows, throwing furniture through windows, almost killing people. They would take me out in a straitjacket. I remember going on a trip with the air force band. I got drunk and kicked all the drinks off the bar in the NCO club. The MPs chased me, hit me on the head, and I ended up in some padded cell. From there they sent me back to the military mental institution in Virginia.

I discovered drugs at this time too — acid and hallucinogens. And then I started attracting people on base who would hurt me, who were, I guess, sadists. I have a heavy masochistic streak in me. These guys would beat me up and take what I owned. I must have been putting out some kind of nonverbal messages. They'd stop by my room, have sex, and then beat me up and take what money I had. This was a pattern set up by my brother. He took my money too, and he was also very violent. With my brother, the violence wasn't actual violence; it was threats. But I saw him beat up other people. Those threats were real. I was not mistaken. He went on to be a gangster in New York City, where he's killed people and been shot many times himself. As a child, I knew that he was dangerous.

I repeated this pattern a lot. I have a broken nose now because this convict out on furlough, who I had an affair with, knocked me down a flight of stairs and broke my nose. I equated this with some kind of weird love. After all, my brother was the first person who ever showed any kind of physical affection for me. My mother and father never touched me.

There's Something Intriguing About Danger and Sex

I was very violent when I got drunk. I would always approach the largest, meanest person in the bar and I would curse him out and hit him, and then he would break my nose or knock me out or try to kill me. I'm not that big a guy. Often, I would come out of a blackout and have people trying to kill me.

People were telling me, "You're going to have to go because somebody's coming over to beat you up. Do you know what you did last night?"

There's something intriguing about danger and sex. It's like this death wish saying, I'm too chicken to kill myself, but there's something satisfying about having someone else do it. Plus, it's walking on the edge. There's a lot of energy, a lot of liberation, on the edge. I'm a people pleaser and I'm so trapped most of the time, but when I walk on the tightrope and everybody — all my enablers, all my perpetrators — stands back in awe, wondering, Will he fall? They have no power over me up there.

Once, on Mother's Day, a bartender eighty-sixed me because I was insulting his patrons. I said, "If I have to leave, everybody's got to leave." So I left the bar and stuck my arm through a very thick, plate glass window. I almost lost my arm. The miracle of microsurgery saved it, but I lost the feeling in one hand, and I will never be a musician again. That's part of the sabotage. I'm afraid of success. I was given the wonderful gift of music and I did everything in my power to destroy it. Alcohol had become more important than music. Today, I'm a waiter and I hate it. I feel like I have all this stuff bottled in me and no outlet.

The Gay Life

After eight months in the military I moved to New York City. That's when I went into the gay life. That's when my alcoholism really progressed. I felt I could drink all the time because I didn't have somebody in the family watching me. My self-destructive relationships escalated also. I was picking up very dangerous, frightening people. I thought that maybe it would be one of these guys that would do me in. I was going to the warehouses, the piers, into these dark trucks. People were constantly mugged in those places. Plus, I started heavy acid and cocaine use, taking it till I passed out, till I really just went off. That was part of my death wish too.

Alcohol eased the pain. As far as incest was concerned, alcohol helped me hide from the pain, stuff it for a while. Then it turned against me. It took more and more alcohol, and sex, to stay away from this incredible amount of pain.

I had never heard of sex being a drug, but few days passed without my having had sex one, two, or three times and masturbating all the time.

I was living in Manhattan on the twenty-fourth floor of this high-rise with an illegal alien from England, straight and alcoholic, and a topless go-go dancer from a well-to-do upstate New York family, also an alcoholic. The guy was a bartender, so I was the only one holding a nine-to-five job. I was intrigued by their life, their ability to go out and party all night. Of course, I would go out with them. So, it was only a matter of time before I lost my job.

Once I lost my job, they all applauded, the party was now about to begin, that is, until I couldn't pay my share of the rent and food. Then they were upset. One night I went into a blackout and tried to kill myself. I tried to jump out of the window, twenty-four stories high. My roommates stopped me. I called my mother in Louisiana. I have no idea what I told her, but she sent me money to buy a ticket. I left my furniture and my apartment and went to Louisiana the following day.

There, I started therapy. I, by no means, stopped drinking because I didn't think drinking was the problem. I just thought I was crazy, which I certainly was. When I moved to Louisiana, I also started to drive. Alcohol and driving, the lethal combination that could make my death wish come true.

One evening, I had taken Quaaludes and had drank a lot, and I was going in and out of blackouts when I left this club at about 2:00 a.m. I drove to this railroad crossing and I either fell asleep or passed out. I went through the crossbar, woke up from the sound of a train, panicked, and slammed on the brake. Only I hit the accelerator and the car leaped into the train. It rained glass on me and sucked the car into the train.

Luckily, I was thrown out. I got a scratch on my neck that bled all over. Hours later, the police found me walking around with blood all over me.

When I told my therapist, her hair stood on her head and she asked me if I was drinking that night. I said that I might have had one or two. She suggested an alcohol rehab program. I went in and they told me I had to attend five AA meetings before they would admit me. Right away, at the first meeting, I identified with people. I heard my story all over the place. I felt so comfortable in AA. I took to AA like a duck to water, and then I started outpatient treatment.

I Drank Perrier and Started Taking People's Inventory in the Bar

I stayed in AA for nine months. I read the Big Book from cover to cover and I thought I had the secret: I knew how to stay sober. So I went back to my bar, quit therapy, stopped going to AA, and I didn't drink. I drank club soda and Perrier, and I started taking people's inventory in the bar. I knew how to solve all their problems. Well, what happened was, the bartender made a mistake and put somebody else's drink in front of me, and I was so busy talking that I grabbed the drink and chugged it. When I realized it was a scotch and water or rum and coke or whatever it was, I screamed, "Oh no, this can't be!" I went on and on and turned around and said, "What the hell, I've done it." And I ordered a drink. All my friends just started applauding; they were so happy I was back.

I stayed out there for another year and a half. During that year and a half, I got three DWIs in four months. By the time I got back into the program, I was going to court a lot and serving time in prison.

I'm sober five years and seven months now. I decided to do it the program's way, by trusting. When I started the court stuff, though, I was angry, furious, and resistant. I had a court date for my last DWI, and I was doing time at the stockade for the other ones. I used to ride my bicycle to the town the stockade was in. One day, I showed up at the stockade and got ready to go to court because they told me they would give me a ride to the courthouse. They called me in with the other prisoners and put me in manacles. Everyone else was in prison uniforms and I was in my civilian clothes, and we get into the van. There's an art to fitting into a van while wearing chains. Anyway, we get to the courthouse, in my hometown, where I grew up, and they put us in a holding cell. The court is designed so you have to go through the public to get to court. They fling the door open and make an announcement, saying, "Step back, step back, the prisoners are coming through!" And there we were, coming through, and there I am, one from the end. And as soon as I step out, wouldn't you know, I saw one of my classmates, plus a whole group of people who knew me. They said, "That's Harold. What did he do?" I saw them and burst into tears. This guy behind me shouted, "Aw, shut up fag." And I started weeping uncontrollably. They put us up in the prisoners' gallery, and I turned it over. I said, "God, I'm yours. I can't go on with this. I'm yours. Here I am, whatever you want." I said the Serenity Prayer and at the end of the prayer, "Thy will not mine be done."

A Chain Gang in Louisiana: My Worst Nightmare

I pleaded guilty and the judge sentenced me to prison. I went back and did my time, and a funny thing happened: the rest of my life began to turn around. I was doing road work; we were digging up ground with the road crew, like a chain gang. This was my worst nightmare and it had come true. One hundred degree weather in Louisiana during the summer!

Anyway, I had mentioned I knew how to sew. I had gone to a fashion institute and learned how to make patterns and sew, so I mentioned it in passing. I came in one morning and the guard said, "You're not going on the road crew. You're going to save state money and repair the prisoners' uniforms." The prison had three major sizes. Guys would swim in these large uniforms, so I put darts in the back and tucked the sides; I would give them designer uniforms. It was hysterical. They brought me a portable radio. Even the officers came in. Their heavy keys would make holes in their pockets, and I would reinforce the material. At the end of my stay, the guys didn't want to see me go and I didn't want to go. But I said, "This is ridiculous. I have to get out of here." I couldn't believe that I didn't want to leave.

Escape from Home

As my father's disease progressed, my mother brought twin beds into their bedroom. When he stopped bathing, she moved him out and moved me in. I was about fourteen at this time. I became her surrogate husband. She started telling me things that normally a wife would tell her husband. She would walk around in the bedroom with no bra on. This became the norm. I had no privacy; there I would be, in my underwear. This went on for years. I moved away from home when I went into the military, and I moved back when I was about to commit suicide in New York. And I moved right back into the bed next to my mother. I moved right back into surrogate husband, confidant.

When I got out of prison, I had a sponsor in AA, a woman who told me not to go back home. "You can't go back there," she said. She told me I didn't have to go back there *that night*. We were at a coffee shop talking, and I thought she was the craziest person on earth. How could somebody just not go home? I was so hooked into this family; it was like trying to extricate a fly from a spider's web, like a fly trying to extricate himself. Somebody else can; he can't.

But I moved in with somebody else that night. The following day, someone went with me and helped me collect my clothes. My mother threw a fit. She felt like she was losing something; she felt betrayed. And I felt that I was disloyal, betraying the family, that I was a bad boy, that I was going to die, and that nothing good was ever going to happen in my life. I come from the background of "honor thy mother and thy father." Oh God, that crap was drilled into my head. It's wonderful if you're coming from a healthy family, but coming from a dysfunctional family, this stuff ought not apply. It's very sick. I have to keep telling myself over and over that if I wouldn't have gotten out of that incestuous, abusive house, I wouldn't be sitting here today. I'd be dead or in an insane asylum, certainly not sitting here without drink or drug, taking care of myself.

Then I started to accumulate time in AA. I started to work. I got my own place. Things kept getting better in some respects, but the incest stuff was not addressed. The drinking was arrested, but the incest stuff got crazy.

Finally, I moved back to New York to be exposed to all the Twelve Step programs. I've tried to address many issues. I work at them one day at a time. I go to AA, which is my primary program. I also go to Al-Anon, Debtor's Anonymous, Incest Survivors, Sexual Compulsives Anonymous, and ACOA [Adult Children of Alcoholics]. It's helping. I'm in therapy for being HIV positive. I have not yet been to incest therapy. I figure this is only the beginning. It's a miracle that I'm sitting here, still being able to go on and hope.

Dismantle the Death Wish

I believe that if I don't address my incest issues, I'm bound to succeed in this death wish via AIDS or some other form. My thing would be to address the incest stuff, forgive myself, and dismantle the death wish so that I can put a life wish there in its place — a life wish that will enhance my immune system. Otherwise, I will forever repeat the self-destructive behavior in one form or another. If I don't deal with incest, I'll survive in my death wish. AIDS would be the perfect way to go because of how I feel toward my genitals — they were so violated. These are parts of my body that, at times, I would love to cut out.

They've created a lot of problems for me, a lot of pain. I used to think that if I didn't have them maybe my brother wouldn't have molested me. I used to think those places were diseased.

I knew, early in sobriety, I had to seek answers to *all* my problems. I was sober, working a program, but not addressing the incest stuff: the death wishes, the sexual compulsivity. I was sober and still acting out, wracked with guilt, remorse, shame, and wondering why I could never get rid of all the anger. I see the anger from the incest as equivalent to crabgrass. You can snap it off at the top, but it just pops up again. You have to dig down and get the root. I would do a Fourth Step with the surface, and all I was doing was snapping tops off crabgrass and the crabgrass kept coming. I see what happens when crabgrass gets out of hand — nothing can grow. You're stifled emotionally, spiritually, and feel hopeless from the snipping. Hope comes in when you get at the core issues.

I found out I was HIV positive around the end of January. I'm a food handler, and they require physical exams where I work. During the exam, they discovered a lesion, a black spot on my brown skin. Two or three weeks later, I took the HIV test and I was positive. Of course, I wrote my obituary. I was dying. The next thing was to jump in the grave. I had buried myself already. Luckily, shortly after that, they started this HIV SCA [Sexual Compulsives Anonymous] meeting. Like there are no coincidences. The support I needed was coming out of the woodwork. I put myself in the right places, and people would say things I needed to hear. The key for me was openness, being open to hear. I was honest enough to realize I needed help, that I wasn't emotionally all right. I was willing to find out the information, to get directions, addresses, telephone numbers — whatever I needed to take the next step.

Around this time, Bernie Siegel came out with *Love, Medicine & Miracles*. I read it and realized that my doctor's attitude toward my HIV status, and AIDS in general, could kill me. So I sat with my doctor and told him my story — about my alcoholism, where I came from, the alcoholic household — and

I asked him how he felt. He seemed interested. I needed to be more than just a passive patient with him. The book, and my background in AA, had me ready to disclose. Now, he sees me as a human being as well as a patient. I asked him to read Bernie Siegel's book. He said several other patients had asked him to read it too. I attend a lot of seminars and forums and read a lot of positive information, and I bring it to my doctor. All of a sudden, I'm not taking my life for granted.

Over Here Are Crocodiles. Over There Are Lions.

All my life my household was chaotic, unorderly, full of confusion. But from an early age, I discovered I liked doctors' offices. They were always so neat and orderly, sterile. And people are there to wait on you, give you attention. Today, when I feel I am needy, I have to be careful that I don't do something self-destructive in order to have someone in a doctor's office or a hospital hold me, touch me, look into my eyes, hold my throat. I feel that pressure every time I walk into a clinic. But that's changing too.

When they found the lesion on my leg, I showed it to my doctor and then saw a dermatologist who did a biopsy. Three specialists looked at the results. Two said KS; one said possibly KS, possibly psoriasis. They took another biopsy and same results: two yes, one maybe. Meanwhile, I'm going to meetings every day, sharing these painful feelings, like anger: I'm angry at this disease, angry at my mother, my brother, and angry at God. I was working what I thought was a good AA program and this had to be some hateful, horrible, cruel joke God was playing on me.

Anger and fear. Maybe more like terror, like walking through something physical, like terror had taken on a physical form. Like being in a jungle with vines in your face and you have to hack them away and try to find a way out. Over here are crocodiles — drinking. Over there are lions — suicide. Oh, I couldn't go there. Then there was my dark side, with a smile, glad that I was HIV positive. After all, there are lots of benefits from this. It's freeing. I was ready to get out of this shitty life. It would be over, and I would no longer worry about where I would move when this sublet is over or have to put up with this unbearable job or struggle with these addictions. It would get me sympathy, pity, empathy, attention — the things I equate with love. I wouldn't have to worry about why I didn't finish college. This was the perverse side I never told anyone about. How do you tell someone that some part of you gets off on all this, doing the ultimate, satisfying the death wish?

A Breakdown or a Breakthrough?

Since then, I've met many other men who are HIV positive, who have AIDS and ARC, and I've heard their experience, strength, and hope. I've healed a lot. I've had a breakthrough. At first, I thought it was a breakdown. People were ready to take me to Bellevue.

You see, what happened was, I was overwhelmed at the Names Project Quilt in Washington, D.C. I was gone two days, came back, and fell apart. The last day I was in Washington, I was going back to see the rest of the quilt. I was leaving from Dupont Circle, where I had spent the night with a friend. On the way to the Metro, the subway, we met three ladies: two old and one young, who didn't know how to get into the Metro. They asked me to help them go to the Elipse. It didn't dawn on me where they were going. I thought that anything they had to say or do was trivial compared to what I was there for. I was irritated by their intrusion. But I helped them anyway and they tagged along with me. When I got off the Metro, they got off. I headed to the Quilt and they followed. Then it dawned on me. One woman turned to me and said, "Can you help me find my son's panel?" Well, I get a lump in my throat. I got a directory and we went to find her son's panel.

The woman, her sister, and her niece had all flown in from some Midwest town to see this panel. The mother started to cry in my arms. She said "Son, I don't mean to burden you; you can leave if you want to." I said, "Ma'am, you're not burdening me. I'm here for this." I told her I was waiting for biopsy results, that I was HIV positive. She held me; we stood there a long time. When we separated, I looked in her face; something had changed. She went back and grabbed her friend and took pictures of the panel.

We stayed together for two or three hours. The mother was overwhelmed by the size of the quilt. Everywhere she looked there were families and clusters. She came from a town so small they didn't have street signs, and I knew when this woman went back she wouldn't fit in the same slot. My life was changed too. She's been in my thoughts for quite awhile, how we touched one another. Love overcomes a lot of things: homophobia, racism, health issues. I never got her name or address.

They left and I was left alone. Then I started to get overwhelmed and, eventually, I broke through. It was cathartic and very healing, like the floodgates had opened up. I had lost my father a year before and never grieved that, and many of my friends have died of AIDS. When the floodgates opened, I was overwhelmed. So much unfinished grief work. Because of this breakthrough, I feel differently now.

This was one of those stories God had His hand in. I didn't realize my purpose was to help those ladies; in fact, I was annoyed that they were bothering me about the Metro. Everything is in Divine order.

I'm realizing more and more that people are in my journey, and people cross my path not a moment too soon. My faith is growing in the Divine scheme of things. This is all a very important part of my journey. I believe I can come out of this; I don't have to die from this. It was in my journey; it was there down the road from the beginning. It was meant to open me more as a channel to connect with other humans. It's hard to put words to this: I can only throw pebbles at it. I feel very good inside now. I really do.

Eventually, the pathology report came back negative — it wasn't KS. My hope was stronger. Only then did I realize the amount of stress I had been under.

My life is pretty amazing now. There's still a lot of uncertainty, but my health has been good. I'm finishing college and I'm going on a dream vacation to Europe this summer. I have a life wish now that's real strong.

TOMMY

Since I was three years old, my mother knew I was gay. I was always sexually active with the neighborhood boys. I never had the chance to come out; I've always just been out. I never understood men who had families and married and then came out in their thirties. A lot of them were my clients.

Two and one half years ago, when I was living in Oregon, I had pneumocystis. The doctor there told me to go to San Francisco, where I'd get better care. I was pretty frightened and flipped out. My family got involved and they were basically pasted on the ceiling. I was using; they were using. It was high drama and I went into a big depression. I thought I'd be dead in a month. I guess it's typical to panic. That was two and a half years ago. In the meantime, I got sober. I've been sober nine months and three weeks today.

I come from a totally dysfunctional family. I left home at thirteen. I spent a lot of time on the streets, a lot of time in a lot of different cities up and down the West Coast, the Southwest, and the Gulf. Since the age of thirteen, I've been in and out of jail and in and out of juvenile detention homes — mostly for prostitution.

My first major offense happened when I was eighteen. I was having a bad day. I had just flown back into Houston from Seattle, and I got into it with a couple of officers. I hit one of them over the head with a bottle of champagne — hurt him pretty bad. As a result, I had to go home for six months and the court ordered me into a youth drug and alcohol program. If I got picked up again, they said I would spend the rest of my time with the big boys.

The second time I got into major trouble was four or five years later. Again, I hurt a guy real bad by hitting him over the head with a bottle of booze. He went into intensive care, and I was taken to detox. They didn't know if he was going to live, or if I was going to be charged with murder. I was in detox for three weeks and in a halfway house for three weeks.

This was my second introduction to treatment. I was twenty-two at the time.

When they let me out I thought, I can't deal with this; I need to go back to California. I was always on the run. The longest time I stayed in one place was maybe a year. I was always afraid. I had a hard time being stable.

I Picked People Who Were Like My Abusive Stepfather

My last series of geographic cures started when I was in Oregon. From there I moved to Los Angeles and from there I moved to Phoenix. After I was diagnosed and went through this panic thing, I decided I'd better make some changes. But I didn't know how to get help. None of my relationships had lasted more than three months, so I figured the solution to my problems was to settle down with one person. I picked people who were like my abusive stepfather. I got into violent situations that I knew wouldn't work out, so it would be *safe* for me. Up until now, it's been the same thing over the years — abusive situations.

The way I understand it now is that I was sexually abused as a child, I sexually abused myself, and I have this sexually transmitted, incurable disease. I've carried a lot of guilt and shame around all my life. I still feel most comfortable in abusive situations because that's what I know. I'm trying to work on that now.

Besides finding the man of my dreams who was going to solve all my problems, my reasons for moving to Phoenix were to cut out the working — prostitution, hustling, hooking — and cut out the drugs. I've always done major drug changes, so this was a familiar theme. When I was twenty-two and strung out on MDA, I switched to coke and alcohol. This time I wanted to get away from the coke and alcohol.

There I was in Phoenix, the place where all this is supposed to happen, and this friend of mine mails me a quarter ounce of MDA. I took two days to go through it. It was just like I never stopped from when I was twenty-two. There I was, trying to get off drugs and stop hustling, and I do all this MDA. Two days later, I wake up with three guys. I had pulled a trick. Everything was the same. I had one client in Phoenix, one in Los Angeles, one in Seattle, and I was living in a drug dealer's house. I wanted all these changes, and in one week, I was set up with what I'd been doing my whole life, the same repetitious stuff. Plus, as much as I tried to deny it, I knew what my health situation was. I was beginning to snap.

So I woke up with these three guys and thought, This is too much. What I did remember of the night was pretty sleazy — I felt awful. If there would have been a bridge in Phoenix, I would have jumped off it. As it was, I couldn't find my car and I had to call a cab. When I got home and walked into the house, I saw that it was a wreck. I had had parties every night, there were needles everywhere, the house was trashed, and I didn't remember most of what had happened over the previous five days. I was in tears and thought, I can't go on like this.

My girlfriend, who I was living with, knew I had AIDS and that we were both alcoholics and addicts — that's never been a secret for me. We cried together and then I called a treatment center. The woman on the phone said, "If you can get here, we'll worry about the financial part later." She really Twelfth Stepped me into treatment. I told my girlfriend, "You've got to take me there." Anyway, Chris was drinking and high, and we kept getting lost and calling for directions. But we finally made it. I had a shoulder bag and that was it. When I left Arizona ten days later, that's all I left with. I had my friends sell my car and everything else, and I paid cash for treatment. I really wanted it. I was real serious about living. I was fed up and I knew I needed some help.

The Head Dooda of the Treatment Center Said, "You Have to Leave."

I didn't let them know for a couple days about my diagnosis. They tested me for HIV anyway — state law. They took my blood, and I said I wanted to talk to my counselor. There were a couple of gay counselors there, and I told one of them I had AIDS. It caused quite a ruckus. The treatment center was owned by a big company from another state, and all the executives flew in, everyone. The staff said they'd have to deal with this sooner or later, but the head dooda said, "You have to leave." They gave me forty-eight hours. I was real fortunate that my counselor was understanding. He found a treatment center that would take AIDS, ARC, and HIV people. Otherwise, he said I could go into a hospital.

That's how I ended up here. Now that I'm sober, I'm *feeling* everything. Because I'm not using drugs, I'm starting to deal with emotional things from my past. That can be depressing sometimes. There are things that I've done that I'm very shameful about. I try not to focus on them. I'm not that person today. It still hurts when people talk. Sometimes I can joke about it, about being a tramp. Other times, I take it in and get offended and really hurt. It bothers me to see people or be around people who are hooking; it really hurts a lot.

My Mother Was Like a Little Girl

Recently, I spent three weeks with my family. That's the most I've ever interacted with them since I was thirteen. My mother is on her third marriage and this one seems to be working. My father, her first husband, and my stepfather, her second husband, were both very abusive. Not only was I sexually assaulted by my stepfather, but for ten years I got the shit kicked out of me and watched my mother get beat up too. He was a manic depressive and an alcoholic. I take after my mother: throughout my use, I found abusive men too.

In addition to abuse from my stepfather, I was also molested in the swim team locker room when I was five years old.

Since I was three years old, my mother knew I was gay. I was always sexually active with the neighborhood boys. I never had the chance to come out; I've always just been out. I never understood men who had families and married and then came out in their thirties. A lot of them were my clients.

Sometimes I feel like I'm a walking time bomb. When I spoke at an NA meeting in Chicago, I broke down and cried — almost for the first time. It's very unusual for me to show emotion. While I was a child, my whole family was very emotional and always yelling or in tears. It seemed like my mother was in tears all the time. So I learned to never show my emotions.

When I was growing up, my mother was like a little girl. She's always been like a little girl to me. She's done a lot of growing herself, right along with me. She and I have a wonderful relationship. She's always been there for me, but she doesn't know how to handle me; I've always been my own person. She's more like my sister than she is my mother. It's real neat for her to finally achieve a happy relationship with her third husband. I'm glad to see her happy. I spent a lot of time caretaking her. I've always felt so sad for my mother. I've always wanted her to be happy because I've seen her in so much pain. And I give her credit. When she left my natural father, she moved into a mother and children's home and put herself through school. Her problem was, she kept picking the same kind of man. It's in her blood to pick the same types.

My father was an identical alcoholic asshole to my stepfather. He beat her up while she was six months pregnant with me. Chemical dependency runs rampant in our family. I started out with marijuana in the sixth grade, and by the eighth grade I was playing around with pills. I didn't get into alcohol until I was eighteen. I was into speed, pills, acid, and all that good stuff first.

My Family and All the Adults in It Were Victims of Victims

I have gotten over a lot of my childhood, done a lot of letting go. I did that when I was about twenty years old. I spent a lot of time carrying all that around, and one day I thought, Just forget it; this is a waste. I understand that it was a very dysfunctional family and we were all victims. My family and all the adults in it were all victims of victims. Truly, they didn't know how to do anything else. It's been just in the last ten years that we've begun to understand any of this. American society is dysfunctional. We're all walking messes. Like my brother: he's forty, he's manic depressive, alcoholic, and really in turmoil.

I don't want to dig up a lot of my family stuff, not at nine months sobriety. I've got plenty of other things to do. I have to deal with Tommy and who Tommy is and Tommy's past life and habits and what Tommy likes to do. I have to take care of my addictions and my alcoholism. It's all the same being an addict or an alcoholic. I don't care if you're into heroin or cocaine or pot, it's all the same to me. I know that I will use any kind of chemical I can to cover one for the other. Look at my life: I came down off the MDA after being strung out on that for years and look what I used in its place — gin and vodka.

John Doe Name Tags on My Hospital Sticker

It's just by the grace of God that I'm alive, because by all accounts, I should be dead. I've overdosed a couple times and awakened to John Doe name tags on my hospital sticker; I didn't know where I was and they didn't know who I was. I've been in and out of jail. I've almost killed two people; I've almost been killed myself. I've been in and out of hospitals. I have been both sexually and violently beaten to the point of nothing. I don't know why I'm still alive. I've gotten thirty stitches in my head. I've had my face kicked in and had plastic surgery on my nose, which was then broken again. I've had my hand bitten — you can still see the scar on my hand from the bite. I've had my eyes stitched back up because I'd been kicked. I've been raped and mugged more than once. I used to say there was nothing better than getting totally out of it and then being dragged down the street by some King Kong — get a high and kiss the pavement, so to speak. I've been in car wrecks, really repetitious stuff. And yet, I'm alive. And now I'm dealing with Tommy. I'm dealing with staying clean and sober. I'm dealing with my AIDS issues.

And here I am. I haven't done anything with my life. I think my life has been real sad. I don't have any skills. I did get my GED, but that's the only education I have. All my education has been learned on the street. I'm living very modestly now. It's really been hard for me to live on a limited income. I get $203 a month plus $67 worth of food stamps. But I manage to do a lot of things that are important to me. I go to the doctor; I do alternative healing things; I meditate. I've gotten into spirituality and begun work on things I've neglected my whole life. I know that I am somebody. I mean that in a positive, self-affirming way. I'm not being grandiose.

Everything that's happened to me in the last nine months has basically been a miracle. I can't believe it. I went from treatment right into this AIDS housing situation, and it's working very well. It's also the hardest thing I've ever done. There are times, now, when I'd like to throw it all away for one last good time: go to Miami and live it up for the winter. I could do it, but I don't know if I'd live through it. I have a survival instinct built into me; we surviving alcoholics do.

I Helped Start a "Working Girls" Drop-In Center

It's real important for me to share, to let people in. A couple of people in the last few weeks, friends in recovery, said I needed to find someone to let loose with, someone to hold me, that type of a thing. I need to let my emotions go. I can't do that yet. Maybe I will. It's an issue of trust. I've never trusted anyone. I don't think anything will last because nothing ever has. I wouldn't let someone hold me; just the thought is very frightening to me. I have to have my walls around me, and I may have them till I die.

But I am getting support. In fact, when I first got out of treatment, I helped start a "working girls" drop-in center for male prostitutes. By doing this, I set up a support system for myself. I know I can go there and I can talk. It's hard to talk about prostitution at AA meetings. But I do get a lot of support at my AA meetings. I also go to NA meetings and to straight AA meetings.

Last week, I was twenty-six and clean and sober. I was diagnosed when I was twenty-four, so I've dealt with this for a long time. Most of the time, I was flipping in and out of denial and moving from city to city. I was going to make sure I wasn't going to die from AIDS. My alcohol and other drug addictions were going to kill me before AIDS was. Now, at least I have a fair chance of letting AIDS get me first. Before that happens, I have a chance to find out who Tommy is.

Actually, AIDS is a positive thing. I'm grateful for it. Most of the people around me are loving and positive. If it wasn't for AIDS, I think I'd still be out there. I put myself in this AIDS housing in order to not deny my AIDS status. I thought the best way to stay present with having AIDS would be to live with other people who have AIDS too.

I've Got My Spirituality Back

My favorite part of the program is Step Two: "Came to believe that a Power greater than ourselves could restore us to sanity." I've got my spirituality back. I'm Jewish and I've become involved with the Jewish community. It's like, how can you be an alcoholic, a street person, come from an abusive family, and be Jewish? Well, come on. My mother came from an abusive family. I've talked to the rabbis and gotten a lot of support from them around the issue of abuse. I've also joined the Gay and Lesbian Jewish Group. Most of them know I'm recovering, and they all know I've got AIDS.

I'm a survivor. I really don't think I'm going to go right away. I know it's a day at a time, but I do plan things now.

JONATHAN

I don't want to be a sick person. That's no role; that's no identity at all. That's why I started calling myself a "gay-activist-singer-songwriter-and-poet," because everyone has to be something, and to be a gay-activist-singer-songwriter-and-poet is a whole lot more positive than to be an "AIDS victim."

I'm the son of two very wonderful people who got married too young. We were rather poor and lived in a two bedroom house. Seven people, a dog, and a cat in a very small house. The only thing I ever heard my parents argue about was money.

I have a longer history of sexually dependent behavior than chemically dependent behavior. I had a lot of sexual experiences in high school, most of them anonymous, most in public places like rest rooms. I went to rest rooms as a kid — started at about thirteen — because it was an easy way to deal with my sexuality. It took care of the desires I felt, and yet I could still get back on the bus and go home and be the perfect high school boy. The people were always older. I was young and cute and thin; they were older and mature — or so I thought.

I knew that because it was public sex, it was wrong or bad. I guess I probably felt pretty bad, but I didn't see it as abuse. I was the one who decided I was going to go do that. Legally it is abuse, but do I feel it was? I suppose I felt like an element of all my acting-out sexual behavior has been abusive. I don't need to single out those years that I was under-age. I don't think the fact that I was under-age made it more abusive; when I got older, it was still abusive. What I mean is, the whole behavior is abusive. It's not loving, caring, and intimate. It was fantasy sex.

He Was Older and Very Dark

One day, while cruising a Target store, I met this rather attractive Frenchman. He lived with three under-aged kids, slept with all of them, and had a lover as well. I hung out with them and went to a gay bar with them. The three kids all attended my high school — one girl and two boys — but I met them through him. When I think about it now, it was a crazy situation — sick. He was older and very dark; that attracted me to him. And there were messages that we had to keep this secret. I always wanted to believe that this was a phase I would grow out of, that it would be different some day. That's really how I saw it. I really believed I'd get to a point where I'd be tired of being homosexual. Then I got AIDS.

It wasn't till I got to college that I learned how well alcohol and addictive sexual behavior worked together. Since my sexual needs were seemingly being met, I didn't seek out any permanent or intimate sexual relations. Unfortunately, now I don't equate sex with intimacy. I don't know what they're like together. I did a lot of drunk, anonymous sex. This was 1981 or 1982, when we were just hearing things about AIDS. Soon, I quit school and spent a year as an intern in a professional theater company. I also worked as a nurse's aide in the psych ward of a hospital; I was supposedly a mental health counselor.

My First Trip to AA

In the fall of '84, I made my first trip to AA. I stayed sober for a few months, slipped, stayed sober for six or nine months after that, relapsed, stayed sober for a year. In some ways, my recent relapse is all about AIDS. In some ways, it's not about AIDS at all, but part of a pattern from the past. AIDS intensifies it, but it's really not because of AIDS. It's a pattern I've had; AIDS is an excuse. I go along emotionally, spiritually, physically, and program-wise very successfully and very happily. And then my will usually takes over; I stop going to meetings, and I relapse. I have never, have absolutely never been able to use anything, any mood-altering substance, and not have severe, awful consequences.

Pneumocystis, Meningitis, and Ativan

I was diagnosed in 1987 with pneumocystis. It took me three weeks in the hospital to get over that and then, almost immediately, I got spinal meningitis. I came away from those two hospitalizations seriously addicted to Ativan, a wonder drug. Take two of those, and everything is fine. That addiction continued for about three months before my doctor caught on to the fact that I was seriously abusing and refused to renew my prescription.

My doctor is learning about chemical dependency. "You've been taking too much Ativan," he said. And I said, "Well, I guess some days I take too much." And he said, "No, no, no. We figured it out here and you've been taking between six and eight a day." And he said, "No more." I had enough to wean off. In some ways, I felt so glad he caught me; I'm glad he's learning about chemical dependency. I thought, Oh God, you noticed; you're not just pushing pills on people; you noticed that I was hooked. Just a little while ago, he told me that he's learned that alcoholic people need to go to AA. "You need to go to your meetings. You know what you need to do." And that's all he said.

Taking the Wrong Bus to Detox

This last drunk started when I was downtown. I had been using for about a month, and then one day, I had lunch at a bar and stayed and drank all afternoon. Much later, I tried to get on a bus to get home, and I got on the wrong bus. I got sick on myself while on the bus, got off, and sat on someone's front step. They called the police, and I ended up screaming and hollering and pounding my head against the wall in the county detox.

Despite my relapses — I haven't been able to do it all perfectly — I'm grateful that I had the program a couple years before I was diagnosed. I can't say what it might have been like if

I didn't. AIDS is an incredible stress. I think I've been fortunate not to have had a lot of infections and to have had the support system I do have. What would this be like with more opportunistic infections, no family or other support? Add alcohol to that, and AIDS would certainly seem like the best excuse to drink.

It's a lot easier to live a day at a time if you know you're going to be around for a long time. One of the most difficult things about living with AIDS is living with uncertainty: the uncertainty of whether you're going to live a long time, the uncertainty of whether you're going to be healthy tomorrow.

When I'm feeling spiritually connected, the only certainty I need is knowing I'm in the care of God and that everything will indeed work out. Chemical use is dangerous because it becomes easier to buy into the fear. Using chemicals deadens those spiritual connections so you can't experience the goodness. The chemicals are saying, I'm making you feel good; you don't need that spirituality.

Balanced Like a Mobile

Someone in AA used the analogy of a mobile when talking about spirituality. A mobile is something that's real balanced; it has many pieces, and they all balance each other. One of the problems I had this summer was I took out that piece that's marked AA, and I stopped going to meetings. I took out that part of the mobile, and the whole thing got out of balance. I justified it by thinking, Well, I'm going to church and I'm doing all these other things, like meditation every day; I've really been taking care of myself, and I don't need AA. I made a mistake. For my alcoholism, the best way to get spiritual and emotional needs met is to be around other recovering people.

I believe there will always be enough grace to sustain you, provided you stay open to it, provided you choose it; there will always be enough grace or love. The days that I drank to excess, I chose not to avail myself of that grace.

214

No Reason to Die

I don't see any reason to die right now; it's all not really that horrible. I don't need to leave. I've known a number of people with AIDS who left because it was just really horrible. AIDS turned my life upside down, but for whatever reason, I have never felt that AIDS has taken away my purpose. I hear people say that because they lost their job, or for whatever reason, they lost their sense of purpose. AIDS is a spirit breaker. It can take away a person's purpose. I don't know why some people mend and some don't. I think, if anything, AIDS clarified my sense of purpose. A lot of that's about my spirituality. There is a God alive in this universe that is greater than these things we experience. That's really the message that I've gotten over and over again. God is greater than this.

I'm going to be around for a long time because other people look for that too. My family, my friends, and the people around me do not look for me to be sick and do not look for me to die. My family realized that it was a life and death situation, as opposed to a death situation.

I don't want to be a sick person. That's no role; that's no identity at all. That's why I started calling myself a "gay-activist-singer-songwriter-and-poet," because everyone has to be something, and to be a gay-activist-singer-songwriter-and-poet is a whole lot more positive than to be an "AIDS victim." So many people with AIDS don't get beyond being an AIDS victim. They don't get past that. I wish I could give that to other people with AIDS: You ought to, now more than ever, be who you always wanted to be, whether you're really perfect at that or not. If you always wanted to be a nuclear scientist, go be a nuclear scientist, or at least call yourself that, because then you won't be calling yourself an AIDS victim.

There's a lot of pressure to get sick and die. As gay people, we need permission to live. It's why I was always a nurse's aide. I did this awful job so I could justify my being alive. I have a lot of anger and a lot of sadness about that.

I have a friend who was one of those people whose life was turned upside down by AIDS, and after that, he never felt he had a sense of purpose. He got diagnosed with AIDS, and his life was over. He expected that because he was a person with AIDS, he needed to be sick; that was his role. He also had a family who expected him to be a sick AIDS person and die. So much inside of me says, Oh, what a shitty role to play.

Part of me is really angry still. It was so fucking perfect; it was just beautiful. I'm really angry that he chose to die and that he did it so picture perfect. He died so incredibly perfectly. He was an actor and it looked like the nicest script he'd ever had. What he didn't get all along was that he really didn't need to die. I don't think he needed to die anyway. I think he really wanted to know what it was like to have his family say, "You're going to be fine." I've heard it from every member of my family. If I got sick and died, they'd deal with that, too, but they don't look for me to get sick and die. My friend really wanted to please other people. This was the one last grand way to please his family and do what they expected. See, AIDS gives you such an opportunity to do that.

It's Easier to Live If People Know Who I Am

I'm so much more comfortable now with being gay after having AIDS. Before gay people come out, it's really questionable as to how alive they are. Who are you? You're a person nobody knows because you're afraid they won't like you. How alive is that? A lot of my coming out happened with my diagnosis. I thought, I am going to come out; it's going to be a lot easier if I do. It's going to be a lot easier to decide that I want to live, that I want to be happy, and that I want to love myself, if I get rid of all that old shit that says I'm bad, evil, and wicked. I needed to claim who I am as a gay person.

You're not going to live with AIDS and have those negative messages in your life. A lot of people think, Well, I guess this proves more than ever how awful, evil, and wicked I am.

I decided that I was going to love myself. I decided I was going to live. Deciding to love yourself and deciding to live are the same things. Coming out is really about accepting, and accepting is really about loving. So the message is, if you've never truly decided that you're going to accept yourself — that you can love yourself, that you can come out — if you've never decided that, then when you get a diagnosis of AIDS or ARC or you test positive, that's the time to make that decision. There's no reason to wait any longer 'cause you're not going to be able to fight AIDS until you've made that decision. You need to love yourself to fight AIDS.

The Third Step Is Good for Living No Matter What

I really like AA because if you go away, they let you go. People cannot care about you if you don't let them. They can't care about me if I don't go to meetings. It's like anything; if you don't let people know what you need, they can't guess, and chances are, you won't get it. After my relapse, people were really concerned and glad to see me back.

The bottom line is that I relate the program to my whole life. The Third Step — "Made a decision to turn our will and our lives over to the care of God *as we understood Him*" — is good for living no matter what you're doing. I really like the words, *as we understood Him*. A lot of us understood a loving, caring God. Why would you turn your life over to something that was going to judge and hurt you?

I understand that the force that is my life is loving and caring and capable of so much more than I could ever do. The Divine part of me is so much greater than the human part could ever think of. It can invent possibilities that I alone could never dream of, imagine, or see. One of them is that I can survive from AIDS. Physical me, earthly me, doesn't usually believe that. But me, combined with that which is God, understands that and knows that that is thoroughly possible. Me with Higher Power, I don't ever separate God from myself. Well,

I do when I make a choice to go get drunk. But I'm never totally separate; God never leaves. That part of me that is good, that is life itself, never leaves. In a phrase, I understand God as, *everything will work out*. It's all part of the whole process. I think the whole universe is on a spiritual process.

You Need God Wherever You Can Find Him

Paramahansa Yogananda explains the Trinity in a way that's so crystal clear to me: Creator God is that omnipresent force in the universe that we can't fully understand or comprehend. The Christ consciousness is that part of the Almighty that we can understand. The Spirit is that part that gives us the tools to understand. It's like, God is too great to understand, well no, not really, here's the Christ consciousness. God is usable, and here's how, here's the Spirit. I see the Spirit as the way people communicate God to each other, whether that's done with music or whatever. When you ask how I understand God, I understand God in many different ways. I understand the God that people talk about in AA and I understand the God that Lutherans talk about. I don't always like those words, but I've felt God. I've felt God in all those ways, so I'm comfortable using the words.

A big part of my message about God is, don't close yourself off to one way or another, especially when you're trying to survive AIDS. You need God wherever you can find Him, and you've got to grab ahold and not let go till you get what you need. You need it from a message therapist; you need it from an atheist father who loves you dearly; you need it from AA; you need it from the church, if you're comfortable with that; you need it from wherever you can get it. It's up to each person to find the balance.

CHAPTER THIRTEEN

Native and New Age Spirituality

MARY

That's one of the big things AIM [American Indian Movement] did for me. It helped me come out of the closet in terms of being Indian, and that included opening up my potential for real spiritual growth. I started understanding that religiousness was not the same as spirituality and that the reason Christianity never worked for me was because it wasn't what was at my spiritual center. I started to let go of Christianity and become more involved in traditional native spirituality.

I think I've always been chemically dependent. I think from the time I took my first drink I've been chemically dependent. It took a lot of convoluted pathways until ultimately I found my drug of choice, which was narcotics. And then I was on a downhill slide. But really it started the day I took my first drink. It was after my father's funeral and I was twelve. I didn't start to drink day in day out; I drank similarly to my grandfather who was a binge drinker. Sometimes nothing for three months. But every time I drank, I drank to get drunk.

I tried different things as I got older because I kept hearing the message from people, "You don't want to be a drunken Indian." I tried speed for a while and I tried marijuana for a while and all of that stuff in a very binge kind of a way until about 1982 or 1983 when a relationship I was in ended and

I was raped. My life was on very shaky ground and I started to drink much more heavily. Then I ran into a woman at the bar one night who introduced me to a whole variety of drugs that she and her brother and some friends did continuously.

I got involved with them and I tried morphine. By this time I had been a nurse for fifteen years and had given hundreds of injections to people. It never crossed my mind to use morphine myself. Once I had that first dose, then it became, well, whenever I had the choice, I chose narcotics. I worked in a hospital and access was easy. That's when I started stealing from hospitals. Toward the end I started using IV drugs. I quickly plunged to the bottom physically. I was totally out of control.

Thankfully, I got sick and ended up in the hospital. I had an infection from using dirty needles. My friends intervened and informed me that I had two choices: I could go to treatment at this place or that place. Saved my life. I wasn't ready to stop myself. I thank God crack wasn't available. As it was, I almost killed myself with the IV drugs. If crack would have been around, I surely would have died. It's not like drinking where you get drunk and pass out and wake up the next day. The high is so short lived. You take IV drugs, you have this initial rush and high for fifteen minutes, and you want more. But it hasn't left your system yet; you haven't gotten rid of it. So, becoming toxic is almost a given when you use IV; it's like taking an overdose every time you shoot up.

So I went into treatment in February of '84. Nobody said anything about HIV to me despite the fact that it was known I had been using IV drugs. My recovery began at that time.

Tell Them You're French

I grew up in a small town; everybody in town was white. I was teased a lot about being an Indian. There was a lot of mocking. Whenever we got together, when I was real little, and played Cowboys and Indians, I always had to be the Indian. And they'd tease me about my grandpa who was Indian.

He lived with us until he died. My dad was white; my mother was Indian. My parents were really into assimilation; they were very interested in not ruffling the waters. They moved out of St. Paul to get away from all that and pretend they were something they weren't.

When I would get in fights in school about my grandpa or when kids would tease me and I would come home and try to tell my mother about it, she would take their side: "Well don't aggravate them. Just don't pay any attention to them. Tell them that you're French." That's what I heard over and over: "Just tell them that you're French." I got no support from my parents and certainly no support from the community. The only support I got was from my grandfather. He died when I was ten and after that I was pretty much on my own. My brothers were into assimilation. They have real light skin and blue eyes, and they never chose to struggle with it as I did.

Then, I felt even more odd after my dad died. The norm in the town was everybody had a mom and a dad, and so not having a dad also made me different.

When adolescence came and all my friends started dating boys and saying they were having this wonderful time, I started dating boys and it didn't seem like that much fun to me. I just didn't see what all the excitement was about.

I learned young that alcohol really was my friend. I could change how I was feeling by drinking. I am an introvert, and I could have a few drinks and be an extrovert, be the life of the party. I could change who I was by drinking. That's something I remembered whenever I got in uncomfortable situations. Drinking was an important part of relaxing, of being social at all.

The deaths of my grandpa and dad were never discussed. I wasn't home when my dad died, but the rest of the family was. My dad died of a heart attack in the middle of the night. I was visiting a friend and the doctor told my mother not to call me. My brothers and mother had four hours together, then they called me. I walked into the house at 7:00 a.m. and the first thing my mother said was, "We have to be strong and we can't cry." So I never grieved.

It was twenty years before I grieved the death of my dad. I never shed one tear during that whole time except in the church when they closed the casket and I became hysterical. So it's become real important to me that my son Jason be involved with my being sick. His involvement is important, and it's important that he knows what's going on. Nothing is hidden. The things that are appropriate for him as a nine-year-old to know, I share with him. I remember how painful being excluded was for me.

Anyway, after my father's death, I remember my mother lying in her bed with the door closed crying and crying. For the rest of my adolescence, I took care of my mother. It was the message I got. I couldn't afford to have her go too. And somehow I felt responsible for her happiness. For the next ten years I tried to make her happy and nothing I did worked; I felt like a failure.

Several years ago, after I got sober, I went back and got my grandpa's death certificate. I remember my grandpa as someone who came and went, in and out of my life. When he was there, he was incredibly important. I asked my mother if he drank and she just wouldn't hear the question. She had three brothers. At least two died of alcoholism and my grandfather died of massive GI bleeding. Well, that was very suspicious, so I went to my mother with this information, and even then she wouldn't acknowledge his drinking. Just like at his death and burial, hardly anything was spoken. One moment he was there and the next moment he wasn't. Once he was gone, my mother rarely recalled him. In some ways it feels like a fantasy, a different point in time. I'm sure it was about the alcohol.

I Was In Total Ozone About My Sexuality

I came out when I was about twenty-four or twenty-five, so I've been out fifteen years. I worked very hard at dating and being this normal heterosexual adolescent, but I was never happy with it and I thought it was my fault, that I was doing something wrong. There was something inherently wrong with me that I couldn't be happy in these situations when everyone else was.

So, before I came out, I struggled. I got pregnant and I got married. The guy I married was from Florida and he didn't want to marry me. He was racist. My mother came to my rescue, one time in her life, and she ran him out of town. During that time, abortions were illegal and I gave myself an abortion and almost died. I was in total ozone about my sexuality. I was not in control of my life; I was just being pulled along; I did whatever my friends were doing. I got involved with this person because my best friend was involved with his best friend. I didn't even like him. I was really allowing myself to be victimized. A big part of it was because I was using chemicals. I had convinced myself that I was going to get married and that I wasn't ever going to be happy and that it was really my fault. The abortion turned me around. I became more defiant. I didn't allow myself to get into situations with men that put me at a disadvantage.

I decided to go to nursing school and had a couple of safe love relationships: one with a seminarian studying to become a priest and one with a priest. Then I fell kind of in love with this intern, as much as a lesbian can. Sex wasn't a big part of our relationship and we had a lot of fun together, until he told me his perspective on marriage, namely, that I would stay home and have babies. I totally freaked out, quit my job, and got involved in antiwar stuff.

Six months later I had a relationship with a woman. That was the beginning of my coming out. At the same time, I got involved in the American Indian Movement. This was the early '70s. I had never denied that I was Indian, but I never did a lot about it either. Then, around the time of Wounded Knee and the Trail of Broken Treaties, I met some incredibly strong Indian people. It was easy to begin living as an Indian person in the world.

My son said to me a year ago, when we were talking about boyfriends and girlfriends and all that, "You know, I have to talk about maybe having girlfriends, because I really don't know what I'm going to be yet. I'm really too young to know whether I'm going to be gay or date girls." He was eight years old. I thought, Oh God, to have been able to say that out loud and get validation for that at the age of eight would have been... Imagine what it would have done for millions and millions of us.

I Combined Twelve Step Recovery with Native American Spirituality

Anyway, as I was saying, I was in the hospital because of an infection from dirty needles, and I was feeling better, and I knew something was going on; people were acting a little nervous. One morning, fifteen people just appeared in my room. They got an Indian woman who works in chemical dependency to help with the intervention. They knew they better have an Indian with them. She was the expert intervener. The other people just told me what they had observed and how they felt about it. Lisa, my ex-lover and the other mother of my son Jason, brought this bag of empty syringes.

On the one hand it was absolutely awful. I was humiliated. I don't think I've ever had so much shame. On the other hand it was like a relief. I was so grateful when they said to me, "You have to stop; you're killing yourself." I couldn't say that to myself, but I knew I was killing myself, and I knew that I couldn't stop. But I really fought going into inpatient treatment. I was terrified and had lots of excuses, but I never doubted what they were saying for a minute. There were points I argued about, but I never argued with the overall issue that I was a junkie. It wasn't an arguable point. The question was, What are you going to do about it? Are you going to get help or aren't you? That was the question, and so I agreed to go to treatment.

I went to a place that combined traditional Twelve Step recovery with Native American spirituality. The actual program wasn't very good, as I reflect back now, but it gave me enough to start recovery. It got me sober and clean. I was able to think more clearly. It gave me some real basic initial tools and got me pointed in the direction of AA, which is really what has saved my life. I couldn't have gotten sober or stayed sober without it.

I have friends who, after a year sober or three years sober, quit going to AA and seem to do just fine, but I'm not one of those kind of people. I really value the program and look forward to my weekly meetings.

For a long time after treatment I tried to live two lives. I tried to do the AA life and tried to do my other life. I didn't want them to mix too much. I was resistant to having any AA friends, so I wouldn't go out after meetings. I didn't want to be that closely associated with AA. And I was mad that many of my using friends, my nonusing friends, and my lesbian friends left me. During the first year or two of AA I really struggled with that.

The Disease Stops Being Your Enemy

During the first years there was a lot of acting as if. But there was something happening because I kept going back; I kept at it. When I first got out of treatment, I went to four meetings a week, then three, then two. But every time I went to a meeting I realized it was the only place in my life where I felt normal. You know the saying, *It feels like coming home?* Ultimately, what I let in was, when I'm with these people it feels good.

I guess I decided that I was an alcoholic and an addict in all areas of my life and that was okay; it's part of who I am, a big part, and unless I start integrating this disease into my life, I'm going to be in big trouble. It's sort of like the perspective I have on AIDS which I learned from the disease of chemical dependency. You can't separate out your disease and set it over there and go on with your life. You have to integrate it, and then the disease stops being your enemy. The disease becomes just another part of your journey. When that happened for me, both with chemical dependency and with AIDS, it was like taking a big sigh of relief. Because then I didn't have to fight it anymore.

I'm not trying to sound Pollyannaish, that chemical dependency or AIDS is my friend. What I'm trying to say is we all have dozens of different parts of what our journey is in this world, and if disease is one of the parts, then it is important that we integrate that into the rest of our journey. There's lots to be learned from it and there's lots of joy to come from it. So I started doing that, and now not all of my friends are in the program, but the majority are, and I don't think about it anymore; it's not a big deal. Most of them do AA and have a Twelve Step program. I'm at a place where that feels good.

I Changed the Family Rules

My going into treatment was very upsetting to my family and we haven't associated since then. What happened with my family was, I changed the rules. My family had set it up, and I had gone along with a system where I was the strong person and I took care of my mother. When I went into treatment and then stayed sober in AA and said that I'm not going to do this anymore, this isn't good for me, the whole family went up in arms.

I started with my mother. Whenever we communicated it was always because *I* called her. I said, "This doesn't feel good; it doesn't feel like an equal relationship. I want to make an agreement that we will call each other." I wanted her to call me sometimes because it didn't feel like she cared. She did call and for about three months she was pretty good; I didn't expect her to be perfect. And then she just quit doing it.

Communication in my family is indirect. If we didn't talk,

she'd say something to my brother about how awful I was because I didn't call her, then I'd try again.

When I was diagnosed in November of '86 with ARC, I talked to her and the new system worked again, briefly. But then we were back to the same old thing where it's my fault that there's no communication. So I made a choice. I decided that this is not okay anymore and I'm not going to do it. It was my decision that messed up the whole system and got everyone mad at me. My mother was mad because I didn't shower her with attention and my brothers were mad because they had a bigger burden. My brothers decided that their perspective was the same as my mother's, and they didn't care about mine. They'd listen to her and never ask me; they chose to believe her. It was real hard at first. Now I'm okay with it. But there are times that it makes me lonely and sad, especially when I'm sick or when I see a thing about AIDS on TV and someone's parents are with a person when he died.

But, on a day-to-day basis, I feel reconciled that my family of origin isn't my family anymore, because in order to stay in that family, I would have to do things that I don't think are healthy. I feel sadness about it at different times, but I also feel empowered by having been able to make the decision and stick with it. I spent so many years not ever making a decision for myself, doing only what my family wanted me to do. I didn't know what having my own feelings was. I didn't know how that felt. All my feelings were based on how my mother was feeling. I never felt it was okay to have a feeling. To be able to do that now, standing firm in the face of a barrage from my family, really feels good even though it is sometimes painful and sad.

Spirituality and Religiousness Mixed Up

When I was so sick last January and almost died, it was clear to me that the opposite of spirituality is addiction, and that it's important to me that when I die, I'm spiritually centered.

Then it becomes essential I die sober, and in order to die sober, I have to be able to live sober. So in addition to all the other motivations to maintain sobriety and stay in healthy recovery, that has become another real important one to me, the fact that it's important to me to die sober.

Looking back on my life, I've always recognized that I am a spiritual person and I have been in greater or lesser struggles around the issue of spirituality most of my life. Growing up, my family insisted we practice at least a social, superficial form of Christianity. For me, that never fit. I would try. I would do everything to be a good Christian: I would go to church, I would go to church activities, I would sing in the choir. I would do all those things and pray at night before I went to sleep, and day after day I'd continue to feel totally empty spiritually. And also torn: When I went to church, I would hear about how Indian people are pagans, that they are not spiritual people. Then I would hear from my grandfather things like, two-leggeds are part of all living things, and every living thing deserves the same amount of respect; we are not to consider ourselves higher than other beings. I would hear that kind of spirituality from him and then I would hear the standard Christian rap about how you're supposed to act and feel in order to be a Christian or religious person. So I had the two, spirituality and religiousness, mixed up.

Until I got into high school, I was going to be a nun. I thought I wasn't trying hard enough to be spiritual and that being a nun would fix that, that would be enough. That's how important spirituality has always been to me. I thought there was something wrong with me that I didn't feel more like a spiritual person. So I would increase my religious stuff, the external stuff that I did. Then I went to an all-Catholic nursing school and became even more involved in church stuff.

All this time, underneath, I was drawn to the spirituality of my grandfather. When I would be in church and I would hear someone read from the *Bible* about man taming the earth, I always thought, Yuck, I don't like that. It caused me pain to hear that because it didn't feel right to me. But, of course, I didn't do anything about it.

That's one of the big things AIM did for me. It helped me come out of the closet in terms of being Indian, and that included opening up my potential for real spiritual growth. I started understanding that religiousness was not the same as spirituality and that the reason Christianity never worked for me was because it wasn't what was at my spiritual center. That sort of expression of my soul was not who I was. I started to let go of Christianity and become more involved in traditional native spirituality.

Of course, because I was using, I felt restricted. There were certain ceremonial things that I never felt I could do. I would never have an eagle feather in my house because there would be drugs and that wasn't okay with me, even if I was the only person who knew that the two were in the same house together. I limited what I allowed myself spiritually in order to keep using.

And then I got into recovery, and that was the next step that opened up for me spiritually. I really began to feel in an incredibly deep way how important spirituality had always been to me, and I became aware of all the many different ways that I and society had prevented that from blossoming. Now, in recovery, I can do all that I had avoided in the past.

There are a lot of things that go on in traditional native spirituality that require having patience and the faith to wait. The most important thing for me to learn was patience. I had to learn to let things happen, to not force them, but to be as ready as I could be within my own self for when they did happen. I used to dream a lot when I was a little girl, and then, because I was using, I didn't dream for years and years. One of the gifts that I was given in recovery was the ability to dream again. Part of my spiritual program was nurturing my patience for that to happen. I believed that it would happen and that it would happen when I was ready, and that to push it or be upset about it was not helpful. And then it did start to happen and I did start to dream.

That's been true in my recovery all along — recognizing things that I needed in my recovery and then working my program with patience until they happen. The American way of *I want what I want when I want it* is not a very spiritual journey. It's not flowing with your own life energy; it's really forcing life. So that's been one of the gifts I've gotten in recovery: to return to the flow of my life's energy.

I Live My Life in a Circle

It's funny, there were some painful parts in doing Step One, but by and large, I love Step One because you don't have to play games anymore; you don't have to hide anything. Admitting that I'm powerless — it felt like a real gift to be able to do that. So much of my life made sense then in that context. My life had become unmanageable. Step One was a point at which I could begin to come back. It wasn't a devastating, Oh-ain't-it-awful kind of thing. It was more of a rejoicing. I saw it as the turnaround point for me. As awful as it was, as awful as my behavior had been, it was also time for wonderful rejoicing because my life was going to be different.

So the spiritual part of my program is critical to me. It's hard to imagine working a Twelve Step program and staying in recovery without a spiritual component. I do daily meditations and prayers that are a combination of both AA and traditional native spirituality. I pray the traditional native way with tobacco. I do traditional native prayers morning and evening; I also include some of the Twelve Step suggestions like taking an inventory for the day and that kind of thing. I think there is something wonderful about waking up in the morning and praying gratefully for the fact that you're alive. It's a great way to start the day. And then I end the day with a reflection.

The Twelve Steps have been rewritten for Native Americans and the concept of character defects is not used. Instead, they talk about ways that you have strayed; it's not so negative. It's not about being a defective person; it's about having lost sight of what's really important and about needing help from the Great Spirit and from the community in order to return to that awareness. So at night, when I reflect on the day, even if I've been terrible during the day — if I've been crabby, unfair, and unreasonable — it's not cause for shame. It's more like, it was wonderful to be alive today, but there were ways I didn't show it. It's hard to put into words. It's not rejoicing in being a crabby person, but it's certainly rejoicing in the lessons that I can learn from reflecting on my "crabbiness." Just like I don't rejoice in the fact that I have AIDS, but I do rejoice in what I'm learning from it. Sometimes we learn more from the things in our life that are hard or that are struggles than we learn from things that are easy and happy.

I think the most important thing in my life is the spiritual journey. I live my life in a circle so everything rotates around that. Things like my health, my romantic life, my job, or those different aspects of my life are important to me, but they don't make or break me on any given day. If tomorrow I wake up and, spiritually, I feel strong and centered and at peace with myself, but I feel terrible physically, the feeling terrible physically is less important because of how I feel spiritually. My whole life doesn't center around how I feel physically.

I see all of this as just part of my journey. We all go along in life and incorporate things into our life, into who we are. Whether it's a wonderful, loving relationship or having to end what once was a wonderful, loving relationship, or getting sick, giving birth, losing a child — it's all part of our journey, part of who we are. In and of themselves they don't have a value; it's how it is for us. So I don't place a value on having or not having AIDS; what I place a value on is how I'm able to incorporate having AIDS into my spiritual life and what effect it has. When the disease was having a negative effect on my spiritual life, I really felt it. When I was depressed because of AIDS, I started living in the past or projecting into the future, I stopped doing daily spiritual meditation, I stopped praying, and my life became unmanageable because I was spiritually adrift.

Now I feel much more centered about AIDS; now I feel like this is the latest thing that I'm incorporating into my journey. Somebody down the block might be dealing with a new relationship, losing a leg, getting married, or having a baby. We are all continually challenged to incorporate change, and for me, it's having AIDS. Now that I've been able to get past the anger and the rage about AIDS, it has become part of life.

When I had to have an IV in my arm and had to walk around in public with my arm wrapped because I had to give myself antibiotics two, three times a day, I said to my doctor, "This is terrible; I will never get used to this." And now, I don't give it a second thought. I'm not making light of it, but I really do feel that once I am able to incorporate something into my life, then it just becomes part of my journey; it doesn't have any more weight than anything else. It may be more present because it requires more attention, but it doesn't have more significance.

I do think that I learned this since being diagnosed, or maybe it's only been since then that I've been able to put it into words. My friends and I talk about this kind of stuff more often than we used to — spirituality, connections, life, death. That's been a gift that I don't know we'd have if I hadn't been diagnosed. There's definitely a different level of intimacy; I think that I get there faster with people than I used to. I allow the intensity to be there if it's there and not hold it at arm's length and be cautious. I just let it be and that feels really good. Even with my AA group, I think we have much deeper level of connection — the core group of us. Living in the present, today, is a challenge, but it sure feels good.

An Ojibway Story

About ten months ago I had a healing ceremony and out of the healing ceremony I learned that even though my doctors gave me six weeks at the most, it wasn't time for me to die yet. There were some things that I needed to do on this plane first. I knew I was not dying, that there were things that had to be done, some of which were talking about AIDS, some were about Jason.

There's an Ojibway story about people who are very sick and they're taken by the hand by some spiritual beings to the edge of a great dark cliff over the water. If it's meant to be that their journey is to continue on into the spirit world, spirit beings from that world come to meet them and walk them off into the darkness. If it's meant to be that their journey in this life is not over yet, then the cloud beings come and open up the clouds and a rainbow appears. Then they are given a message about their lives, about how to be in this life, and messages they might want to pass on to other people. That seems like what happened to me. I went to the edge and the spirit beings didn't come.

I had never seen a double rainbow in my life, ever, and I've seen two double rainbows and three triple rainbows since last January. So I think I'm on the right track. And my recovery continues to be a really big important part of that.

Society Tears out the Spirit of a Person Through Disrespect

You know, we're told that if you're a gay or lesbian person, you can't be spiritual. Everybody, all living things, are spiritual and it's for us to find the right language to be able to express our spirituality. Maybe it's not Christian and maybe it is. Maybe it's a kind of language that nobody has spoken before; just because there aren't any words for it, doesn't mean a person isn't experiencing spirituality. It makes me so sad when I hear someone say, "I'm not a very spiritual person," because what they're really saying is, "I've never been permitted to find my spirituality." What happens is, it's beaten out of us.

233

If you don't express spirituality in a certain way or demonstrate it in a certain way, it's not okay. We take it on as our shame that we don't know how to speak appropriately about spirituality. But really it's society trying, again, to force people to fit into certain kinds of molds so that the few at the top will be able to run things smoothly. The sad part is that thousands and thousands — gays, lesbians, women, Native Americans — lose that sense of themselves, lose that critical center out of which everything else springs.

In the Indian way, the spirit is the most important part of a person. Stifling or hiding or putting our spirit in the closet is really hiding the essence of who we are. It's how we relate to everything else; it's how everything else relates to us. And that's why in traditional native culture, gays and lesbians were not ostracized, were not shunned, were not ridiculed or murdered. They were accepted, very often becoming important spiritual people within the community.

The belief was that the Great Spirit took a lot of time preparing a spirit that was different from the average person. The Great Spirit gave a little extra attention to that person. If anything, gays and lesbians were thought of as special people because it was considered that the Great Spirit turned a flash of attention more on them. And we don't question our Great Spirit. If the Great Spirit chose a person to be gay or lesbian or in any way different, then that was a gift.

How a person sees him- or herself in relation to other living things and to the great energy in the sky is really important, and to say it doesn't count because it doesn't fit standard society is a form of murder. Society is tearing out the spirit of the person through disrespect, and we feed that, those of us who are alcoholic and addicts. In order to fill that hole that's been created by that disrespect, in order to make it go away, we try to fill it with alcohol and drugs. In order for us to recover, filling that hole has to be a spiritual quest. One of the things I got when I graduated from treatment was an eagle feather. I've had it for five years.

We Can't Do It Alone

I really need the Twelve Step program. It becomes more important to me the longer I'm in recovery. Just to be in the presence of other recovering people is nurturing. What a wonderful feeling, just to sit in the same room with people and to be able to say we are in fact doing it. It makes you want to laugh; it's such a wonderful thing.

I don't think I'd be alive to deal with having AIDS if I wasn't first dealing with my alcohol and drug addiction. It's not something I can set aside and not think about for a while. It's like being diabetic: if you need to take insulin every day, and you just decided you were going to stop worrying about eating sugar and not take insulin for a week or two, well, you'd be dead. Chemical dependency is a life-threatening illness, just like AIDS. If a person relapses after being diagnosed with AIDS or ARC, and a person dies in that relapse, did he or she die from AIDS or ARC, or was it from chemical dependency? I think that's open to question.

I think AA was right on target when they started groups of recovering people. We can't do sobriety alone and I think that's true for AIDS too. We can't do it alone. Thank the Great Spirit we don't have to.

LINDA

I don't think there is failure. Maybe I would consider it a failure to give up and feel like a victim or not even try, but death isn't a failure, and illness isn't a failure. . . . When I was in the hospital the last time, I had a near-death experience which was pretty amazing. It was very clear to me that death is just a breath away from life; it's just another beginning.

My father was a workaholic. He built a whole empire. He recorded and produced a lot of fabulous music. I was always driven to succeed and do well.

I always got attention by becoming ill. I often had pneumonia as a child — that was the number one way to get attention. Number two was by being bad and number three was by being good.

My mother was not available at all. She's a very quiet alcoholic. Even to this day, she's unable to show emotions. She'll go home and cry about me having AIDS, but she doesn't have the heart to talk to me about it, which is sad.

My father had a fierce temper; he was violent a lot; he was very cruel. He took a lot of it out on my mother, so she was busy protecting herself from him. He hit my sister a lot, but he didn't beat me. He would come up and scream and shake me, stuff like that. We all had some really nasty nicknames that he'd given us as children. "The slut" was my nickname, my brother was "the garbageman," and my sister was "dummy."

There were also sexual overtones in my father's relationship to me. It never became physical, but he was very seductive.

Our whole family did a lot of drugs together because it was the cool thing to do. It was fun for a while, doing drugs with the family. My father introduced me to a guy who shot me up for the first time.

I Spent the Next Ten Years Getting High

I jumped right into using heroin when I was about eighteen. I was involved with a band that my father had been working with and the head of the group had been a junkie for many years. I was all bowled over by the excitement of it all, going on the road with a lot of famous bands and stuff, and I got right into it. I sang background vocals and I danced. I tried some regional cures, like coming back to New York, but I just got deeper and deeper into it.

Finally, my family found out and put me in a mental hospital, but, of course, that didn't work. The second I got out I was looking for drugs. I spent the next ten years getting high. I ended up in the street, you know, all the heroin horror stories: I was prostituting and worked for a ring that cashed phony prescriptions for morphine. We all were a tough bunch of characters. I was very lucky; I was never really hurt, and I was in a lot of bad areas. Part of me really wanted to get clean, but there was a really big part of me that didn't, that loved the job, the excitement.

Finally I got on methadone and stayed on that for a year. I hung out with people like the Rolling Stones and went to their doctor to kick, to get off of it, and I got better.

I got a job at a TV station and I worked my way up to a top management position, which is really unheard of. No secretary gets promoted like that. But I kept relapsing, and they kept holding my job for me because I was good at what I did. By the time I had my last relapse, which lasted for three months, I knew I had to stop. None of the prior hospitalizations or rehab efforts worked because I was playing at getting straight; I didn't really want to stop. But before my last relapse, I got married and I started feeling better about myself — good enough to hope for a decent life. It's a matter of wanting and I wanted it.

I had been on the streets, sleeping in the gutter. To go from that to this job and getting married, all that improved my self-esteem to the point where I could really see myself having a life without drugs. In 1984 I went into treatment for the last time. I really knew I wanted to stay clean. That's when I started to go to AA meetings. And OA. I had an eating disorder too; I was bulimic.

Anyway, I was in the rehab for five weeks and they thought I was doing really well so they let me out. That's when I started to go to meetings regularly. The fellowship became very important to me, my sponsor was great, and OA was also really good for me at this time too. It's very hard to get over an eating disorder because you change physically. Your digestion starts going backwards, so you can't keep food down. It's tough.

I got very involved in the program right away. I had a tough sponsor at the beginning and she told me to borrow her faith since I didn't have any faith of my own. And it worked. At that time I still didn't consider myself a spiritual person.

It was rough the first couple years. I did my Fourth Step and it was sort of like a purging exercise, releasing all the self-pity. I had felt like a victim my whole life. I was very lucky to have done that Fourth Step about a month before I became ill. I guess it was the spring of 1985 when I developed the Epstein-Barr virus. It's connected with the AIDS virus — a lot of people with AIDS get it. I got it like a ton of bricks. I was in bed a year and a half with a lot of terrible, painful symptoms. I knew in my heart that I had AIDS, that I was HIV positive, but I was afraid to get the test. I finally went and sure enough, it was positive.

During that period of time when I was in bed, I started to get involved with the work of Louise Hay, Bernie Siegel, crystal healing, the Seth material, and other channelers. I started on a very strong spiritual path. I went to all kinds of psychics and healers, anything I could find that I thought would help my spiritual growth and my physical healing. And I started speaking all over the city. This was 1986, and I was still feeling pretty lousy. It's been rough for me. A lot of people have AIDS and they feel good, but I have a lot of symptoms and I don't feel good.

Spread the Message of Hope

I went to Mexico to get Ribavirin, which didn't do me any good, it just dropped my blood count, but while I was down there, I got deeper into the whole spiritual side of things. Then I went to a meeting in San Diego with this woman who channels the spirit of Christ. She told me I was in my last lifetime and all this good stuff, and that I was going to heal. Then I went up to LA and I met a guy named Scott Gregory, a doctor of Chinese medicine. He's got a book out and has worked quite successfully with a lot of people with AIDS, using natural therapies. A good friend accompanied me on this trip. She's a filmmaker. We decided to go ahead and make a documentary about the people who were thriving with AIDS, or at least who, if they died, had grown a lot and healed themselves in other ways before their deaths. I've been working on that the last year and a half, and it's terrific; it's really coming along. It just became very important to spread the message of hope to people. And, I was doing quite well.

Then in February of last year I got pneumocystis and developed full-blown AIDS. That just blew my mind. I had quit smoking, I had changed my diet, I was meditating, and I was praying. I was doing everything — getting acupuncture — everything I thought could be done, and none of it had worked. It had gone to full-blown AIDS and that sent me into depression for quite a few months. I felt ashamed. Here I was talking about healing and it wasn't happening to me. So I backed down from doing all that work and resented the fact that I had worked so hard and it wasn't working for me.

This September, I ended up in the hospital with liver failure and dementia, which was awful. I was hallucinating; it was like being in a blackout. It was terrifying. I was yelling at people; I thought there were old people in my room wheeling themselves around in chairs, and all kinds of stuff. They told me they wanted to put a Hickman catheter — one they use to feed you, it goes right to your heart — in me. I didn't understand and they didn't really talk to me about it and what ended up happening is they let some first year intern do the procedure and he messed it up. They kept cutting me and putting it in the wrong place, and I wasn't anesthetized properly, so I felt the whole thing. I was lying on the table screaming. It's a terrible feeling to be at the mercy of doctors who are incompetent and who aren't sharing with you what's going on. I'm still not over the feelings. It was hideous.

One thing I learned: it's very important to have a partnership with your doctor. Some people do the spiritual side without exploring the medical, but I believe it's important to cover it all. So I found a new doctor and I still have the same doctor; he saved my life.

The Drama of Having AIDS

They put me on AZT because apparently AZT is very good for dementia. I had been one of those people who would go around talking about how AZT destroys your bone marrow, it's poison, and it ended up helping me a lot. I'm off it now because my white blood count dropped down to nothing, so I'm very, very vulnerable at this point. I had developed this tuberculosis-like disease — it goes into your liver, your bone marrow, your bowels. You have high fevers, bad night sweats; it's an exhausting and terrible disease. They put me on an IV drug — I still take it three times a week — and that cleared things up. I was really ill during that hospitalization. They had to get nurses around-the-clock. I still have nurses about three or four times a week, but I'm better now; I've improved.

I know I've done the emotional and spiritual work and there's really no reason why healing can't happen for me. I'm working now on what's standing in the way of my healing — like not wanting to go back and get a full-time job, like loving the attention and the drama of having AIDS. And that's kind of where I'm at right now. I want to get involved in things, but I have to watch my energy real carefully. Sometimes it's like waiting for the other shoe to drop. I know that I'm open to anything because I have no fighting equipment, but I try not to stay in that space.

The Steps Saved My Life

I was lucky to have gotten through the Twelve Steps of AA and NA very early in my recovery and have used them all the way through my AIDS-related health problems. It gives me a way to deal with being isolated a lot, being in bed a lot, being in pain a lot. I use Steps Three and Eleven often, turning it over as much as I can and spending time in prayer and meditation. I also use the First Step. I am powerless over what is happening; I can take action, but I can't count on the results. You can do what you can to heal it, but you're powerless over the fact that you have it.

I've had to go on narcotics which, because of the program, brought up some guilt, but I've resolved it. I know that you have to do what you have to do, and that I'm not meant to be living in pain. And, thankfully, the desire to abuse it has been lifted. I take just what I'm supposed to take and that's it. I have a doctor coming in to do an experimental treatment on me and because my pain is bad today, he's bringing me narcotics; he'll give me an injection. Sometimes I feel funny about it, but the addict in me still hasn't come up.

The Steps saved my life. My friends bring me an AA meeting here once a week. I'm really lucky I found AA before I got AIDS.

Death Is Just a Breath Away from Life

I read a lot of Stephen Levine and Elisabeth Kübler-Ross, who both work with terminally ill people. I have resolved, for the most part, my fear of death. When I was in the hospital the last time, I had a near-death experience which was pretty amazing. It was very clear to me that death is just a breath away from life. It's not this big deal; it's just another beginning.

I believe in reincarnation and I believe that we're here to grow and learn and become as loving and spiritual as we can be. And sometimes it has to be through pain. That seems to be one of the biggest ways that we humans learn. I believe that when you get symptoms or opportunistic infections it's for your learning and for your greater growth.

A lot of times when people work with Louise Hay's concepts, they feel guilty if they don't heal themselves because they judge they're not doing it right or they don't love themselves enough. I came to understand that that's just not the way it is. Sometimes we may have agreed upon things before we came into this life and we don't really know why we go through things. Like Louise says, the spoken word and thoughts are very powerful, but this is a hell of a disease; even she doesn't know the answer. She thought she did when she was first dealing with AIDS, but now she knows she doesn't. A lot of people have become very spiritual and loving human beings and died anyway; it is such a rough disease. So, I'm more at peace with that possibility. I don't think there is failure. Maybe I would consider it a failure to give up and feel like a victim or not even try, but death isn't a failure, and illness isn't a failure. That's a very hard thing to get into your head because when you're ill and physically feel rotten, it feels like you're doing something wrong.

I never felt that my body was my enemy. From the beginning, I felt that it was all one picture, that my mind and my body were connected. When I have a relapse of some sort with the disease, I take full responsibility. I always take a look at what's going on emotionally and mentally and see what kind of work I can do — as well as seeing my doctor and taking whatever medicines he prescribes.

It's All in My Heart

I don't run to psychics anymore. I have a good friend who channels. He's done some channeling for me and has given me a lot of suggestions. Some of them I listen to and some of them I don't, because I feel that it's all inside you. It's all in my heart, and from the beginning I've always known, even medically, what's right for me. I knew it was time to come off the AZT a couple weeks before they took me off it. That's a good feeling — to know that I know.

I've eliminated most of the stress from my life. I had a very stressful job before I became ill. It was very stressful and I've learned to just eliminate it all, all the extra stress. There's nobody in my life anymore who is negative. I can spot negativity right away. I don't allow that in my life. And I try to stay as calm as I can. It's not always easy. I mean, I woke up this morning a little depressed. I thought, Well, okay, here's another day; what are you going to do with it? I still have that Horatio Alger work and reward kind of thing.

I know that I'm healing because I'm not running fevers anymore; I'm not having night sweats anymore; so sometimes I feel like I should go get a job. But I know I deserve to take this time to heal. Even when I'm not desperately symptomatic, I still deserve this time for myself.

I don't know what led me to a strong spiritual path. I was lucky. I have a good Higher Power. I absolutely believe that you have to have spirituality to deal with this. First of all, you're facing death — I'm in my thirties and facing death every day. You never know when you wake up in the morning if you're gonna find lesions or pneumocystis; you're vulnerable, and you have to have something to believe in.

New Age spirituality and the Twelve Steps, it's all the same thing; it's all the same principle. That's why it works together so well. The only thing that I find is — I don't want to sound like I'm putting the program down — but I find that in a lot of meetings there's too much focus on what's wrong, instead of on how to make it right. I think a lot of people in the program are very hard on themselves. I've spent a lot of time learning how to be good to myself, easy on myself, nonjudgmental.

CHAPTER FOURTEEN

Treatment

KEVIN

I was always the sickest one in the family. Most of the first grade, I was home with strep throat. I had pneumonia as a child and was always in and out of the hospital. I was always the one with something wrong with me, every single year. I think it's directly related to being abused and being told I was no good. If you're not feeling wonderful about yourself, if you're not feeling healthy about yourself, I think you're open to being infused with a disease.

I was born into a middle-class family. We were never hurting for anything like shelter, food, or clothing. But things were not harmonious in our home. My dad was gone a lot working, and when he wasn't working, he had a lot of social clubs he was involved in. As a child, I was abused physically by my father and abused verbally by my mother.

Every time I sat down at the dinner table I had to listen to my father tell my mother she was a horrible cook. There was always something wrong with the meal. Having to watch my mother shrink to that every night was horrible. And there was always something one of us kids had done. We were dunderheads; we would never amount to anything because we were all stupid. I sat to my father's right in the kitchen or dining room, always to my father's right. He was right-handed, and if there was something that didn't please him, I got it. It felt like I was hit by my father every single day of my life. A lot of fat lips went unnoticed by teachers at school and other people.

There was always fighting going on with Mother and Father, and with us kids and Dad. My mother and older sister fought too. My mother dished out a lot of verbal abuse. She threatened physical abuse and hit us with the belt a couple times, but nothing compared to my father. "Wait until your father gets home!" That was scary and abusive on her part. If she told Dad, he would carry it out. I denied my mother's abuse because she was abused by Father. In therapy, I was taught that she was an adult and could have stopped it. She was as abusive as he was. I wanted to excuse her, but she was an adult.

I also lived in fear of my father's guns. I have no idea how many guns he had. He owned pistols and shotguns. And because of how angry he was, I always lived in fear that he was going to use them on us. Some nights it took me a long time to get to sleep because I thought, Oh my God, Daddy's really angry with us tonight. He's going to get one of the guns out and shoot us. Kids have wild imaginations. With the things that go on in the world, and with news reports of fathers going berserk and killing entire families, well, I thought, That's our family.

I was always the sickest one in the family. Most of the first grade, I was home with strep throat. I had pneumonia as a child and was always in and out of the hospital. I was always the one with something wrong with me, every single year. I think it's directly related to being abused and being told I was no good. If you're not feeling wonderful about yourself, if you're not feeling healthy about yourself, I think you're open to being infused with a disease.

There was never a time in my childhood that I remember as happy. I remember hating my parents a lot.

Something Was Different About Me

Around tenth grade, I was introduced to marijuana. In eleventh grade, I started learning how to smoke it and to drink alcohol. I would go to Howard Johnson's and order tequila sunrises and those high school drinks that everyone seemed to really love and would get sick on real fast. I don't know if my parents ever had a clue until I borrowed the family car, went out drinking with a friend to a basketball game, smoked all through the game, and went to a party. My friends drove me home in the family car, deposited me on the front steps, and rang the doorbell at three in the morning. I was severely punished.

I had another year of drinking and doing dope in high school, and then I chose a college as far away from home as possible. I needed to have an excuse to not come home on the weekends.

The town I grew up in was a pretty sheltered community. I didn't know what homosexuality was. I had an idea I was different; I didn't like women, but I didn't know what that meant. I knew something was different about me and something was wrong because I didn't do all the other things normal boys did. I was called a sissy or a fem from day one of the first grade till I graduated from high school. It made me feel inferior. I obviously didn't fit in, and I felt separate from everyone else. And I didn't have anywhere to go with it. When I was being called names, who did I have to talk to at home? My parents weren't available to talk to about things like that. Plus, I think I felt shameful. Do you go home and tell your parents how shameful you feel about the way kids are treating you at school, only to be further shamed at home? I was already being shamed at home by my father about not helping out with the gardening, the car, or other "male" things.

The one thing that amazed me in my childhood was that I was allowed to take cooking lessons. I wasn't allowed to take ballet because it was a sissy thing to do, and my father wouldn't let anyone in the family drive me to ballet lessons. My father was not going to have anyone in the family grow up to be a dancer because that was a sissy thing to do. If I had wanted to take track, if I'd wanted to be a swimmer, certainly I would have been driven to those activities, but not to anything that wasn't "male." It wasn't just what happened in school, it happened at home too.

In high school, I just did marijuana and alcohol, and maybe something out of my parents cabinet, like Valium. In high school, using allowed me to stay farther away from my family, which allowed me to feel like I was doing something for myself. It also made me accepted in school. Up until tenth grade I was an introvert, but when I used drugs I became an extrovert. Before, I had two or three friends; when I used drugs, I had lots of friends. I also drove. A lot of my popularity was based on the fact that I had the drugs and the car. I think I always had a problem growing up thinking that I had to buy affection. It was natural; people seemed to like me if I gave them something. It was a theme all through my life, still is. Now I know that I don't have to give people things to be liked. I'm liked because I'm me.

Just Don't Tell Us You're a Queer

In college I became known as a person who was a go-between between the user and the dealer. My profit was I would take a little off someone's bag, which seemed to satisfy me. After awhile, the dealer would give me a little coke, or I got special deals. If a gram of coke was $100, I sold it for $100, but *I* got a gram for $60 because *I* was special. I was real popular because I knew where all the drugs were. If you needed some acid, call Kevin, and Kevin was always ready to get it for you — at his own expense. I was used. Now it makes me feel sad and angry that I didn't recognize it. I never thought of myself as being worthy of anything. To be popular, I threw lots of parties, big beer bashes with lots of drugs. I have numerous stories of what I did in college to try to win the affection of people.

During this time, my mother read about the drug raids at my school. She said, "Well, we don't care what you do as long as you don't tell us you're a queer." This was right at the height of learning about my homosexuality, of my being able to connect a word with it, of my experimenting with my sexuality. I thought, Oh fuck, what am I going to do? I dropped the phone from my ear and counted to ten and thought, Well it's okay then if I do drugs, just as long as I don't tell you I'm gay. I said, "Mom, you know me better than that."

After the drug raids, I cooled out a little and realized that things weren't working for me in college. The drugs were crazy; the sex stuff was crazy. I had one quarter left of school, and I thought, To hell with it. I moved to Kansas City and started selling drugs. Nothing changed in Kansas City. I hadn't quit doing anything. I did lots of crazy things down at the bars every single night, and then I got fired from a job for stealing to buy more drugs. After that, I started working in a restaurant and fell into a crowd of heavy users. We drank and did drugs all day long.

I Feared for My Life Every Single Day

Soon, I met a guy, and I allowed him to move in with me. It was a real abusive relationship. I learned what it was like to be a battered "wife." I think, because of the abuse I got from my father, it seemed natural for me to accept Tim's abuse.

He would threaten to kill himself, and he was always unemployed. In order to make a scene, he would make up lies that I was going out with someone else. When he was sober he was a sweet, charming man. When he was drunk, he was physically abusive. He drank constantly, and I drank right along with him. I never knew from day to day if he was going to threaten me with a knife, or what. I feared for my life every single day.

When we got evicted, that gave me a way out. I didn't know how to get out up until that point. Plus, there was security in the relationship too. I came home and felt safe at the same time that I was in danger. It was a weird thing: I've got security because I've got him and always have someone to sleep with, and even if he beats me up, it's okay; he's still there.

Later, I started taking Tim's violence out on others. I'd blast someone for no reason. I'd kick people. I became violent when I drank, very violent.

I spent all of my time at the bars. If I wasn't working, I was at the bars. If I was off work at 11:00, I was at the bar at 11:10. I didn't spend much time getting to know people, and I didn't spend any time getting to know myself.

Then I had a two-year relationship with Sammy. We moved in with each other right away. No courtship, no dating period, no time to get to know each other. It was a tumultuous relationship and very violent. We hit each other a lot. Around my birthday in '85, we had a fight to end all fights, and he left me.

October '85 I was tested for HIV and came out positive. That created a lot of turmoil at work. One of my "best friends" was manager. We did everything together; we drank together and coked together. I told her, and she freaked out and told the general manager. In turn, I was laid off. I fought it and won an out-of-court settlement.

A Blackout and a Felony Charge

I usually made good money. In fact, I was probably one of the top paid waiters in the city. So I had a lot of cash from tips. I would walk in the bar, see a handful of friends, and put up a round. I continued to buy my friends. People liked me 'cause I bought cocktails and always had coke. When it came time to pay rent, I was always late and always scrambling. I was making tons of money, but I could never figure out where my money was going.

One night I was walking home from the bar, really drunk and in a blackout. The next thing I know, I'm arrested and in a squad car. How did this happen? My hands are cuffed behind me, and I'm screaming and pounding on the window, until a cop comes and bangs my knees twenty times with a billy club. It hurt like hell. Supposedly, I broke an eight-by-eight-foot plate glass window. I spent the night being verbally abused by the cops. They were harassing me because I'm gay. They put me in a holding tank with the rest of the drunks, until I was taken into a holding tank by myself where I was stripped and left naked for hours.

I was given a felony charge: criminal damage to property. I had no way to defend myself. There were no witnesses, and I was in a blackout. *Operation de Novo* took over my case; they promote rehab programs for alcohol offenders. I went to see their counselor. I've always been belligerent around authority, and the man at *de Nova* reminded me of my father. He said, "You have a drug problem." I said, "No I don't." I was real defiant. Then he said they could throw me back to the courts and I could go to jail for a year and pay $10,000 for this offense. I said, "Let's talk."

We made another appointment for two weeks later, and he said I should stay sober during that time. Two weeks later I met with a woman, and she asked, "Well, did you stay off alcohol and chemicals?" And I said, "I did have two glasses of wine; it was my roommate's birthday." Of course, I didn't admit to all the coke I did, or any of the pot. She said, "Obviously, you can't abstain." Which was true, I couldn't. So I said I'd go through treatment. Because of my sexual orientation she sent me to a gay and lesbian treatment center. She figured I needed to be in a safe place.

More to Life than Despair

In the first twenty-four or forty-eight hours of treatment, I realized that I was an alcoholic. I started reading the Big Book and related to the stories. I could see the consequences of my use. Hearing other people talk about what was going on with their lives made it easy to see what was going on with my life. People began looking up to me; I began looking up to myself. I began gaining my self-respect.

I realized there is more to life than despair, going to the bar, drinking a quart of scotch, and snorting cocaine. The first AA meeting in treatment I went to, I said, "I'm an alcoholic." It was real scary for me. When I heard people say, "Hi, my name is so and so and I'm an alcoholic," I thought, Boy, people can really say that. I knew that's what I was, so I decided not to hide it. I'd taken this giant step, and I was fearful because I was saying something that I had felt for fifteen years.

It was also hard to allow myself to have feelings. In treatment, people could see when I was getting ready to have feelings. Someone said he could actually watch me start to cry; it took time for it to happen. He said it was beautiful. I didn't think it was, but I've seen it in other people, and it is — there's a beauty to someone's tears. I spent thirty days in treatment.

My first roommate after I got out of treatment used, so that became an unsafe situation. My second roommate, well, it's amazing when you get sober, you aren't able to tolerate behavior that you put up with when you used. The further away you get from chemicals, the more aware you become of your feelings, and the less you're willing to put up with. I started creating boundaries and sticking to them. Finally, I said I wanted to move out on my own. I learned that I can be safe in a place by myself without having to have thousands of roommates. That was about six months ago now, and I've really enjoyed learning more about myself. I'm enjoying having everything my own. It's peaceful; I've gotten more serene.

People Really Do Care

Most of the summer I was sick with bronchitis. I got over that about midsummer. Then, toward the end of August, I thought I had a relapse of bronchitis and told my doctor. I had night sweats, coughing, shortness of breath. He took an X-ray, and I ended up in the hospital with pneumocystis. The first week in the hospital I don't remember. Everything happened so fast. I recovered pretty miraculously. I guess I was very sick; it was real scary. I don't know how much I allowed myself to feel; I pretty much allowed myself to remain numb.

There were times I was overwhelmed with gratitude at how much support I was getting. As far as support from people is concerned, I compare the pneumocystis with the time I spent in the hospital with hepatitis. When I had hepatitis, I was still using and in a lover relationship. We never allowed each other to have friends, and he never came to visit. It was a miracle to see *that much* of a change. Now, in sobriety, I'm available to myself, and therefore, to other people. I'm totally overwhelmed by the support and the friends I have.

One big difference is that I'm asking for support, not just waiting for it to happen. I've always thought that everything ought to be handed to me on a silver platter. That's not the way life works. I have to do a lot of the work to get where I want to go. It feels good to do that. I think part of the reason I'm feeling as well as I do now has to do with the positive way I approach things. A lot of that came about when I was in the hospital and people came to see me. I thought, Oh wow, people really do care. I need to care for myself. I don't think, until the pneumocystis, that I really did. Since the pneumocystis, I've learned that I have to take care of myself; plus, I want to.

I think being part of a Twelve Step program, AA, has helped me in my recovery from pneumocystis. I've learned that it's a one day at a time process. I can't look too far into the future. I can only do for myself, today, what I can do, and that's going to be good enough.

Before I went into treatment I joked that I would play the game, play by the rules, do what they wanted me to do, and when I got out of treatment, I'd have a big party and I'd show them. As it turned out, I didn't have to show them — I had to show myself. I was feeling so good about myself that I made a decision that I didn't want chemicals anymore. I made a decision that I didn't want to feel like a piece of shit anymore. I made a decision to continue to go to AA after treatment. I also knew I had to make a lot of time for it; I had to take a lot of nights off from work. In addition to AA, I also went to treatment aftercare for six months. After treatment, I only worked two or three nights a week. I learned that things would work out financially, somehow. I was learning from other people who had similar experiences that I was not alone. Without the meetings, I don't think I would have learned that.

I went through a gay treatment center. I don't think a straight center would have been as effective. I would have had to take time out to say I'm gay. I would have had to spend time getting over the fear of telling people I'm gay. Being brought up gay is a big problem; you have certain feelings that are different. A gay treatment center gave me an automatic opportunity to feel safe with whatever I needed to do in treatment. For example, I came out to my parents in treatment.

At the beginning, I went to gay AA meetings also. It was a matter of safety for me. I could relate to other gay men. Just the large number of recovering gay men helped. Otherwise, I may not have stuck it out.

I think when I discovered I was positive and heard those messages that said, *once you get AIDS, you're going to die,* I believed them. When I was just HIV positive I thought, Well, I'm going to get AIDS, because I've been exposed to the virus; it's inevitable. Well, it's inevitable that we're all going to die someday of something. A great number of people are living with AIDS, telling their experiences, giving people hope. It's not just the medical field that helps you survive, there are other things you can do too. That's what gives me hope — the positive side, not the medical, fatalistic side. I hear of people who have no hope and deteriorate rapidly. They do that because they've never been given the hope that they can live with AIDS. People are living a long time because of what they're doing for themselves. People are surviving. It's not as fatalistic as we are led to believe.

JOHN

That's how I was able to cope with being abused — ten joints per day or more. On my typical school day, I got stoned before school, stoned at lunch break, and stoned after school. Then I came home and fixed dinner for my mother, she'd go to bed, and I'd smoke dope on top of the dog house. Then I'd masturbate myself to sleep and start the whole process again the next day. I was a lonely, scared, unhappy little boy. You would think my mother would have noticed how stoned I was.

When I first came to the Twin Cities, I had just graduated from St. Olaf College. I had a very active chemical dependency going with pot, and I had a lot of problems. I was pretty immature and had some growing up to do. I had a lot of dysfunctional ways of behaving. I was twenty-two. That was four years ago.

I know, now, that most of all, I had to detach from my sick family system — especially from my mother, she was the hardest. I reached rock bottom one day at work. I simply collapsed and cried all day. I wanted to commit suicide, but the only thing I had was Drano — hydrochloric acid. I thought that would probably be a really painful way to die. That was the only thing that kept me from committing suicide that day. It sent me a signal though. I thought, Gee, maybe I need to do something; it's not normal to want to kill yourself.

So I went to employee assistance, and they sent me to a therapist. Right away he said, "We need to make a contract that you will not use mood-altering chemicals." The next Saturday I was with my boyfriend, and I got loaded, stoned. I tried staying straight for another week and the same thing happened. When I came back the second week he said, "Okay, which treatment center do you want?" He gave me two outpatient options. I checked them out and chose to go to the one that offered dinner. I continued to work full time, and every afternoon at 4:30 I hopped on the bus, had dinner with these people, and then we had these really tense, difficult, hard sessions where we all got our shit out. I went there for thirty days and ended up with a tentative grasp on the First, Second, and Third Steps. Plus, I was sober. Then I started to go to meetings, lots of meetings.

At the same time, I found another therapist. He and I spent three years together. He helped me with my family. He helped me understand how cruel and abusive my mother was to me. He helped me understand that my mother had abused me badly when I was a child — physically and emotionally. Like so many people who have been abused, I had all kinds of blinders on. My denial system was very strong. It took me a long time, but he helped me recognize that part of the reason I was so dysfunctional as an adult was because I was so badly mistreated when I was a child. We worked through a lot of the specifics around that. There was the usual stuff, she beat me and sexually abused me, and my father sexually abused me too.

My mother didn't have any boundaries. She discouraged me from ever having any friends, because she had no friends herself, nobody ever called. When I developed a pot addiction, she turned her head. She never noticed. Everyone else seemed to know. Her philosophy was: ignore it and it will go away; hold it in and it will go away. That's what she told me to do when I got angry. She taught me to be rigid, constricted, closed, and uncommunicative. It's a pretty typical abused kid's story.

When I got out of treatment then, I had a lot to learn. Fortunately, I started that process with a great therapist. First, we worked in individual therapy and later in group therapy. I was also doing a lot of healing work in Twelve Step programs. One of the corollaries of an abusive family system is, don't trust anyone. Twelve Step groups have really helped me learn to trust. I'd recommend Twelve Step groups to anyone. I found a safe, nonjudgmental place where I could talk about myself. It was safe for me to do that. It took a long time to realize it was safe. The groups also provided me with some real concrete role models — old-timers. Old-timers are great.

I figured out that people are going to love me only if I am

willing to love myself. I didn't figure it out intellectually. It's something you have to learn in your heart. If *I* think I am pretty neat, others will too. When I was a child, I learned to hate myself. When I was in treatment, I would say things to my counselor like, "I'm such a mess; I don't know why you bother trying to do anything with me." He would say, "John, that's your low self-esteem talking."

It took another couple years of therapy and a lot of meetings for me to get to the point of loving myself. Now I know that I'm pretty neat. I like me; I love me. I've got a lot of skills, a lot of talents, and a lot to offer the world. Even as sick as I am now, I still feel I've got a lot to offer the world. Here I am. That's my attitude.

My mother has no idea I'm this ill. As far as she knows, I'm the way I was a couple months ago. I realized that my mother's not going to change, and the healthiest thing I can do is detach and not be around her. When I get around her, she makes me crazy. I get enraged. She doesn't respect my boundaries. It takes a lot of energy to defend myself against her constant intrusions, and I can put my energy to better use. I can seek out people who don't do that. I have very nice, wonderful friends and lots of caring acquaintances who I talk to instead. In fact, I've developed a whole new family system. I have *uncles* in my family system: Peter, my doctor; Donald, my therapist; and Richard, my priest. They care for me a great deal. Each one offers different things. I can't say enough about my doctor, my priest, and my therapist.

Growing Up Gay in This Society Is Abusive

My new family is validating, supportive, and nonabusive. I think we all need some kind of family like that — support to get over the trauma of childhood. Even the most well-meaning parents don't realize they're abusing their gay children. What would not be abusive for a straight child, could be for a gay child. Moms asking their sons, "Why aren't you dating girls? Susy down the road likes you." And you want to say, "Oh Mom. I don't want to date Susy. I want to date Jack." I think growing up gay in this society is inherently abusive. I've never met a gay person who has escaped the scars.

A fair amount of laboratory research has shown that when you stress out rats, their immune systems break down, particularly when you don't give them any control, when there isn't any way to get away from the stress or modify it in any way. So as a child, when dependent on one's family, it's hopeless if Mom and Dad are abusive. The little boy ends up totally stressed out with a weakened immune system that he carries into adulthood.

Recently, I ran across a little chestnut that made a lot of sense to me. If you're an abused child growing up in an abusive family system, you have three options: you can kill yourself, you can go crazy and become mentally ill, or you can develop an addiction or compulsion to something. Fortunately, most of us develop addictions. In a way, that's the safest path. It's a horrendous consequence, and we've all got horror stories, but you know, it's better than dead or the Thorazine shuffle.

That's how I was able to cope with being abused — ten joints per day or more. On my typical school day, I got stoned before school, stoned at lunch break, and stoned after school. Then I came home and fixed dinner for my mother, she'd go to bed, and I'd smoke dope on top of the dog house. Then I'd masturbate myself to sleep and start the whole process again the next day. I was a lonely, scared, unhappy little boy. You would think my mother would have noticed how stoned I was. I started smoking in the tenth grade and continued smoking till the day I left home to go to college — she never noticed.

When I started college, I tried to cut it out. I actually realized that it was not helping my academics. Brilliant. My abstinence didn't last very long, although I didn't smoke as much because my emotional pain was not as great — I was away from home. Nevertheless, I never stopped smoking all together. Then, in my senior year, my dope habit really took off. I became known around campus as the little gay drug addict. Still, I don't know what triggered such use. Maybe I realized that I'd blown my wonderful opportunity at St. Olaf. Maybe it was because I had no friends. Maybe it was because I was struggling with coming out. Whatever, the pressures got worse, and my response was to smoke more dope. People who are chemically dependent usually don't have many tools to solve problems in their lives. My response was more drugs; that was my tool. When I left school and got to the Twin Cities, I got crazy pretty quick. That's when I tried to commit suicide and came into the program.

God for Me Is a Hunky Gay Man with a Mustache

I've been sober for almost four years now. My four-year sobriety date is in November. I want very much to get a medallion. I hope I'm alive at that point; I don't have much time left. My body told me that. You know, you just know. As I deteriorate, more hope fades. I am dying; I don't think there's any question. How much longer? As long as I can manage, but that's for God to know. I'm Episcopal. I basically view God as a warm loving creator. I also see God as a hunky gay man. God, for me, is a hunky gay man with a mustache who's incredibly cute and who takes good care of me. I shared that with Father Richard, and he thought it was a wonderful image.

I really don't know what's going to happen when I die. I've read lots and lots of books, but I don't know. I've come to the conclusion that it's different for each person. I'm not afraid of death; I'm very accepting of it. I've gone through a hellish process to get to that point. I'm about as serene as I've ever been in my life.

Like last Tuesday: I've been the secretary at St. Edward's Church, I take minutes, write them up, and distribute them. I recognized that I was too weak to continue and I resigned. I was very sad. It was something I enjoyed doing; it was a neat part of my life. The people were wonderful and I'll miss them. It was very painful to have to quit. I started crying as soon as I got in the car. I got all the way home and Mark was there; he helped me. I cried all the rest of the evening. I don't know when I've ever felt such pain in my life. It felt like my entire life was unraveling a thread at a time. Earlier that day, I cried on the phone with Bob, the hotline coordinator at the AIDS Project, because I had to quit there too.

In terms of the activities I like to do, my life is becoming smaller. It's been a very painful process. The nice thing about going through things like that is you do get through it and come out the other end. You discover what the program has been saying about getting the emotional shit of your life together, and you really do get serenity. There really is a reward at the end and, for me, it's serenity. I mean, I get kind of irritated with the Republicans on TV, but it doesn't get me upset. Not much disturbs my serenity.

They say no pain no gain. I'm not sure I buy that, but if you don't have much pain, maybe you don't have much character. It's kind of like the Velveteen Rabbit: You've got to be handled a lot by a lot of people. You've got to have all the sharp edges smoothed away. I don't feel like I've got any sharp edges anymore; they've all been worn away.

I've Been Active. I Didn't Smoke Myself to Death.

When people find out they are HIV infected, one of the ways they comfort themselves is with drugs. Several of the people I know with AIDS do that. They manage to get their doctors to prescribe them tranquilizers, or they use alcohol, or smoke a lot of dope, or get addicted to pain pills, and that's how they cope. And you know, it's not good for their bodies and certainly not for their minds. What usually happens is they die pretty quickly; they don't live very long and don't accomplish very much.

A lot of people figure, Why bother? I know one person who

said, "I've got AIDS; I'm going to die," and he stayed stoned all day long. He didn't live very long. That's the kind of tragedy we can prevent.

People who are HIV infected don't have to lead their lives that way. The tragedy is, he could have been of so much value to other people if his life wouldn't have been snuffed out the way it was. I've been tremendously active as a volunteer doing all sorts of things, including talking about the experience of having AIDS. I've made a difference in people's lives and left a mark in local AIDS groups. I couldn't have done any of that if I would have smoked myself to death.

AIDS doesn't necessarily have to kill people. No one knows why some get the virus and never develop AIDS and some end up in the hospital with pneumocystis. I seem to be one of the people who succumb to the virus.

I think my chemical abuse hastened the onset of my illness. I supposed if I had not had the immune stressing situations I had, I would merely be positive and not be sick, or I would have developed it later, or it wouldn't have been as severe. One of the cruel ironies of this disease is, it hits people who already have one or two strikes against them.

The Twelve Steps Can Be Used to Deal with AIDS Too

Steps One, Two, Three, Ten, and Eleven are my day-to-day Steps. I've done the others, and I feel at peace with them: I've gone through making the list of shortcomings, talking it over with somebody, humbly asking for forgiveness, being willing to change, making a list of persons I've harmed, and making amends wherever possible. I think I've cleaned up my garbage, which is part of the reason I feel so serene: I don't have any backlog. What I try to do is keep it that way, and the Tenth Step is a wonderful way to do that.

But more than anything, I think the principle message of the program — and this goes for AIDS or alcoholism or other addictions — is, *you don't have to do it alone.*

I think the Twelve Steps, the program of Alcoholics Anonymous, can be used to deal with AIDS too. Step One says, "We admitted we were powerless over alcohol — that our lives had become unmanageable." We're also powerless over the AIDS virus. As a person with AIDS, I know that what is going to happen to me is not entirely in my control. My task is like the task of any alcoholic: I have to recognize the parts I can be in control of, and I have to recognize the parts that are not in my control. I have to use the Serenity Prayer and pray for the wisdom to know the difference.

Like alcoholism, there's lots of unmanageability with AIDS. When we're very sick and unable to come and go as we please, life can feel unmanageable. Unmanageability is last Monday, when I wanted to take my lover Mark out for his birthday. We were going to have a marvelous time on the fiftieth floor at the Orion room. We had a corner table reserved. We both put on our suits and got as far as the parking lot, and I said, "Mark, I feel just awful." I was a bright shade of green. That's unmanageability. I felt horrible; I was beside myself; I cried.

But there was a lesson to be learned: If you can't do it the first time, try again. On Wednesday night, we had a wonderful time. It's that kind of tenacity that I think is so critical in fighting this disease. Sure, the disease wins a round or two here and there, but I can win a round or two also. The disease may ultimately win the war; but I'm going to give it a battle. We had a marvelous time. Mark had steak and lobster; I had scallops and raspberry sauce. The entire city was spread out at our feet. It was a fabulous evening. We want to go back there again. So, you win a few and lose a few. I pray for the wisdom to recognize what I can control and what I can't.

If life gives you lemons, you make lemonade. I'm just trying to live my life one day at a time and be the best AIDS patient I can be. I am a professional person with AIDS. I call myself the AIDS Project's resident AIDS victim. We mean that tongue-in-cheek, because I'm not a victim at all. When you hear the media talk all the time about AIDS victims, what they mean is people who have no control over their lives, who have no power, who are not able to change anything and might as well hang it up and wait to die. That's what victim implies. Well that's not true. It's also unfair to a person with AIDS to be given that kind of message because there are things those of us with AIDS can do to make our lives better. There are things we can do to live longer and be more productive. The media, and everyone else who call us victims, denies that. It makes me so sad. The complete lack of understanding these Neanderthals they put microphones in front of have, astonishes me.

You Don't Have to Do It Alone

My advice to people with AIDS, or people afraid of getting AIDS who may have a problem with alcohol or other drugs, is: As far as chemical dependency is concerned, what works for everyone else, works for us too. Go to meetings or get into treatment. And remember, *you don't have to do it alone.*

STUART

After snorting for a period of time, the heroin starts tearing the tissue in your nose. . . . So we decided to skin pop. . . . But then I was watching these guys who were mainlining, shooting it in their system. While I'm waiting to get high, they're high already. Shit, I'm waiting; these guys are high; I'm gonna try one time. Why do we always say, "One time, that's it"? So I tried it one time, and I was off and running. I was about nineteen in New Jersey.

I'm forty-two years old, I've been married three times, and I have three children, all from my first wife, two boys and a girl. My profession was sales, when I was not using drugs. When I was using drugs, it was breaking and entering. I was diagnosed with AIDS on December 25, 1987. My opportunistic infection is TB.

I was born in Atlanta, Georgia, and I moved to New Jersey when I was nine years old. My father never came to New Jersey. He abandoned the family once we moved to New Jersey. He was supposed to have come later but he never came. My mother basically raised six of us. I was a country boy moving to the inner city, to the concrete jungle. I wanted to fit in, see, I didn't know anything when I first came to the city. The biggest thing in Georgia, where I was from, was dipping snuff. I came to New Jersey and I needed to fit in; I felt alienated so I started to people please. *Oh shit, give me some of that. Oh, I'll take it.* And I would drink the most so they could see that hey, I'm the bad guy. Sick as a dog, but I wouldn't let them see me sick. I carried that role on. I was glad that marijuana came around 'cause the alcohol was getting me so sick. When the marijuana came out and people started leaning towards marijuana, I started smoking it. I didn't have to worry about throwing up and getting sick.

You Won't Get Hooked If You Snort It

So then the heroin came into play — snorting it. I said, "No, I don't want to get involved in that." They said, "Come on man, it won't hurt you; you won't get hooked if you snort it, only if you shoot it. Come on, try it." I snorted it and got sick, extremely sick, so I thought, That's that with heroin. But my peers had transferred to another drug, from the alcohol to the marijuana and now to heroin, and if I'm gonna hang out with the guys now, you know, I'm thinking that, Hey, I gotta do what they do or else I won't be accepted, you know. So I started to snort. Then I thought, I'll never shoot it; I don't care what they say. After snorting for a period of time, the heroin starts tearing the tissue in your nose; your nose starts bleeding. So we decided to skin pop. You don't go directly into the vein, and it takes about ten or fifteen minutes before you feel the effect of the drug. But then I was watching these guys who were mainlining, shooting it in their systems. While I'm waiting to get high, they're high already. Shit, I'm waiting; these guys are high; I'm gonna try one time. Why do we always say, "One time, that's it"? So I tried it one time, and I was off and running. I was about nineteen in New Jersey.

I never realized that I had a habit until about three months into my using. I was using every day and never had a crisis where I couldn't get it. One time something came up and I couldn't get it and I was sick. I wondered, What the hell is wrong with me? Do I have a cold or what? I went to one of my friends and he told me, "Man, you got a habit." I said, "A habit? What do you mean?" He said, "You know, you're hooked." That scared the hell out of me. *You're hooked.* That's how naive I was, you know — you're hooked. So we bought some drugs, I shot the drug, and I felt better. From that point on, whenever anything, any ailment came up, I knew what to do.

Let's Make a Deal

After awhile of shooting, I was convicted of various felonies: breaking and entering, possession, sale, robbery. They were experimenting on drug programs back in the '60s and they came to me with "let's make a deal." They said if I was willing to go to a drug program and plead guilty to use, they'd expunge the other charges from my record. The program would last a year in upstate New York. At that particular time, I was at my low. I had ran the gamut as far as burning my bridges: stealing from everyone that was close to me and robbing and sleeping in the street — the whole thing. It sounded good to me, 'cause I didn't have nowhere to go.

I ended up being in there two years, and while I was there, I was devoted. I never used; I followed the program; I did what was required of me. After the first year, you come from upstate and you're housed in Manhattan and you get your "wings," which means you're allowed to drink. You see, it was a program basically designed for heroin addicts. After a year of therapeutic treatment — I did what I was supposed to have done in the program, you know — I was allowed to drink. I started working with the staff and we'd go out and drink. Nothing wrong with drinking. Dope was the real problem; heroin was the problem. Alcohol was cake. It's that damn nasty heroin — leave that alone. So I thought, Cool, all right.

I Became a Muslim

So I stayed clean. One of the reasons I stayed clean as long as I did was because I became a Muslim. I didn't do anything; for four years I was totally clean of everything. I didn't smoke, fornicate — none of that. We had a program that I believed in. That was '73. In '75, Elijah Mohammed, the founder of the program, died. His son, Wallace Mohammed, took over. He revealed to the people in the program that reverse racism was being taught. He revealed the structure and foundation that we were building our lives on was not Godly, it was man-made. It was not Islam, it was "Hislam." Wallace took the structure away that we were leaning on for support. When he took that structure away and started building another structure, we got weak, 'cause the foundation that was keeping us strong wasn't there anymore.

When that was taken from me, I started back using again. I started experimenting with cocaine and pills. I'm quite sure you know cocaine is not habit forming. That's what they told me; hey, that's what they told me. You remember that? They told me this! Yeah, it's not habit forming, so what the hell? So I still had some morals and a conscience, but since I wasn't messing with anything that was detrimental or habit forming, it was all right, cocaine.

Then I ended up coming to California in '77 and got a very good job selling burglar alarm systems. I was very successful. Bought a brand new car right off the show-room floor. Had money — money in the bank, money around the house. I had gotten off cocaine when I moved, but I was still drinking. Now, with all this money, I started getting back into the cocaine.

With Cocaine, You're Never Satisfied

I started shooting it and the money started to drizzle away, drizzle away, 'cause when you shoot cocaine, it's an all day thing. It's not like heroin. You get a $25 bag of heroin and you're set for the day. You can find a corner and sit in the corner with a $50 bag — or whatever your shot is, whatever it takes for you — and that's it. Leave me alone, give me a soda or whatever, something sweet, some chocolate, and leave me alone. But with cocaine, you're never satisfied. You never reach that point. One more bag. You just spent $300, but you know you're gonna want one more bag.

Finally, I went into a program out here in LA I was in the program for a year. My sincerity was there and I ended up being on staff, and to celebrate my becoming a staff member, champagne — Couvoisier!

I'm working outreach and doing intake, and I'm the counselor at the group meetings. I was very happy with the job, but that alcohol, after a period of time, broke down something, some defenses I had. When I got drunk, anything goes — Yeah, what the hell; try a little of this; it will be all right. After a period of time, I got weaker and weaker and weaker, knowing all the time if I got into drugs what'd happen. It was harder to say no when I was drunk. The next thing I know, I went back to the drugs and I lost the job.

Freebasing — I'm Not Putting It in My Arm

This time I was freebasing. The thing about freebasing is, I'm not putting it in my arm. And you've got your elite people doing it — Richard Pryor. You're with money, hey, hey, Natalie Cole. I could start a list; it must be all right. I started freebasing cocaine and that was the worst bottom I ever hit. I mean, that took me out, totally out. It took more money to maintain than I ever could come up with. I would do damn near anything. That's when I started to do male to male sex. It got to the point where, when it came to hitting that pipe, I had no scruples. Once you hit that pipe, you get that obsession, and the only way that obsession is relieved is by hitting that pipe again. That's how the mind does cocaine. If you shoot it, or any other way, there's something inside of you that can quiet that craving, but with freebasing, I couldn't reach nothing inside of me to quiet that craving.

So I had to go out and do something to get more money to continue to get high. So one night I drank a lot of wine, and this person called and told me, "Come on, I want to give you some cocaine on credit." And that's the dream — on credit, on credit! So I go over there at 3:30 in the morning, and I'm living in a part of LA they call "the jungle." In the daytime people are reluctant to walk there, and it's 3:30 in the morning and I'm walking through alleys to get this cocaine. They got these guys outside — they call them the check squad — that check people and take what they have when they go by the dope houses. People can't go to the police 'cause they're burning dope. So they hit me in the head and robbed me.

I went to the hospital, and the doctor said that a fragment from my skull went into my brain and would create seizures. I couldn't drink or use any street drugs with the medication 'cause it would induce a seizure. I'm in the hospital and I'm so close to death there's no way I'd go out and drink and use drugs. But once I got out, I started to come up with my own program of sobriety; you know, I'm not gonna do nothing hard for me. Within four weeks I was drinking and using again, and I ended up having a seizure. The paramedics came and got me and I was in a coma for twelve hours. While I was there, I decided to share about various problems that I was experiencing — night sweats, weight loss, diarrhea, swollen lymph nodes, and other various complications. The doctor explained the symptoms related to HIV infection and asked me if I wanted to take the test. He gave me the test and it came back positive.

Everything Fell into Place

After that, I talked to some people and they told me about AA and that there was a program in upstate California. It was a ninety-day program that gave an individual a chance to get away from the rigors of the city. Clean air and a chance to get your head somewhat screwed on straight so you decide which direction you want to go. So I went there. After the ninety days were up, they asked me if I wanted to continue in a recovery setting until I could get on my feet. I could have left and moved in with my family and my mother — I had places to go and all that — but I didn't want to go back to the dependency-type setting. I wanted independence. I figured if I come into the program here, I would get a chance to work, get my own place — be self-sufficient and independent. So I said I wanted to continue in the program, so that when I finally leave, I will have my own key to my own place, my own furniture, my own job, my own car. I won't have to go to the family and lean on them. So I came to this half-way house. It was the best choice.

There is no doubt in my mind that God is in my life. I have turned my will over to God, and I know without a doubt that God is working in my life. I came here and everything just fell in place. Here, I get a chance to focus on first things first and not worry about extraneous stuff. The director here is understanding about AIDS and allows me to go out on speaking engagements, sharing about my AIDS, and they understand the Twelve Steps here.

I'm Powerless over Alcohol

I didn't recognize that alcohol was a problem till I came here. If I'd never come to Alcoholics Anonymous and went to another drug program instead, I would still be using. I'm powerless over alcohol; once I start drinking alcohol, I do not have any control whatsoever over my actions; there's no telling what I might do. I'm totally powerless. Once I take that first drink, it's over with. There's no stopping me.

I needed a program like this to see the picture, to get the clarity. I needed to hear other people's stories, stories that I could identify with — man, that's me. I stopped running. I stopped feeling that uniqueness: Oh shit, if they only knew; they don't know what I'm going through. Instead, I start hearing these stories and, Oh well, now what Stuart? Listen to that. Where you gonna run now? I needed to hear those stories. That's why I love going to meetings. I've been affiliated with AA now two years. I've been clean and sober for two years, and I love it.

If I wanted to find an excuse to drink, this AIDS is a damn good excuse. I could use this and justify the hell out of this, but that's not a reason. This is not a reason to drink or use. I know there's no reason that I can come up with that could justify me drinking and using. I have an excuse. I have a lot of excuses. You know, I can get on the pity pot and start poor me, poor me, pour me a drink. But that's not what it's about today for me.

Today, emotionally and physically, I feel good. I have my ups and downs, but I feel very stable. What's helping me is the Twelve Steps of Cocaine, Narcotics, and Alcoholics Anonymous. Today, I'm dealing with my disease through understanding and trusting God. And through acceptance. Today, I accept the fact that I have AIDS. I'm not fighting anymore. I realize that I have AIDS and I accept it. I'm dealing with my disease through honesty with myself, through caring, through sharing, through loving, through giving, and through getting up off my ass and living.

CHAPTER FIFTEEN

Abusive Childhoods

LEWIS

As a child, I was very spiritual. I had an imaginary pink elephant that I used to talk to all the time, and the only thing that the elephant used to say to me was, It will be all right; it will be okay. One night, in one of my father's crazy alcoholic rages, he said, "Little boys don't see pink elephants." And he grabbed me out of bed by my hair. . . .

My grandmother is a compulsive gambler. So my mother grew up in a world of feast or famine. One day there was loads of money and the next there was no food to eat. She was the last child of three, and she was a child of the depression, which didn't help things any. My grandmother's family came from Russia. They were Orthodox Jews, and all of the children married either less religious Jews or they married into other faiths. In that era it was unheard of. My great grandparents were the kind of people who would actually go through the whole routine of sitting shiva and mourning children who married out of the religion. My grandmother married an Italian. In my mother's home, there was no sense of spirituality. They were what I call gefilte fish Jews; they celebrated the holiday, but it had no importance or significance.

All Twelve of My Father's Brothers and Sisters Were Alcoholic

My father's parents died when he was very young, so my father was raised by two older sisters who were very stern women. My two aunts sent him out to work when he was about thirteen. There was a message that I got from my father as a child that discipline was a way you showed children that you loved them. He went to work in a bread factory. He was a bread slicer, and he sliced off one of his fingers on one of his first days on the job. All twelve of my father's brothers and sisters were alcoholic. So both my parents came from very dysfunctional homes, from families that were not affectionate, emotionally open, or available.

My mother and my father met and fell in love. I've had the opportunity to go back and read some of their love letters, and I think there was a genuine love there. My father went into the service for World War II, and before he went overseas, he wanted to marry my mother. So she and her sisters got on the train and went down to Ft. Hood, Texas, and they got married. Reading these letters has given me a great deal of compassion and understanding for him. That was an era of great expectations. We recovered from the depression, we were victorious in war, and he was really looking to come home and start a family, become successful, and build something.

However, my mother basically was, and is today, so codependent with her family that she has never established any boundaries of her own. Her family always came first, before my father. And so my parents had a number of battlegrounds. One, my mother agreed to raise her children Catholic. At that time, there was an actual contract that people signed. So religion became a battleground.

My father's alcoholism was of a violent nature, and as a result of that, I was totally dependent on my mom for whatever security I thought I might have; therefore, I was allying with her. I went to church because I had to go. It was a church of the Catholic God who was a punishing God, who blinded you, crippled you, and was very vengeful. So here I was: I was dependent on my mom for whatever safety, or certainly for the alternative to violence, and if I went to church on Sunday, then, according to her I was this dirty little Catholic bastard. If I didn't go to church on Sunday, then my father was in a violent alcoholic rage. There was just no winning on that battleground.

My dad was a milkman for twenty-five years, and so he was used to carrying bottles of milk between his fingers; as a result, his hands were enormously powerful. So when he would smack you, you were being smacked by a real instrument of power. The violence took all kinds of forms. The earliest violence I remember was at age four when I saw my father trying to strangle my mother in the bathroom. The violence directed at me involved lots of cuts. My lip was opened a number of times; my eye was cut open a number of times. I was beaten at times to a point where my face was swollen beyond recognition. It was that kind of stuff where a punch or a smack from someone else was nothing, but a hit from him would leave my arm black and blue. That was the kind of violence that I'm talking about.

My Parents Fought Bitterly over Sex

So that was one battleground, the religious battleground. Another very important battleground in my household was a sexual battleground. Today I understand what was going on; I did not understand what was going on then. My parents fought bitterly over sex, chasing around the room, all kinds of craziness, screaming about why do you deny me, and this and that.

I was turned into a surrogate husband. I knew the most intimate details, not only of what was going on in the bedroom, but what wasn't going on in the bedroom. I knew that not only from her, but also from him. Whenever I was in either of their company, all I heard about was the other. For years and years my father accused my mother of being frigid. He used to tell me how he would work so desperately to please her, and there was just no getting through; she would never do anything to please him. I used to think, Well maybe it's the smell of alcohol on a drunk's breath? Which came first, the chicken or the egg? I spent a lot of time in therapy sitting on a couch trying to figure that one out.

What I later came to understand is that my father was actually a gay man who was trapped by society. He married because that's what men did then. He wasn't being satisfied. Not only did women not do things like give blow jobs in those days, but he didn't want to be with a woman; he really wanted to be with a man. But I didn't understand any of that at the time.

If I Told Anyone, He Would Kill Me

I was an obese child; food was my first compulsion. A number of times my father got into bed with me and just told me to lay there, and he massaged my chest and was probably masturbating while it was going on. I was told afterwards that if I told anyone he would kill me. I believed him. And then I got into this whole crazy thing with him in that I really believed that if somebody would just give this guy a blow job, we would wind up with some peace in the house. I really thought maybe that was my responsibility to do that. It wasn't until I got into my healing work that I began to remember all the instances where I was sitting in the bathtub being bathed as a child, and he would be standing at the toilet masturbating. I came to understand that every conversation I had with him, which was about my mother not giving him a blow job, he was covertly saying to me, that's what I want *you* to do.

My parents lived the typical codependent existence: they neither shared with each other any of their feelings, nor did they have any concept of joy. Whatever social life they had revolved around my mother's family. There was a great deal of animosity and anger and bitterness about that. My mother's mother and her sisters became the fixation. I think a lot of that anger was anger he had at his own mother and older sisters, who were extremely controlling women. Here he was, married into a situation with horrendously controlling women.

So my dad really never knew any sense of joy or peace. Life for him was a terrible drudge. When he died in 1983 and they were about to close his casket, I remember thinking to myself and saying to him, "Pop, I'm glad you're finally at peace." He knew so little peace in his life; I was happy for him that he was out of it.

I Made Myself Invisible

If you read the book *Codependent No More*, that was my parents' marriage. In essence, I learned that in order to survive, I had to control everything in my environment. I couldn't take risks; it was always better to go with safety, because I had so little of it in my life — even in terms of relating to people. Obviously, choosing safe people is a healthy thing, but I would choose people who were safe because they were emotionally dead or emotionally unavailable. Taking the risk to open myself to someone who was emotionally available was just unacceptable; it was just too frightening; it was something I didn't do.

In this household we had no rights; we had privileges that could be taken away at any time. Nothing was consistent, ever, and none of the rules made any sense. In order to survive, I made myself invisible. I need to say that because it's a very important part of AIDS for me. What did being invisible mean? I remember the day clearly, when I was about seven years old, that I decided I was going to do everything that I could to be perfect. I told myself that I would never express anger. It was just too risky in that house, and nobody would listen to it anyway. I learned that no matter what, you must never rock the boat; you do that by being invisible, by not expressing your own needs, your own feelings, your own emotions. Instead, you just push it all down, and you rationalize and justify. You go around the circuit and get your needs met by the side door. That's what it was like as a child.

In my attempt to be perfect I tried to excel in school, which I did. I was pushed into a progressive education system, which meant that I skipped a lot of years. I went from second grade to fourth grade, from fourth grade to sixth grade, from seventh grade to ninth grade. This was a feather in my mother's cap. This was her symbol to the outside world that she was okay. Because she had this brilliant son, she was okay. The reality is that the tests to get into that special program I had to retake because I was just borderline. My mother was a school crossing guard; she knew the principals and everybody else, and she pushed them to retest me. So with a little bit of nudging, I was taken in. If I got an eighty-five, my mother wanted to know why I didn't get a ninety-five; nothing was ever good enough. So that was another message that came through: *nothing you ever do will be good enough.*

I didn't fit in because of my age, and because I was peculiar. I was a very large child; I was almost ten pounds at birth. It was a very rough birth for my mother — her cervix got crushed on the way out. A lot of guilt was thrown onto my shoulders for that, as if I did it intentionally. I was also a very precocious and active child. And I grew very quickly; so by the time I was in kindergarten, I was already five feet. By the time I was in sixth grade, I was nearly six feet. I was this huge kid who was like an infant. I had this big body, but I was this very little spirit.

My first way of dealing with the pain was by eating; I tried to eat it away. I had always been this big kid, so no one made too much of a fuss about it, except when I got into sixth grade and I had a teacher who was extremely cruel. Once a week, a girl and I had to go fetch the scale and get weighed in front of the entire class, because according to this chart, we were heavier than we were supposed to be. She didn't factor in that I was the height of an average man. Every week this went on. The humiliation was horrendous. When I came home with that kind of pain, the only way my mother knew of showing affection was through food. So I would go home and complain about being big and heavy, and she would sit me down to eat.

The first real signs of food abuse, though, did not show up till I was around thirteen or fourteen and I had to go for a physical for summer camp. My blood pressure was too high, so the camp wouldn't take me. My mother's great uncle, who was a doctor at the time, said to her, "He has to go on a diet." I always loved this guy because he really stuck up for me. So around thirteen I started the battle with food.

When I say that's the first compulsion, that's not true. I think the first compulsion was work. It was instilled in me at a very early age that it was not good to relax; you were not a good person if you sat and did nothing. We were all meant to work, work, work.

About the time I began to discover that I liked boys, the food addiction really kicked in heavy. When I was coming into my own sexually, it didn't help to be in a world that revered thinness. Here I was, this really obese queen — talk about painful. My second or third year in high school I was riding the subways and hitting the tearooms for sex. By the time I was in college, I ate from the time I got up in the morning till the time I went to sleep at night. And in between, I was having sex. If I connected with someone in the tearoom, if somebody showed me the slightest bit of affection, that was more than I could stand; it was overwhelming.

Weight Watchers for Teenagers

At age sixteen, I reached my peak weight; I was up to about 320 pounds. My blood pressure was so high that I couldn't climb to the top floor of my college buildings without collapsing. Finally, my great uncle said that if I didn't lose some weight, I would be dead in six months. My mother said, "Give him some pills to control his appetite." But my uncle said, "Not with blood pressure like this; he'll have a stroke in a second," and he wrote down on a piece of paper where one of the first Weight Watchers groups was starting for teenagers. He said, "Go there." I did and it was the first place I ever felt at home. I felt like I fit in; I felt like I belonged someplace. I had a wonderful sense of humor, and I worked very hard at being liked. I was sixteen and coming out of the closet at 320 pounds.

I was in college already, and all of my friends were driving. Of course, my father's answer was, "You're too young." So I took the car without permission. I drove to an embankment, and I put the car into neutral and floored the gas. I was going to drive off the embankment. That was my first spiritual awakening. I started to cry; I knew that I didn't want to kill myself. I thought I did, but I didn't. I went home and I told my mother that I thought I liked boys and I needed help.

So my mother sent me to a psychiatrist in New York. I was told that under no circumstances should I dare tell my father, 'cause he would kill me. A year or two before, he committed physical incest with me and said, "Don't tell her or I'll kill you." And now, I had my mother telling me, "No matter what, don't tell him; he'll kill you. And if you do tell him, I'm gonna get caught in the middle, and I'll kill you." It was like everyone was gonna kill me.

So my mother sent me to a shrink. I got a sense one day that this guy was telling her everything that I was saying. So, I made up my mind to tell the most absolutely outrageous story that I had ever heard about her. I got home that night and she wanted to beat me within an inch of my life. That's how I knew that as soon as I left the office, he'd call her to give her a report. Very professional guy.

That was the day I told my mother that I was cured. I had lost 120 pounds in Weight Watchers, and I looked wonderful. My whole life was about to blossom.

He and My Father Had Been Lovers for Years

There are some other things I need to go back and fill you in on. They were very significant things.

I did not speak until I was about four. I understand, now, that the reason was, when I was about one and a half years old, I saw my brother sexually abused. For many years I had a recurring dream: I saw this black man sucking this little boy's penis. I thought it was a black man. It wasn't. Sometime ago I looked through childhood pictures and saw it was a man in black; it was a priest, and I saw my brother standing there holding his crotch with a most horrendous look on his face, and I understood it all.

This priest, who was my father's cousin, was the guy who, when my dad died in '83, called me three weeks after my father's death. He thought it would give me comfort to know that he and my father had been lovers for years. This was the priest that my mother would go to for marriage counseling every time my father left home.

He Beat Me Till He Got to the Point of Altering Reality

Another thing was significant in my childhood. The worst physical violence that happened between my father and I happened as a result of my coming home and catching him in the act. My first cousin, this gay cousin who's an alcoholic, well he and my father had an incestuous affair that lasted about ten years. This was someone my age, my father's nephew.

Anyway, what happened was, for ten years, every Saturday I was given money to go to the movies, and my mother chose to work on Saturday. She knew what was going on. The times when the violence against me was the worst was when I would come home and catch him. He beat me till he got me to a point where he was altering reality. He would focus his anger on how I scratched the freshly painted wall, or some other nuttiness. That became what the beating was about.

The incest was the cause of the last beating my father ever gave me. I came in and I caught them, and later that afternoon he accused me of having sex with my cousin. My cousin and I had never touched each other. My father started hitting me.

Finally, my eye was bleeding and my mouth was all swollen and twisted, and I just made up my mind. Something in me said, I don't care if you kill me; I am not going to tell you what you want to hear, because it never happened. And he went to hit me one more time and I picked my foot up and I kicked him between the legs. He laid there on the floor for a while, and then he told me to get out of his sight. The next day I was terrified; I roamed the streets because I did not want to go home. No one had ever challenged my father's authority. We used to go through these insane things as kids where he would sit me, my mother, and my brother down, and if that wall was white, he would beat us until we said that wall was brown. He needed to assert this authority.

The next day, I came home and he was sitting there with his bottle of Canadian Club. He told me to sit down, and I figured, This is it; I've had it. I sat down and I thought my heart was going to pop right out of my chest, and he said, "The only reason why I'm not going to kill you is that you're the first person who's ever had the balls to stand up to me." Well, for whatever alcoholic logic there is — thank God, because God only knows what would have happened — from that day on he never touched me.

I clued my mother in that if she stood up to him he would back down. It took her years to get the message. But one night my father started this riot over something, and my mother just went into the kitchen. She came back with this frying pan of hot oil and she stood over his lap, and she said if he said another word, she was going to pour it. He shut up, and from that day on he stopped bullying her.

"A Big Bruiser Like You Having a Coke?"

I graduated from college when I was about nineteen, and I really wanted to be an actor, but my parents said, "You'll never make it; you'll starve; you'll never be able to feed yourself; you'd better teach; you'd better have something to fall back on." I got my teaching certificate, and I stopped being an actor. I became a teacher.

My teaching life was really a place for me to catch up with myself. Emotionally, I was fifteen or maybe younger. I taught in a high school and the kids were my friends. They were the friends I never had as a kid and it was a great time for me.

I did not have my first drink until I was twenty-one, because I said I wasn't ever going to become an alcoholic. I was not going to be like my father. I was in a bar in Miami and I was embarrassed into my first drink. I had on a football jersey and I ordered a coke, and the queen behind the bar said, "A big bruiser like you having a coke? Why don't you have a drink?" So she fixed me a rum and coke, or something, and I missed my plane home. It was love at first sight. For a while, the drinking was predominantly social drinking. With that socialization came experimentation with drugs and the stuff that went with the culture. You took mescaline to go dancing, that kind of stuff. I smoked pot, I used to do some THC, and on Fire Island, I did some acid.

During that period, sex was anonymous. I was living on my own here in Manhattan, and it was the world of the discos and bars.

My Father Stopped Drinking

I'll go back a little bit; 1968 was a very big year. My father stopped drinking; he bottomed out. Unfortunately, he went to a shrink who treated him as if he had a nervous breakdown and they substituted Librium for the alcohol. He became a Librium addict. But, at least in 1968, the abusive behavior stopped. It was really a time for amends. It was a time when I came to know him. I got to see the gentle side that was on the other side of this alcoholic. He would never admit that he was an alcoholic. I'm sorry that he never made it to AA meetings. The alcohol made him a very ugly and violent man. He was actually a very gentle and sweet soul, and I was very fortunate that from age eighteen on, I had a chance to get to know him. And he really tried to make amends; he tried to be there for me.

My father never gave me a problem about being gay. Every lover I had, my dad always came to our homes. He was always supportive; he used to help us move. So a lot of the healing work with him happened before he died, which I'm extremely grateful for.

The First Time I Ever Felt Good About Being Gay

My drinking and drugging was progressing along its course. I had decided when I was about twenty-four that I was ready to go to law school. Law school was the college experience that I never had. Law school happened as a result of the first gay cruise that they did in 1973 or 1974. It was the first time I ever felt good about being gay. I met such wonderful people who were positive, who were successful doctors, lawyers, writers, and artists. I came back from that cruise, I ended the relationship I was in, moved out of his apartment, got my own apartment, and started making applications to law school. I began to work on the process of feeling good about myself.

It was the first time that there was a spiritual connection for me. As a child, I was very spiritual. I had an imaginary pink elephant that I used to talk to all the time, and the only thing that the elephant used to say to me was, *It will be all right; it will be okay.* One night, in one of my father's crazy alcoholic rages, he said, "Little boys don't see pink elephants." And he grabbed me out of bed by my hair and said, "You show me where there's a pink elephant up there. I never want to hear another fucking word about it." And I never said another word about it. That was the violation of my spiritual boundaries, the only ones left to be violated.

John Was a Caretaker

My second year in law school I met a guy who was my exercise instructor at the Y. We had had one or two dates. He had a great big apartment, and his roommate was moving out. So I thought, This is great. This guy is not a drug addict, not an alcoholic, he's very stable, he's older than I am, and he's settled. It will be a nice quiet space for me to study in, the rent is right, and he loves to cook. I moved in as a roommate with no intention of getting intimately involved. I'm still involved with him.

I was teaching at the college level, part time, in four different schools at the same time. I had four shopping bags in the back of my car with the curriculum and the books. I literally used to make up a chart and schedule when I would eat, where I would go to the bathroom; that's how crazy my day was. I was smoking two and a half packs of cigarettes a day, I was drinking coffee and sugar like it was going out of style, and then, of course, I would start to shake. So I went to a doctor, and he said, "Here's some Valium; you'll be fine." That was the beginning of my bottom.

I would come home at night and John would give me a drink, and my dinner would be waiting with this bottle of wine; it was all just a gorgeous set up. He wanted to get involved, and I would come home and there would be very lavish and expensive gifts. It was consuming so much of my energy to push him away, to try to keep that boundary up, that I finally got involved with him. And I just thought to myself, What a great set up; anytime I feel insecure, anytime I want to have sex and smoke a joint and sniff some poppers, John's there. On top of which, he's cooking for me. Talk about safety.

In recovery I've learned a lot about intimacy, and in so doing, I came to love John very much. His caretaking, probably in its own way, saved my life and helped teach me how to care for myself.

"You're Not an Alcoholic, You Just Don't Have Any Discipline."

I very quickly crossed that magical line where I was alcoholically addicted. I drank alcoholically for the next two years. Every time I said, "I have a problem; I want to get help," John would say to me, "You're not an alcoholic. You just don't have any discipline or control; you're immature." This little voice in my head kept saying, No, darling, you are definitely an alcoholic, and before it gets worse, why don't you get some help?

There was a tremendous amount of pressure on me. Here I was in law school, which is stressful enough as it is, and I was teaching in these four schools. They could do a Marx brothers movie. There were times when I would grab the wrong shopping bag, and I would wind up with the wrong curriculum, and the people would be looking at me like, what on earth is he doing? I remember, once, I gave out the wrong final exam, and they sat and answered the questions. Can you imagine?

I moved in with John so that I could save money, but the next thing I knew, I was living this lifestyle that was beyond my means. After all, if you're lovers for ten months you have to act out fantasies and set up house together; that's what people do. So I just got caught in that grind, and law school stopped being what I wanted it to be.

We're now up to about '78. My drinking progressed for about another fifteen months. John kept telling me I wasn't an alcoholic. Then he went away on business, and my bottom came in a hot tub. I was drinking champagne, sitting in a hot tub, boiling away, and I thought I was going to drown. I'm way more than six feet tall and I was sitting in a four foot tub. I called AA the next day. That was eight years ago. My recovery started the minute I walked into an AA meeting. Except once, I've never wanted to have another drink since.

When I Left the Baths, I Felt Suicidal

I had two years of sobriety under my belt when I started to act out all the sexual stuff. It was at the same time that I started to go to ACOA [Adult Children of Alcoholics]. I would go to ACOA meetings, and then I would leave the meeting and go to a porno theater and act out for hours. That's how I would zone myself out.

The pain that started in '83 from the sexual compulsion was overwhelming. There was no feeling that was as painful as what it felt like after going out on a sexual binge. This was no longer what I wanted in my life. I wanted to be with somebody on an intimate basis; I needed to be held. Yet, anytime I was in any emotional pain, I used sex to relieve it, particularly if the stuff was related to an ACOA issue. If I had a client who hauled me on the carpet because I didn't do something, and I started feeling not worthy, like I'm fucked up, not perfect, I would leave the office and head to the baths. I would act out there for hours, and when I left the baths, I felt suicidal.

For me, the sexual compulsion was much worse to put down than the Valium or the booze. I did about a year and a half of SCA [Sexual Compulsives Anonymous]. That was at the very beginning, when it first got started. I used to go three times a week. I was still going to my ACOA meetings; I could deal with the ACOA stuff if I went to the SCA meetings.

In SCA, I started dating. It was very difficult because I had one foot in this relationship I was unwilling to give up, and this other foot that really wanted to get out and try to experience intimacy. My sex plan called for no anonymous sex, no bathhouses, no backroom bars, and no porno theaters. Nothing anonymous.

The Family Rescuer

In '83, my dad died suddenly in a brutal accident, and I was thrust back into the role of caretaker. My older brother is completely dysfunctional. In his dysfunction, he abandoned his wife and child. My mother and father had taken on their support. After my father died, my mother had a hard time doing this. I could now be the family rescuer by being not only my mother's surrogate husband, but my sister-in-law's surrogate husband and her child's surrogate father. I dove right into it. I was very fortunate in that I had already started in Al-Anon to learn about codependency.

I was very busy rescuing, and resenting it horribly. I was doing it because I thought I was finally going to get all this love from my mother. Yet, I was hating my sister-in-law and my mother. To my brother's kid, my mother would say things like, "When you graduate high school, Uncle Lewis will buy you a car. Whatever college you want to go to, Uncle Lewis will send you." It was that kind of insanity.

I took everyone on a family vacation down in Virginia, and one thing led to another, and it all blew up. I was in a parking lot, and I threw the car into park. My sister-in-law had already left on a bus with her kid, so I was with my mother. I left the car running in the middle of the lot and went running to a bar. I was going to get drunk to show her just how crazy she made me. Instead, I ran to a phone booth and called my sponsor. He was great. He said to me, "Go out and buy a pack of cigarettes and go walk around the parking lot. I'd rather see you smoke than drink." He had enough sense at that moment to know that if I hadn't had some release, I would have drank. I finished up that vacation with my mother; I insisted on it. And I really began to express how I felt about being set up in this role.

I came back and I really dove into Al-Anon. I knew, for the first time, that my primary illness was codependency, and that I had to start working on the issues of my mother. Al-Anon was wonderful, because I was really encouraged to make a life for myself.

I Was a Codependent Magnet

When that bottom happened in Virginia, I also had been experiencing a bottom with a lot of people in the program. I was the codependent magnet; I was able to find other people in the program who were reflections of every area in my life, areas that I didn't want to look at.

I now had this second home in Connecticut. I started getting connected to the program out there. There's something very special out there; the meetings are very small compared to meetings here in the city, and it's really a very spiritual place.

So, I began opening up out there. Much of my recovery was about this egotism: being the person with the answers, instead of being the person with the questions. I had so much self-esteem wrapped up in having it together that it was too difficult for me to let people know that I was a mess.

However, my greatest spiritual experiences came as a result of being completely vulnerable. In 1986 I started working the Eleventh Step. I began to feel like I was just adrift somewhere; I was really lost. I felt like I was in a rowboat, and I knew that the program and my faith in God were keeping me afloat. I had oars, but I didn't know where the shore was. I had no idea how to row or where to row to.

I had this feeling like I was just floating. It was a very scary feeling 'cause it was the first time in my life I didn't know where the fuck to go, what to do. Every day I got up and put one foot in front of the other, and I would get on my knees and pray. I prayed every day, and I would meditate, but nothing came. I don't think I've ever experienced a time in my life when there was so much nothingness.

Thank God for my sponsor in OA, who became my AA sponsor and my Al-Anon sponsor. He suggested this wonderful church in Brooklyn where a lot of program people went. It was a Catholic church with two very flamboyant priests. I found a home for myself in this wonderful place, but I still just felt like I was floating.

The church had a program on alcoholism, and one day, I volunteered to be a host at lunchtime, to sit with a table of people from the community and tell my story. I was sharing with this woman this feeling of floating and not knowing where to go, and she said, "Oh, have I got somebody for you." She steered me to this woman who helps people with spiritual direction, especially people in the program. I went to see her, and my life has not been the same since. She started to do private spiritual direction with me. She taught me how to pray. I had never read the Bible before, and she picked out all the sections where God said He loved me, He loved me unconditionally, and He forgave me for everything.

My whole life I felt that I was not good enough; if only I could work hard enough on myself, I would be enough, I would be okay. I used to see Jesus as this Being of perfection. If I worked hard enough, I'd never get to be like Him, but it was something to aspire to. One day, she had me read something out of the Bible and meditate on it. When I opened my eyes, I said, "Gee, I am just like Jesus. That's why He came, why God sent Him here. We're supposed to find out what it is to be a human being." It was extraordinary. It was like a light bulb had gone on in my head.

My T-Cells Were 70

In the summer of '87, I got a phone call from the doctor asking me to come in. I had gone through a regular six month physical, and he told me my T-cells were 70. It turned out that they were 370; they had dropped the three on the lab sheet and they incorrectly typed it. I'm sorry that happened, because at the time, the doctor was one of these conservative guys who did not believe in aerosol pentamidine.

When I got the wrong T-cell count, I had been planning a dream trip to China. I proceeded to throw caution to the winds and went. And I have to say, except for those first few days after being diagnosed — when I went into a panic and drove to the cemetery — I haven't had a frightened day since. I'm not afraid of dying; I'm afraid of debilitation, but I'm not afraid of dying. I really do believe that God's taken me this far, and I'm not going to be abandoned at this stage of the game.

So I went to China and came back, and the day after Christmas, I felt like I had the flu. I didn't call my doctor who I had been seeing for AIDS. I called my old family doctor, 'cause I had such denial. He knew nothing about it and he prescribed a strong antibiotic that's very immune suppressing.

So after eleven days, when my fever started to strike, I thought, I better get into my AIDS doctor; this ain't no flu. I was going to go in that afternoon, but on the way into work, I lost my breath. I couldn't walk; I had to grab hold of the street post. I went in and they did a bronchoscopy, and it was pneumocystis. I was given a prescription and told to go home and take it, and if I made it through ten days without an allergic reaction, I'd be over the hump. I got the typical drug induced hepatitis from Bactrim™. My temperature spiked to 106 degrees. I had to be on intravenous pentamidine for eighteen days. It took the first week and a half to get me off the reaction to the Bactrim™. I prayed every day.

I Felt Like I Was Washed in Hope

One day in February, I went to church and one of the priests told me he had been saving something for me. He gave me an article, an interview with Dr. Bernard Bahari. It was like the same experience I had the day I got down on my knees and asked God to help me stop drinking; it was exactly the same experience. I felt like I was washed in hope. From that day on, I have not had any doubt that I am gonna survive this illness. I read this article and it just transformed everything for me. In bold letters in the center of the article was a quote from Bahari that said, "In a very <u>short</u> time, this will be a chronic disease which is manageable." They had underlined the word *short*. From that day on I had absolutely no doubt that I would be a survivor.

I came in one morning and I said to my law partner, "I will never again work more than three days a week, ever." I decided that I wanted to spend as much time as I could out in the country, because I feel wonderful out there. It's a place that personifies my growth and my being well; it's a place that's very light.

In April, I went to Key West and saw that I could travel. I started to meet people, I started to come out of the closet about AIDS, and I started to listen to other people and hear what they were doing to get themselves well. I made a commitment to work at this too.

I came back and started to spend four days a week in the country. It took me from April until July to get to a point where I could get up in front of an AA meeting and be a channel for God's words and hold absolutely nothing back at all. I talked about my AIDS diagnosis and the most amazing thing began to happen. All the hugs, all the love that I walked around so desperately wanting, started filling my life.

I Should Buy a Mommy Doll and a Daddy Doll

I started to be open to people and listen to what people had to say. I felt that I had given up the control and was asking God what His will was for me. I was trusting that the Spirit would lead me to the right people. Extraordinary things were happening. All of the incest stuff that had remained covered for years started popping out all over. I was in a toy store one day, and I felt that I should buy a mommy doll and daddy doll, so I bought them. My sponsor said, "Well, let's go to the beach and play with them." We went to the beach, and then all of this stuff started to come out. The details began to gain significance. The stuff with the priest molesting my brother had never come up before. The pain of the emotional incest with my mother started to surface.

My mother brought some of my childhood pictures to me for my birthday. Looking at these pictures started unlocking more stuff. I decided to go through this ritual on my birthday, and what I did was, I burned my Fourth Step, gathered the ashes, and decided to go down to the beach and scatter the ashes into the ocean. I've always felt that God lives in the ocean.

I spent hours down on the beach cleansing myself. I thought that our program teaches us that we're not supposed to be angry, so I had made that decision. I thought I was supposed to get to forgiveness and unconditional love, so I was Gentle Ben. I wasn't angry, I was forgiving everyone: I forgave my mother; I forgave my father; I forgave everybody. And I went down to the beach, and it was extraordinary. I've never felt so spiritually connected to my dad, ever. I was really able to finish with him. I was able to tell him not what he *did*, but what I *felt*. Through that process, I was finally able to tell him that I loved him. First, I got to the forgiveness, and then, I got to the love. No matter what meditation I do now, the only thing that comes up for me with him is love. I really have finished my work with him.

I did this thing with my father, and I thought, Now there's still work that has to be done with Mom. I meditated, and I prayed that day and that night, and I was really directed to draw a picture of myself with finger paints. I drew a picture of myself with all this red inside and all this yellow trying to get in. The next day, I was given very clear instructions to draw again, and this time, I was to draw all of this light, this yellow from my heart that was sealed in red, trying to get out. I had no idea what it meant.

Then I went to a meditation group and somebody suggested that I go and see this woman who does channeling work. I carried my pictures under my arm, all rolled up, and I walked in there, and she started going into a trance. She described to me my two pictures under my arm in detail and began to explain to me my whole life. She didn't miss a beat, from the incest I witnessed as a child, to the violence, to John. She went through all of it. She described the pictures and explained, "This is all the rage buried in you. That's what your AIDS is. It's anger incorrectly directed at self. Your only hope for survival is to get this rage out of you. Your glimpses of joy are fleeting; you can't own it until you own the anger and the pain." It was just amazing. She gave me specific homework to do to try and get to the anger. This was a life and death thing to me. She knew that there was no more rage at my dad, that I had finished that.

I started keeping a journal; I started writing affirmations. I would do fifteen minutes of work every day opening the throat chakra, but no matter how hard I tried, I could not get to the anger.

The next person I was led to was a woman in the program. She heard me share one day, and she recommended that I go to Florida to this codependency rehab.

I decided to go ahead, so I booked myself a bed, but before I went to Florida, I decided to do a Louise Hay workshop. When Louise did the anger releasing part of the workshop, I thought, Jeez these people are all nuts; they're really sick. I'm beyond this; I don't have any anger. That's how deeply buried the anger was. I went from Louise's to the airport and checked into this facility, and they were just wonderful. It was the best experience of my recovery. They were so skilled. I had filled out a twenty-five page questionnaire giving them the most intimate details of my life, and they designed psychodrama experiences specifically for me.

They encouraged me to allow it to be a spiritual experience, because I was always afraid that if I let the anger out, I would never be able to regain control, and my survival depended on being able to control everything around me. Finally, when my anger surfaced, it took three or four people to hold me down. The only thing that didn't happen was my head didn't spin around and green bile didn't spew out; it was an extra-ordinary experience.

So now I'm home and there's more work to be done with my mother. It's a process, a wonderful, magical process.

CHIP

My life really fell apart at thirteen. My mother put me in a mental institution because she was afraid I was going to become a homosexual. I was the youngest of 1,100 patients in this mental institution. They took this young boy and put him in a ward with 350 men who were between forty and death.

My life, since my diagnosis with AIDS, has been a very growing time. It's been extremely painful for me, because I've really had to look at a lot of the things that kept me drinking and drugging. I just spent four months in the hospital, where I was introduced to Bernie Siegel's meditation tapes, which have been extremely helpful. Before my diagnosis, I knew about Louise Hay and I used to meditate and go to Unity Church. I was very glad that I already had a program, and that AA had taught me how to live my life one day at a time.

When I was finally diagnosed, it was almost a relief. I wasn't crazy; there was a basis for what was going on, and it was acceptable for me to think about committing suicide. But when the doctor said, "You have AIDS and you have six months to live," my attitude was, Don't tell me I'm gonna die. In lots of respects, I gave myself permission to live. I've tried to keep looking at it in that vein.

I came from a fairly decent home. My father was the head doctor at a hospital in Washington. Then there was the divorce. After the divorce, my mother had to go to work. My mother was a teacher. My life really fell apart at thirteen. My mother put me in a mental institution because she was afraid I was going to become a homosexual. I was the youngest of 1,100 patients in this mental institution. They took this young boy and put him in a ward with 350 men who were between forty and death. Some of them had been there twenty years.

I became a ward of the state because my family refused to take me. I stayed there till I was eighteen. I learned very quickly what homosexuality was, and I learned how to manipulate, and I learned about alcohol.

You have to remember, then, homosexuality was considered a mental illness, just like alcoholism was considered a mental illness — and they locked you away. I'm sure that I had tendencies — I wanted to take ballet lessons, and I liked to play with dolls — but I didn't actually have a homosexual experience until I went to the hospital.

It amazes me, actually, how sad I was as a child and how desperate I was for attention and recognition. Everybody in the neighborhood loved me, but the only person I couldn't get close to was my mother. My father had passed away. There were three boys; I was the middle child, and I was my father's favorite. He died within a year of the divorce. I blamed my mother the only way a child can blame. If she knew he was going to die, why didn't she stay with him another year? I didn't want to believe any of the things my mother later told us. She said that he drank too much, and he had a girlfriend.

And I was different. I was a very creative child. I skipped the third grade and the fifth grade in school, so obviously I had some brain power. My mother just didn't know what to do with me.

They Took My Birth Certificate and Erased My Name

I spent the better portion of the next ten years feeling extremely invisible. It was as if, at thirteen, they took my birth certificate and erased my name — erased everything about me. I'm not necessarily pleased with the person that I decided to be. Obviously, I didn't have healthy role models. There's anger, which I've only been willing to admit in the last two years. For a number of years, I've felt that the anger was so consuming that if I ever exploded I would end up in a corner going blub, blub, and that would be the end of it. Anger is an unacceptable emotion as far as I'm concerned. I've always been one of those people who felt that if you go from *a* to *b* to *c*, that *d* has to follow, and that you can talk things over; there has to be a way that you can talk things out. It doesn't always work, but that's my philosophy about it. Screaming and hollering never solved anything.

In the mental institution, they used to spit at me, curse at me, and kick at me. It was a very violent situation. I didn't think about it at the time particularly, but I'm very aware of it now — not everybody could have been strong enough to survive that. I took a bad situation and made the best of it. Unfortunately, I sent myself down the river in lots of ways, because that's what I had to do. For years, I justified like, I didn't have to have a curfew, I didn't have to worry about going to the prom, or I didn't have to worry about the kids in school calling me a fag. I believe in God, and I think that He gave me a sense of humor. So I can look back at some of that with a great deal of humor. And, it made me real strong.

My first suicide attempt was at sixteen. Obviously, I couldn't have been too happy. It didn't dawn on me, when I tried to commit suicide the second time, that there was something dreadfully wrong with a twenty-one-year-old who wanted to die. I went to bed with my hands out of the bed, so I wouldn't get blood on the bed, so they would think I kept a clean house.

When I was eighteen, I left the mental institution, which was a very protective environment, and moved in with five black guys in Brooklyn who had $100-a-day heroin habits. I was the only white person on the block. I went from that to picking potatoes in the fields. Again, I was the only white person. I spent my twenty-first birthday in jail for robbing a liquor store. I did six months in jail. While I was in jail, they decided I wasn't just your average common criminal and they offered to send me either to automotive school or beauty school. I chose beauty school. I've been a hairdresser now for twenty-seven years.

I think by the time I was twenty-three that I survived more than a lot of people survive in a lifetime. In some ways, I felt that my life was already over, that there was nothing else that I could do.

I Seduced an Attendant on Each Shift

I had my first drink at thirteen in the mental institution. I had sixteen martinis on my sixteenth birthday, and by the time I left the hospital, I was drinking a quart a day. While I was in the hospital, I learned very quickly how to manipulate. I seduced an attendant on each shift and threatened them. If they didn't give me the alcohol, I would tell the doctors what they did to me.

I quickly learned that I had something they wanted. The sexual aspect of it was not always pleasant, but it was what I knew. I don't think I knew how valuable youth was, but I certainly knew the value of sex. I also remember, at some point, rebelling and refusing to have sex unless they kissed me. I was desperate for some affection, and under those conditions — be it an employee or patient — they were just interested in quick releases; there was no romance involved.

What makes it sad for me is that I accepted it; I didn't know better. There's a little voice in my head that sometimes says that sex is very beautiful and very natural. I don't think I will ever know about that.

One of the things I'm really angry about is my lack of education. I think that children should have some rights, some things that they're entitled to. For years, people used to introduce me as the boy with the beautiful ass. On a number of occasions I thought, Don't they care what's going on up here in my head? The truth of the matter is that they didn't.

By the time I was twenty-three, I was being kept by a very brilliant man who read, wrote, and spoke seven languages fluently. Some of my anger is directed toward him; I know, now, that he really just wanted an ornament. He didn't encourage me to go to school; he paid my bar bills. When I was twenty-three or twenty-four, he bought me a house for $90,000. My attitude was, you're not sticking me in the woods away from my friends in the bars. I sold it for $110,000 and thought that I did well. To a twenty-four year old, $110,000 was a great deal of money. All it afforded me was the opportunity to buy clothes, to drink, and to party.

I was always chasing him away. I would say, "Give me $5,000 and get out of my life. Go away." I think that I knew then that I was an alcoholic. I had a knack for dressing up the outside and what you saw was what you got. I was very insecure, so I had to have the Gucci watches and the fur coats and the big rings to show the world that I was as good as they were. I was successful at that for a long time.

There are times when I can say all this and I think, It's just the facts. There are other days when I *feel* it. Sometimes it's devastating to me to think that somebody had to survive all this, and for what? Then it amazes me that I've been so unhappy for such a long period of time, and for a lot of the time, I didn't know it.

I remember the first couple of hours when my mother put me in the hospital. First of all, I thought they were taking me to the electric chair; I thought they were going to kill me. I couldn't imagine what I had done that was so terrible to deserve this punishment. When my mother refused to take me out, I decided then and there that nobody would ever know what was going on; I would never allow myself to be in a position where somebody could hurt me like that again. I very quickly learned how to be what people wanted me to be. I've really started working on that the last three years. My therapist used to say to me, "You know, you come in here, and you tell me something three weeks after the fact, after you figure out how you should feel about it, what you think I want you to feel about it, what's the correct way to go about it." I've finally gotten to the point where I can associate the feeling with the fact.

From $100,000 in December to Vagrancy in April

Anyway, I stayed with this man for five years. By the time I was thirty, I had gotten another $100,000 for a car accident that I was in. I actually got the cash in my hand in December of that year, and in April, I was arrested for vagrancy. That was more than twenty years ago. I moved into the biggest house in town with a six-car garage, a swimming pool, a stable, and a circular driveway. Three months later, I was living in a $13-a-week room with plastic drapes on the window and a big cigarette burn in the floor. I thought, Well, you have your ups and downs.

The one thing that was consistent was that I knew that something was wrong. On my own, I continued to always go to therapy of one sort or another. For a long time my attitude was, I know something's wrong; you tell me what it is; I don't want to participate. That's one of the things that AIDS has done: it makes a person participate in his or her life. Sometimes, a little begrudgingly.

My real downfall started about ten years ago. I was involved in a fifteen-year relationship that was a disaster. I was busy being what I thought he wanted me to be and trying to make him into what I wanted him to be. I used to be one of those people who could make things happen. If I didn't have a job, I'd say, "I'm going to get a job this afternoon," and I would go get a job that afternoon, and that was that. I had that kind of self-confidence. James had a very strong, domineering personality, and I lost who I was in that relationship. In 1976 I went to AA because of him, to save the relationship, but I just kept losing myself. It just got worse and worse, and after four and a half years of sobriety, I started drinking again — to the point where I was drinking around-the-clock.

Since then, I haven't been able to put a year together. Last year I drank one day out of the year, the year before that I drank two days out of the year, and I drank twice this year. One of them, if I'm real honest about it, was a suicide attempt. I shot drugs, which is something I had never done before.

Alcohol Is Going to Get Me Faster than AIDS

At the moment, my concern is that since my diagnosis, everything seems to have switched off alcohol and switched onto AIDS. I know that alcohol is gonna get me much faster than AIDS ever will. That's the choice that I have; I do have a choice. I guess you can tell from my past history that I didn't always make the right choice. But they're the choices that I made. Louise Hay says we need to take the word *should* out of our vocabulary; we did what we did, and we're doing what we're doing, and that's the best we can do.

This last year was probably the worst year of my entire life. I became afraid of people; I questioned my own ability to do anything; I became non-functional. There were periods in my life when I would become lethargic, when I didn't want to work, and I didn't want to play. I usually was able to turn it around and continue forward. My pattern seemed to be that I would make great messes and then spend a period of time cleaning them up: not going to work for a week and not calling, and then I'd spend the next two months working fourteen-hour days to show everybody how wonderful I was again.

But this time, I couldn't pull myself out. I was angry that I spent fifteen years with a person who didn't know whether I took sugar in my coffee, that I thought so little of myself that I allowed this to happen. Lots of days I thought that I would just lay there and starve myself to death. I didn't think I deserved any better; a single room occupancy hotel was exactly what I deserved.

I was tired; I was tired of the lies; I was tired of the deceit. I was trying to let go of the things that I felt were no longer working because the pain was just too great. I couldn't dress up the outside anymore and go sit in the front row at AA meetings and pretend that everything was fine. I distinctly remember sitting at a Sunday meeting thinking, If I stand up and fold my clothes and put them on the chair next to me, this chair will be empty. I have a lot of trouble with verbal communication, telling anybody that things aren't fine; it's been one of the reasons I've gotten drunk, why I've had such a hard time breaking that pattern. If I drink, they'll know there's something seriously wrong.

It's Very Difficult to Be Thirteen and Fifty at the Same Time

I think that my alcoholism, and whatever drugs I did, were about self-loathing; it was a slow form of suicide. And I think that there's a direct correlation with AIDS. I was looking for another thing to manipulate with. I mean, I'm older, so I no longer have sex as a manipulative tool. For years I had, Oh, poor little Chip was in the mental institution; we have to be nice to him, be gentle, be sweet. Then I became an alcoholic and it was, Oh that poor boy is drunk; we have to do what we can do to help him. Then came AIDS and I thought, Oh, boy, what more could you ask for? They all came at the right time, and the right age, and the difference is, now I don't want to use it as something to manipulate with. I think it's very difficult to be thirteen and fifty at the same time. My reaction today, to many things, is that unprepared thirteen-year-old's reactions. And it's okay; I can allow myself that. It doesn't mean I have to like it; it's not comfortable.

There are days when I think I'm not going to be able to tolerate the emotional pain, that the thing that's going to kill me is a broken heart. I worry that I'll never really know what love is, to be nurtured and be accepted for who I am and what I am. It won't happen because of my fear of not letting people who want to do that, do it. There's a little tiny voice that says, I don't deserve it; I've gotten exactly what I deserve.

I make this all sound so grade B movie.

I Can Create a Better Situation for Myself

I think most of us drank to survive, to make things bearable, but at a certain point I have to say, I'm responsible for my drinking. I became the victim very early in life; it was a role that I was comfortable with, that I held onto for a very long time. No matter what positive steps I did, I always, eventually, fell back into thinking, Poor me; look what James is doing to me; look what life is doing to me; look what my mother did to me; I'm just a drunk; I'm not going to be anything.

I made a lot of it happen. A lot of the negative stuff that happened in my life I orchestrated, and then I sat in the middle of it and thought, If I didn't have this job, this wouldn't have happened, or if. . . . The truth of the matter is, I created the jobs and I created the situations. Whatever it was, I created that. I'm just now seeing that I can create a better situation for myself. And that's where I want to be today. It's hard; there are some old tapes that ask, Why bother? But obviously there's a stronger tape that says, Keep trying.

To Parrot the Words Doesn't Do It

For years I've heard people say, "I'm grateful that I'm an alcoholic," and I'd think, What's wrong with those people? They're grateful they're an alcoholic? When they diagnosed me with AIDS, I was really grateful that I'd already had a program that taught me to live my life one day at a time. Whether you're an addict or an alcoholic or a person with AIDS, if you live your life by AA's guidelines, then you'll have to have a better life. Period.

So I need to work at my program with some more diligence. We have this expression, "You have to work for it to work." Showing up just isn't enough. I need to call people before I take a drink. I need to follow suggestions. I could quote you all the slogans and the sayings, but to just parrot the words doesn't do it; you have to really live it. Without being too hard on myself, I'm really doing okay. I go to individual counseling for alcoholism twice a week; I go to an alcohol group for people who are HIV positive or have AIDS once a week. I go to AA meetings, and I'm now co-chairing a meeting here at the shelter.

Being diagnosed with AIDS was the first time that I was willing to participate in my life. It gave me a direction; it made me want to live. It made me take my alcoholism much more seriously, maybe take life more seriously. I started reading self-help books; I started looking at my spiritual side. I started looking at things that I was lacking, the things that made me uncomfortable, the areas I needed to improve.

I haven't always been successful at working AA. Once I found AA, I thought it was always there, so I could go and and get drunk whenever I wanted, go back to AA, and it would be there. Once I was diagnosed with AIDS I decided, I can get as little out of this as I want, or I can get as much as I can absorb. I want to absorb as much as I can, and that means being alcohol and drug free.

ALLISON

My father was murdered and my brother just died of AIDS, and I thought, You're next. The three of us, we did everything the same way....

The more I made, the better my career got, the more I drank. Then, a very famous woman hired me as her backup singer.

I grew up in an average southern town in Mississippi. I always called myself a black American princess because I went to boarding school and I was a debutante. I went through all of that down South. My mother and my father were divorced, so I would spend holidays here in New York with my mother, and I'd go to school down in Mississippi.

The beginning of my secrets was incest. I was first incested at eight years old by my aunt's husband, and I was fifteen when he tried to kill me. That's when I came to New York. I was already drinking when I was fifteen. I came home drunk one day and told my mother about the incest.

They Sent Me Down South

My parents sent me down South because my father was in show business. He was a womanizer and he was an alcoholic and he was off doing his thing, and my mother was working very hard to hold the house together. Two of my sisters died of pneumonia. Then I came along and had pneumonia, and I almost died. My mother said she couldn't lose one more. She had this sister in Mississippi who was doing very well, who could fit in that world down there, and so my mother gave me to her. My aunt and uncle had me from the time I was an infant.

My best friends were boys; they'd come over to play with my dolls. I find it so ironic that as a child, before I was even in the first grade, my playmates were two boys. And here I am, forty-three, and I'm still always around gay men.

You know when little boys say, "I'll show you mine and you show me yours?" I did that with this neighbor boy. We both were beaten brutally for it. My legs were bleeding, and my uncle said, "Don't you ever do that, don't you ever let me catch you doing that again." A few years later he incests me.

When I was fifteen, my uncle called me a tramp and a slut. He was strangling me from behind. My aunt pulled him off of me and told him, "Stop that; she isn't worth it." I could feel myself like leaving my body. I was struggling to get air and I looked at her and I looked at him, and I thought, I'm not safe here. I'm not safe here and I'm not coming back. My neck was all wrecked where he had dug into it. I knew I was going to be going to New York in August to visit my mother and the rest of my family, and I said to myself, I'm not coming back.

He used to write me notes and leave them on my bed, sexual things. I saved one 'cause I knew no one would believe me. I saved it for proof; I hid it. When I got to New York for my regular summer vacation here, and I was drunk, I told my mother what was happening. I said, "I even have proof." She called my grandmother and told her to get the proof. My grandmother got the proof and tore it up and said that my aunt didn't need to see it, that it would hurt her.

So that's kind of the way it was. I was this debutante and it was real glorious and all this sickness was happening. My uncle was a preacher, and I'd sit in church and look at him preach, and I'd pray for his soul.

Secret Number Two

As a teenager living in New York, I was hiding bottles, drinking, and dreaming about a career in show business. My father and my stepfather played in a band. My brother was a musician, too, so I had all these male musicians in my family.

Then I met this woman who had dreams about being a radio disc jockey. Because there weren't any women disc jockeys in New York, we left New York and went to Providence, Rhode Island. She and I lived at the YWCA. She would do her show at night, and I would work at the Y during the day as office manager and sing the Holiday Inn circuit at night. We had rooms across the hall. That was secret number two. We didn't want people to know that we were lovers, so her room was across the hall. We'd sneak into each other's rooms at night and mess the other bed up the next day.

Then I won this talent contest. Out of 1,000 people, I won. I was brought to New York, and I started doing TV stuff and opening acts for all these major people. And they sent me to Australia where I starred in a musical. I lived in Australia for two and a half years. They set me up in an apartment that was just gorgeous. It was in Sydney, in a place called Elizabeth Bay, overlooking all the yachts. The first thing I did was stock the bar with liquor. Next, I bought this marijuana and I rolled all these joints and I put them in the cigarette box. When I came home from the theater, I'd bring an entourage, and we'd drink and smoke these joints and take acid. Well, they took acid; I was too paranoid to take acid.

That went on for two and a half years. I was asked to leave Australia 'cause my visa had expired, and I was no longer there making money for the promoter who had brought me there. I wasn't making money for him; I was making money on my own. I had done a TV show and I had records out, and this man wasn't getting any of the profits. Plus, I was doing all these demonstrations. I was protesting South Africa. I had gotten all political. And everything I was doing, I was doing drunk. So I got a little letter from the government saying, you may leave now, you have no permit.

A Very Famous Woman

I went back to the United States and did some more theater, and I started doing really well. And the more I made, the better my career got, the more I drank. Then a very famous woman hired me as her backup singer. The first tour that I went out on, somebody asked me if I wanted to do some cocaine. They took this mirror off the wall, put it on my bed, and dumped all this cocaine on it. That's how we divided our cocaine. We'd take our hand and just divide it and then just sort of scoop it up into some plastic. That was in 1973, something like that. For five years I was doing cocaine and drinking and being exposed to all these major stars, major money, major fast lane and just getting more and more lost.

I was also being real promiscuous. I had sex from one end of the map to the other. We'd just come out of the '60s, and it was like, be yourself, be yourself, and so everybody was just doing everything. The disco era was coming in, and with it, the after-hours clubs. The backup group that I was with formed our own group. I had a record out with them. That young girl from Mississippi who dreamed about performing, well it had happened. The group only stayed together for a year because two of us were drinking and drugging so much. One of the women didn't drink at all, and how she handled it, I don't know.

Top of the Charts

We broke up and I went out on my own. The very first record I did went to number one on the disco charts. It was a fluke. I was freebasing in the studio at three in the morning, and they said, "I'm going to pay you one thousand dollars, or you can sign and get royalties." I said, "No, I don't believe in this record; I don't believe in your company; give me the money." I wanted to get more coke and go to California and really become a star. I got to California, and the second week I was there, I heard that song on the radio.

So there I was, my dreams were coming true, and I was becoming more insane. By this time, I'd met another woman who I fell in love with, and she started to manage my career. She was an addict too. She was shooting heroin, and we were both on the pipe and drinking and fighting. We fought; we scratched; we pulled hair. I was thrown out of a moving car. I lost teeth; it was just a horror. We were horrible to each other, and every dime I made, I would give her 50 percent. I had three albums out now and they had all done very well. I was traveling to Europe, I was getting a name, and I was trying to get away from this woman. I thought she was my problem — her addiction to heroin. I knew my addiction was kind of out of hand too.

Murdered in a Blackout

In 1984 my father was murdered while he was in a blackout. My father and I were close — when I'd see him. He and I drank together. He was in New York now, and he would play every now and again somewhere, and so we would sit in his clubhouse and drink and talk about the old days for him and the old days for me. He'd smoke marijuana and I'd do coke.

My brother came to my house one night I was living in a brownstone and I was doing real well. I was sitting on the floor and I had all the windows open and I thought, This is the most beautiful evening of my life. I remember being distinctly grateful that night, because I had all the drugs and all the liquor I wanted. I was alone in the house and it was quiet; there was no lover there to bug me. It was real windy out and it was a beautiful night, beautiful life, beautiful people — I had everything. And there was a knock on the door and it was my brother telling me my father had been murdered. My father died in a hotel room after having picked up a woman. He had all this money. They had a bong and reefer, and she robbed him and shot him in the face.

The Discos, the Poppers, the Crystal, the Cocaine

I used to work in the Keys a lot. By this time, most of my work took me to gay disco clubs. People were using poppers and crystal and cocaine and acid and mescaline and every drug imaginable. When they'd send me a contract, they'd ask what I wanted and I'd say, "I want cocaine and liquor. Have it in the car; have it all in the car when I arrive. Don't even wait to take me to go get it; have it in the car." And they would do it. It even got to the point where one club said, "Well, can we pay you in cocaine?" And I thought, Oh no, this is it; this is the Billie Holiday story, and I sort of chuckled and I thought, Oh well, why not?

Around this time, I called home, and my mother said my brother had been very sick and needed to go to the hospital. When I got home, he had pneumonia, and they took him into intensive care. This was in January. He never left intensive care. I was told that they thought he had AIDS. We had to wear masks and gloves and gowns. I would go to the hospital with my vial of coke, my Bacardi in my purse, and Valium, and I would be there around-the-clock. My brother only wanted me and my mother, 'cause we were the closest ones to him. We had the same lifestyle, he and I.

He had all these tubes coming out of him and a respirator. He'd look at me and kind of smile 'cause he was really crazy about me. I was the baby; he was the oldest. We did the same things. He died in March. I was still very high and I couldn't stop crying. He was the closest member of my family — he and my father — and now they were both dead.

My father was murdered and my brother just died of AIDS, and I thought, You're next. The three of us, we did everything the same way. I lived in hotels, picked up people, woke up with men, women, you know. There was the drugs, the police. I'd gone to jail in Dallas, Texas; it was all that kind of drama. And here my father was gone, and I thought, Allison, that could've been you, easily. Someone could've shot you and taken your pay in any town in the USA, and you could very easily get AIDS, you know.

I Thought the Whole World Drank Like I Did

One night after my brother died, I was walking down Broadway, and I was really broke by this time. I had lost my apartment, and I was living in a hotel with a girlfriend. It was like three in the morning, and I hadn't washed my face in I don't know when, and I had mascara down my face, and my cousin said, "You really need help." And I said, "Well, yeah, I do." I thought he meant because I couldn't stop crying. He told me about a therapist who would see me. I said I don't have any money. He said we could probably work something out.

So my cousin called me the next day, and I went to see this therapist who told me a lot of my problems would probably be lifted if I stopped drinking. He asked me about how much I drank and I said, "I don't know, like everybody else." I thought the whole world drank like I did. He asked me how much coke I did, how much pills I did. By this time, I was drinking this stuff called Majorska, this vodka that costs $1.09. The liquor store salesman told me, "Don't buy this, it's gonna rip your lining. It's the worst stuff." And I said, "Give it here. That's all I can afford." I couldn't afford the Valium anymore, so I was knocking myself out with Nyquil or Excedrin PM®. My high had gone to such a low — the bottom. From being this diva, from taking the mirror off the wall and putting it on the bed and doing coke, from saying, "Yes, I want this Courvoisier and Absolut," to doing this Majorska.

My girlfriend, another singer, lived a block away. I would run over to her house at two in the morning, and she'd put vodka in a mayonnaise jar for me. This diva is now running around the block to get vodka in a mayonnaise jar. She would pass me Excedrin PM® in an envelope, that was part of the package. She gives me the Excedrin in the envelope: the vodka in a mayonnaise jar, and all of it in a little brown bag that she'd hand me out the door, and I'd say, "Thank you," and I'd leave. I mean, I was really broke.

I was beginning to listen to my therapist. He said, "I'm sure you can't have just one drink." I thought, I'll show him. I said, "Well, I won't drink." I left his office, which was walking distance from my house. I passed a liquor store, and I thought, "Well, I'll just buy the liquor now. I'll pick up a bottle of wine. I don't drink wine. I mean, that's not liquor to me; that's like buying beer. I don't drink beer, there's no alcohol in it. So I picked up this wine, and I sat it up somewhere in this room, and I thought, "I'm not going to drink it until 6:00 P.M." I'd wait until the hour when people have drinks in the evening, you know, after work. Anyway, by 1:00 P.M. the bottle was empty, and I was out. I could never postpone opening a bottle. After that I would be in the Nyquil, the Excedrin, or I would try to get credit. I used to hustle large amounts of cocaine from dealers by telling them I would thank them — something really flowery — on the back of my album.

My therapist told me about an AA meeting that a lot of people in show business go to. He figured I would enjoy that; I'd relate. I went to this meeting and it was all show business people. They were all white, and everybody seemed to be working and looking fabulous, and I thought, I can't take this; I'm feeling really inferior here. I started going to another meeting where people had low bottom stories. I didn't hear anything about show business, and I felt right at home. Women were sharing about rats in the crib, and I really needed to hear that. I wanted to hear the worst horror stories possible so then mine wouldn't be so low.

After two months of these meetings, I got a call to go to England. I took my mother. I'm such a people pleaser. I thought, I'll take my mother, I won't drink, I'll go to meetings, and I'll be a good little girl. They told me alcoholism was not a moral issue, but I didn't hear any of that. If I took my mother, I'd be a good little girl, and I'd go to meetings while I was there. I took my road manager too. So he and my mother and I went to England. I was getting my life back, and I thought, Oh, AA is fabulous. Two months sober. This was in 1985, right after my brother died.

Anyway, we're on the plane in executive class. Not first class, but in-between, right? So, it's all free champagne, and I'm sitting between my mother and this man, and they're both drinking. I had two months of sobriety. They told me, "Don't go on this trip," and I said, "Are you kidding? I'm going; I'm getting my career back. AA is really wonderful."

I got to London, I went to some meetings, and I took inventory at the meetings. I thought, I know they speak English, but I don't understand a word of what they're saying. One of my famous lines is, *not enough black people here*. And I certainly didn't see any black women, and didn't black people drink anymore? That was always my safety button to push when I wanted to drink again. I'd run into color or sex or something like that.

Finally, one night I went out to the bar with my manager. I said, "I'm just going to go out; I'm not going to drink. I'll just go out with you for an hour, and if I feel uncomfortable, I'll get in a cab and come home." We went to this wine bar and I stood next to the bar watching people. It was real dark, and even though it was a gay club, it was very mixed, you know, men and women, and everyone's kind of dancing together. I watched all these bodies; everybody looked happy, sexy. I was standing there, and I said, "Just one glass of wine." And then it was over. An hour later he and I were arguing, 'cause I was one of those argumentative drunks.

I took a cab to Heaven, the biggest club in London. "Take me to Heaven," I said. I got to the club, and that's all I remember. When I came to, I was lying facedown in my vomit on this white carpet in this dark room. And I looked around, and as I lifted my head up, the room was spinning around, and I thought, Oh God, wherever I am, please don't let the person here be a murderer or a rapist. As things came into focus, I realized I was in my house in London. Through the grace of God, I had gotten home.

All day I was feeling sorry for myself, and for my mother who had to take care of me. I thought, How could you do this to your mother? Oh my goodness, and I cried. I tried to go back to meetings, but it didn't work. I meant to stay clean. I swore, I prayed, and I said I would not take another lick of anything. But a week later I was right back there, trying to be a part of the whole thing. I started sneaking drugs; I didn't want my mother to know.

Little Pea-Like Knots Around My Neck

On the trip back to the United States, I remember feeling these little pea-like knots around my neck. I remember waking up in the middle of the night being paranoid, feeling my body and thinking about my brother, thinking, Something is the matter; I have these swollen glands.

Back in New York, I started going to meetings, and I started hearing about how alcoholics really need to get a physical because we did a lot of damage out there. I was sitting in a meeting, within my first ninety days, and I shared that my hearing was weird. Then someone said, "You don't have to do anything alone in AA. In AA, you're not alone anymore." And I thought, Yeah, but I can't let you know my real fear. I came in the room sharing that I'd been in show business. When I started, I wanted to be "somebody" in AA. I wanted to be "somebody" so much that it kept me from being honest.

Months went by and my glands started getting larger, much larger. In the meantime, I'm living in this hotel with my girlfriend, and I was getting these wigs to hide my swollen glands. I had such denial, I mean, alcohol and drug addiction is a disease of attitude and denial. I was going to this Central Park West specialist who told me that most alcoholics, usually older in years — not young alcoholics such as myself — suffer from periodic gland swelling. He told me that as soon as I cleaned up, as soon as the alcohol was out of my system, the swelling would go down.

So that was very comfortable for me. I was supposed to come back in three months, so I did. The swellings had not gone down. They were actually getting bigger, and I was getting swellings in other areas, in my breasts. I thought, Oh I've got cancer; that's comfortable. I preferred cancer to the thought of having AIDS.

I had no one to talk to about my fear of AIDS. I wouldn't get a sponsor 'cause I didn't want to have to deal with being honest. I didn't tell my girlfriend either.

This was going on almost a year into sobriety. I was still working in the clubs; I was performing; I was doing benefits for people with AIDS; I was at the United Nations. I've done all of these incredible things for children with AIDS, for people with AIDS. AIDS, AIDS, AIDS, you know, and here I am thinking, Oh my goodness, when are you gonna get some help? I finally went and got myself tested, but I never went back for the results. I kept telling myself they must be tumors; I can live with that.

Finally, I went to this cancer specialist. I was thinking, Even if you think it is cancer, you better take care of it. He said, "You have lymph gland swelling, lymphadenopathy, and you better go and see if it's AIDS-related." But I didn't.

You're as Sick as Your Secrets

One day I was sitting at a meeting, and I heard, "You're as sick as your secrets." It just hit home. I grabbed a woman in the meeting, a lesbian. She had a lover, and they were very popular in the group, and I knew they could keep secrets. I asked her to go with me to the pay phone. I used a pay phone to get my test results. She waited outside the phone booth, and I was told, "Yes, it's positive. Come see me." I hung up the phone, and I broke down in the street. I went to her house, and I begged her to please not tell anyone. Then I asked her if she'd sponsor me.

Still, I didn't tell my lover. I didn't want to have sex anymore, and I didn't want her to touch me. She thought there was somebody else. Then she started thinking it was the program, that the program was teaching me that homosexuality was bad, that I was going through some moral adjustment. I just let her think what she wanted to think. I never tried to make her feel comfortable.

In my second year of sobriety, my lover still didn't know about my HIV diagnosis. It was beginning to kill me: living in this one room with this secret and this woman and no lovemaking and no honesty, while AA talked about being honest and willing.

Whenever anything came on TV about AIDS, I'd switch the channel. Because my brother had died, my lover thought that I was being emotional about him. Finally, I was losing friends to the disease, and I wasn't telling them about my diagnosis. I was going to visit them, and I wouldn't tell them. Three years ago my friend, who has since died, had shingles. I also had shingles. He was doing a lot of cocaine and crack. He had pneumocystis, he had holes in his side, tubes going out of here and there, but he was still trying to find one more way to get high. I told him to be strong and hang in there, that he could do it, but I never once told him that I was doing it too, that I was fighting this battle with him, that he wasn't alone, that I wasn't getting high to cope.

He died never knowing. If he was suspicious that was one thing, but he never heard it from my lips. The hospital called and told me he was dying. I was there with his family; he had just died and just before they were going to zip him up, I looked at him. I could feel his soul was somewhere in that room. I talked to him, 'cause I figured he heard me, that he hadn't gone very far. I said that I was sorry that I hadn't talked, hadn't shared with him.

After that, I started sharing about this disease. I speak at a women's prison every month. The first time I shared my HIV status was in a meeting at this prison. Women came over and whispered that they were diagnosed and were scared to let people in the prison know. Every time I went back, it was the same people. New people would come, but a lot of the same people were there.

In a prison, people are deathly afraid; they're ostracized when in jail. They get no medical attention and their diets are poor. So they whisper, and I give my phone number, and they'll call me up at home and share.

One woman whispered to me, "I have thrush; I don't know what to do; I don't know who to talk to." I remember reading letters in the PWA newsletter from people in prison and how painful it all is, and here I was sharing with someone. So I thought, Maybe this is what it's all about in the end anyway. My whole life I've been carrying a message in my music, "Yeah baby, give me good loving; yeah baby, come on over here." All these old cliches in my records were meaningless. But here I am now, really carrying a message.

Working a Program

I'm still in therapy. I go to an HIV meeting, I go to an HIV/ARC private therapy group, and I go to one-on-one therapy. I'm getting acupuncture and chiropractic care. I'm working on a screenplay with someone in the program, and I'm learning to say no to people-pleasing things. I'm starting to let go of guilt, because guilt will kill you. I'm trying to be honest about what I want to do and about what I'm feeling. I'm not just doing things so that people will think nicely of me. I'm constantly looking at new medical options, and I go to an AA meeting every day. That's how I keep clean. I have sponsors. I still don't have the sponsor that I know I need, and sometimes I wonder if it's because I'm getting so much therapy or whether it's still the lack of trust from being an incest survivor.

Now my lover knows about my HIV. It's been about six months, and she's been loving and sexual with me. I thought that she wouldn't want to touch me and that she'd be mad at me for getting this. But no, she kisses me on my lips.

My mother doesn't kiss me anymore. It's a hug, and her head is off my shoulder. It hurts, but I'm living with it; I'm working through it in all my groups. That's the importance of support groups: I get to hear how other people are coping. I find I'm not unique or alone. I always thought I was unique because of my incest issue and it was so easy to feel unique as a woman with ARC. When I go to support groups, I identify with others, and I don't feel separate or alone or terminally unique.

CHAPTER SIXTEEN

Lost Childhoods

BERNIE

My world opened up when I was about ten years old. I met this twenty-four-year-old guy who lived down the street, and he turned me on to my first mixed drink, my first Quaalude, my first joint, and gay sex all the same night. And I thought, This is wonderful; this is what life is all about.

I started drinking and using when I was real young. Alcohol was part of the family. I grew up enjoying Cold Duck at Thanksgiving and other holidays. I always ended up overdoing it and passing out. My earliest memory of alcohol is my father coming home from work and having a drink. I thought this is what being an adult is about: coming home, relaxing, and having cocktails.

I didn't like being a kid at all. I wanted to be an adult. Why? I don't know. My world opened up when I was about ten years old. I met this twenty-four-year-old guy who lived down the street, and he turned me on to my first mixed drink, my first Quaalude, my first joint, and gay sex all the same night. And I thought, This is wonderful; this is what life is all about. I thought at that point that I was all grown up, so I started the process of running away from home and hitchhiking in order to be around gay people. They would sneak me into bars; I went to the first gay bar in Orlando, Florida. By this point, I was probably around eleven or twelve. I hadn't even reached puberty.

The Cycle of Running Away, Drinking, and Using

That started the cycle of running away, drinking, and using. My parents did everything that they could to try and control me. I was incorrigible. The police would pick me up and take me home, and I would leave that same night. It wasn't because I had a bad family life; it was because I wanted to drink and use and be around gay men. I'd be truant, so the police would see me during the day, and they would pick me up. My parents would call them and report me a runaway, so they would stop me. I'd be out late at night, wandering around, being picked up by men, doing that type of stuff — parks, tearooms, etcetera. At that time, in that part of Florida, there was only one gay bar, and the gay people congregated in the park. That was the only place there was to really congregate during the day.

At fifteen, my mother asked me if I would consider going to a hospital. I really didn't understand or know what it was for. I think my parents wanted me to get over being gay, and they knew that I was drinking and taking drugs. What I was going there for was never really discussed. But I think at that time, at fifteen, I had hit a bottom of sorts. I'd had enough of doing what I was doing. My life consisted of drinking and using and sleeping around.

So I went into a psychiatric hospital in Florida. There weren't any chemical dependency hospitals, and no one ever talked about drug addiction or alcoholism that I remember. I didn't know what I was there for. I just knew they didn't like the things that I was doing; I was there to change. I was in the hospital about a month when the doctors decided that there was no sense in me being there. I was doing the same things as before, only now I was coming back to the hospital instead of home. They thought the best thing for me to do would be to go to this private hospital in North Carolina which was a locked facility. For some reason, I agreed. I ended up spending thirteen months in there. It was this very elite, private hospital, and again, as I remember, nothing was ever discussed about my chemical dependency.

They put a male nurse in charge of me, and I was supposed to talk to him all the time — one-to-one communications. He was gay and I fell in love with him. I tried to get him to let me run away from the hospital and move in with him, which fortunately he wouldn't go for. I ran away from the hospital once and found the only gay bar in Asheville, North Carolina. After three days of drinking and using, I didn't know what to do, so I went back to the hospital.

I left the hospital and I went into a halfway house for emotionally disturbed kids. I stayed there until I ran away and hitchhiked across the country. I thought, If I hitchhike across the country, I'll get it together. I had no skills to "get together," but I didn't know that then. So I hitchhiked from Florida to Canada and back.

Raised By a Lot of Drag Queens

I should explain that, basically, I was raised by a lot of drag queens. People always took care of me. They'd sneak me in the bars. I knew the owners of the gay bars and grew up with the whole gay environment in Florida. So I kind of got in everywhere and did all this stuff, and I was drinking and using the whole time. They would sneak me in and hide me from the police. I'd hide in the dressing rooms of the drag queens, stuff like that.

Waiting for Sunrise on the Beach in California

At seventeen, I decided it was time to get it together again and move to California. I thought, Everything will be different; I'll leave all this stuff behind me; I'll get a job. I'd never worked. I didn't realize that you couldn't live like I did and work too. It just never dawned on me. I brought a friend with me, and our first experience in California was a good example of how prepared we were. We thought we'd go to the beach and watch the sunrise like we did in Florida. We didn't realize that it doesn't rise here: it sets here. So we got a gallon of wine and went to the beach and waited for the sun to rise. I passed out and was woken up by the paramedics, because nobody else could wake me up. That was in my first week, and it got worse from there.

I had enough money to get an apartment, so I got an apartment, and I started looking for work. I got a job and lost it, and I got another one and lost it, 'cause I couldn't get up in the morning. I was still drinking and using like I had always done. Finally, after about a year of getting jobs and losing them, I found a job that enabled me to drink and use like I wanted to. I started selling costumes on Hollywood Boulevard. I didn't have to start work until 10:00 A.M. The people who owned the business really enabled me to continue my using behavior. They were in their sixties and adopted me as their son — me and all my problems. They were wonderful people, and they tried to keep me from drinking and using. They tried to guide me and direct me. I managed to keep that job for eight years.

The job gave me some stability. I worked enough to pay my rent and buy alcohol and drugs. They used to pay us at noon on Friday. I was supposed to work the rest of Friday and Saturday. They would pay us, and I wouldn't show up for three days. I'd go drink until my money was gone, and then I'd come back to work. They allowed me to continue that; they were incredible enablers. At the same time, they taught me a lot. I learned the industry, I learned how to sew, and I learned a lot of good skills that I didn't have before. I'm really grateful for those people; I don't know what would have happened without them.

I was ending up in jail as a public drunk all the time. I would go to the bars and drink till I could not physically drink anymore. If I didn't have the money, I'd steal drinks. Then I would try and walk home. Often, I couldn't walk, so I'd get arrested. I don't know how many times I woke up in a padded cell with no clothes on. I rationalized it in my head that it was no big deal, 'cause they let you out the next day. The truth is, it was a big deal.

Then I decided to get a car, and I thought I wouldn't drink and drive. That lasted maybe a week. I'd have these accidents while in a blackout.

My Last Drunk

One day — my last drunk — I decided I would go to happy hour at two in the afternoon. I don't know what happened. I woke up in jail; the police arrested me for weaving. But I must have had an accident before they arrested me, because the windshield of the car was smashed, and there was brick in the car. I must have hit something and driven away. About three weeks prior to that, I had gotten a jaywalking ticket, which had turned to a warrant. I had paid the jaywalking ticket but the payment was not in the computer yet. So for the drunk driving, they let me out on my own recognizance; for the jaywalking, they kept me in jail. This time, I didn't get out in the morning, and it made a bigger impression on me than all the times I'd been in jail before. I was taken to county jail and ended up spending five days there for jaywalking. It made an impression on me. For the drunk driving, they told me I needed to go to driving school and AA meetings.

So I'm one of the people who got to the program of Alcoholics Anonymous through the court system. For me, it worked. I was used to doing everything my way. I called the drunk driving program, and they told me I had to go to one meeting a week for ten weeks. I asked, "Well, can't I go to one drunk driver's meeting a night for ten nights?" I wanted to get it over with so I could forget about it and drink. They said I couldn't do that.

Then I called AA. According to the court order I had to go to six AA meetings, and I asked if I could go to one a day for six days. The woman said, "Honey, you can go to as many meetings a day as you can get to." And I thought, Oh good, I'll go to three a day for two days, and I won't ever go to AA again. I knew for many years that I was an alcoholic, but it never occurred to me to go to AA. I used to pray for the day when I didn't want to drink, but I always wanted to, so I never tried to quit. It never dawned on me to go to AA.

So I went to the drunk driving school, and I started going to AA meetings. On a Monday I went to an afternoon meeting and it seemed all right. That night I went to another meeting, and at that meeting, something happened. I don't know if somebody suggested it or if I made the decision on my own, but I know I decided to go to more meetings than I had to go to. Two people came up to me that night: one of them bought me a Big Book and one of them gave me his phone number. The guy who gave me his phone number kept calling me and taking me to meetings. The guy who bought me the Big Book did the same thing.

On Friday, one of my new friends took me to a meeting, and the people at the meeting needed a person to have a commitment there. He nudged me, and I raised my hand and took the commitment. A commitment means you commit to bring the cookies, to do service work for the meeting. You take the commitment to do this service work for an extended period of time. So I took that commitment. I hope, today, that I have the amount of willingness that I had then to do what people suggested, 'cause I really feel that's what saved my life.

That was the start of what I call my God shots. There have been many God shots since then. After two months of sobriety, they needed a new secretary for that meeting. From my experience in the program, it's very unusual that someone with such a short amount of sobriety gets nominated as secretary, but I did, and I accepted it, and it was wonderful.

I call that my first God shot because I had just met somebody in a bar, and I thought, This is a marriage made in heaven. He didn't drink, he just smoked pot, and I thought that I could say no to pot. I said no for about a week, then I took one hit off a bowl. I felt horrible. I realized, for me, I had blown my sobriety. I didn't know what to do, and I was secretary of this meeting! It happened to be a Friday night, and I thought, Go drink. You've blown it now; you might as well really enjoy yourself. Then I thought, You may not live through it this time. Then I remembered that, as secretary, my responsibility was to unlock the door for the meeting. I know if I just had that cookie commitment they could have done without cookies. So I call that a God shot, because I really feel that that commitment as secretary got me to that meeting.

I went home, I told my closest AA friends what I had done, and they said, "Go to the meeting, and you tell the rest of the people what happened." I was due to take a ninety-day chip, and all I could do was envision myself taking a chip, but knowing that I had blown my sobriety. So I knew that I had to tell everybody what I had done and start over. Walking through that fear was not nearly as bad as I thought it was going to be. And that's been my experience all throughout my sobriety.

My Sponsor Got Drunk

The next major event in my sobriety was my sponsor drank. He was the person who bought me the Big Book, took me to all those meetings, and got me to take a commitment. He's still drinking five years later. The direction he gave me is what's keeping me sober today, so it's very hard to see him not follow his own direction. I volunteer at our central AA office here; I put my name on a phone register. He called AA one day, for a Twelve Step call, and out of all the thousands and thousands of names in Los Angeles, they just accidentally matched us up together. They gave me this phone number to call, and I thought, This number sounds familiar. I called and it ended up to be him. I talked to him, but he continued to drink and use.

Nobody Knew a Lot About AIDS Five Years Ago

Somewhere during my first year of sobriety, I agreed to be a participant in a study that UCLA was doing for AIDS. They were taking a lot of blood tests. I really didn't know a lot about AIDS; nobody knew a lot about AIDS five years ago. I continued testing with them every six months, and it's been going on almost six years now that I've been a part of this study; I still go. Finally, they gave me the result: I tested positive. They suggested I talk to my doctor, and I did. I didn't get upset; I didn't really know what it was. I didn't start getting concerned until people I knew started dying.

The Judgment You Receive from Taking Pain Medication

The next major event in my sobriety was my lung collapsed for the second time. I was still drinking and using the first time it collapsed in 1981. About two years ago, it collapsed again, and they had to take it out. It just happened. I was opening a file drawer in the middle of the afternoon one day, and it collapsed. No reason. They call it a spontaneous pneumothorax. That was hard, because I had to take pain medication; you can't have lung surgery without taking some type of medication.

The other difficulty was the judgments I received from taking pain medication. At least, here, a lot of people have opinions about that. What I did is the best that I could do. When I left the hospital four days after my surgery, I didn't take any medications with me. I feel I was lucky. I was on morphine the whole time I was in the hospital, IV and oral, and when they took me off, I didn't have any withdrawal or craving or anything like that. I hear a lot of people get a craving. I didn't, and I really feel that was a gift.

My lung condition got me going to my physician regularly — monitoring my helper and suppressor counts. I take AZT and acyclovir, and now, pentamidine. My physician felt it would be better for me to start an early preventative treatment before I got sick. As a matter of fact, my helpers were in the thousands when I started taking AZT, which is unusual, or it was then. I've been on AZT about a year, and my helper counts have dropped, and so my doctor started me on pentamidine.

I Talk Back to Myself

Although my health has been good, the thing that has been difficult is readjusting my thinking as changes go on in my body. I can get new test results and feel physically the same as the day

I get negative results, but my emotional state is not the same. So I make an effort to have a conscious connection to my physical feelings — to talk back to myself — letting myself know that I am okay, that I am healthy, and that the results are what the results are, and that I need to continue to do the best that I can. When my helper count dropped, and the doctor started me on the pentamidine, I was upset, and so I decided to take a day off. That began a pattern: When I get stressful news, I take a day off and readjust my thinking. I look at my head like gears. I get new information and the gears get thrown out of whack, and I need to readjust the gears. That seems to sum up the process of my sobriety: readjusting my thinking regardless of what the news is.

Friends dying around me has been difficult. My best friend died and a lot of people I know have died, and that's required a lot of thinking readjustment. When my best friend was very sick, I was very upset, but it wasn't until then that I realized I had the capacity to feel like that — that I saw the positive side. I had no idea that I could have those feelings, being upset and caring about another person, totally, unconditionally. We had no sexual attachments; it was purely on a friendship level. It was a negative experience that turned out to be a gift — that I was able to see something like that in myself. I went to a meeting and cried during the meeting, which is something I haven't done, or don't do often, but it was a wonderful experience.

I use the program around my health. It's the acceptance of things I can't change: this is the way it is and I have choices on how I want to act. I have a lot of choices of how I feel. I can feel sick and become sicker, or I can get up and do what I need to do.

Another difficult thing for me has been what I call *contrary actions* — doing sick things and being healthy. I go to the doctor every two weeks and give blood and take tests. I'm taking the AZT and pentamidine, and to me, those are sick things. Yet, I'm healthy. I make the separation between doing sick actions and being healthy, because I caught myself buying into being sick by doing those sick actions.

I Met Somebody Last Night

I guess when I stopped going to the park and doing risky sexual behavior was when I broke through the denial that I was HIV positive, that it really was a life-threatening situation for me and other people. I don't know how to explain it clearer; I just know that when I stopped doing that behavior, I broke through some type of denial.

I think that's true with chemical dependency too. When we truly break through our denial, we stop drinking and using, because that's killing us. I think that's what happened with my sexual behavior. Now I have to act responsibly. It's difficult. To get involved with somebody, I have to let them know what's going on with me physically, let them know that I'm positive, that I'm taking medication, but that I am also healthy. I have to let them know all that stuff so they can make choices. I have to talk to them, which is a real first. It's difficult to say, "Hi, my name is Bernie, and I am HIV positive." But I think that, for me, it's the only right thing to do.

I feel that way about dating. Dating may lead to a sexual relationship. So if I'm dating somebody with that possibility in mind, I need to be honest from the beginning, not ten minutes before I get into bed with him. Consequently, because it has been difficult, and also because I haven't found anybody I've really been interested in, I've not been in those situations. I don't know. Maybe I'm withdrawing. I don't know the answers to some of those things right now.

I met somebody last Friday who I like. He's an attractive person, and we've talked a few times on the phone. When am I going to talk to him? How am I going to talk to him about what's going on? So, it's something that I am looking at right now. Am I going to talk to him, or am I going to run and not call him anymore out of my own fear? As I shared earlier, my experience is when I walk through those fears, it's not nearly as bad as I think it will be.

A Punk Rocker in Gay Country Western Bars

The bottom line is, the program saved my life. It probably would not have been very long until I was dead, either from the drinking and using itself, or from being run over by a car because I was passed out in the gutter, or from having my throat slit because of my behavior toward other people. What does the program mean to me? It's my life.

It comes down to that willingness I had my first week. I think I'd reached the point of being sick and tired of doing all the stuff I was doing, and I just couldn't do it anymore. I didn't know before I came to the program that there was a way not to do it. When I came into the program, I was doing everything possible to keep people away from me. I had purple, green, and blue hair; I wore a collar around my neck. I looked like a punk rocker, and I was going to country western gay bars 'cause I wanted to sit and drink and be left alone. I came into the program and people came up and said hello to me despite how I looked. That made a big difference. It seemed like they were people who just cared. They didn't want anything.

At first, I tried my same old games. That one guy I talked about, who called and picked me up and brought me to meetings, I thought he wanted my body, which he didn't. I'd get in the car and move a little closer, and he still wouldn't touch me, and I couldn't figure it out. He didn't want anything. He may have been attracted, but he didn't act on it. He was responsible. I tested the waters with the program, and I found good results.

I Don't Have the First Cigarette

I now have three years without cigarettes, and I miss cigarettes a lot. I would love to have a cigarette, but I think it through. I use the AA program with cigarettes; I don't have the first cigarette. In the same way, I don't go to the park, not once. Because if I go once, then it's all over. I don't go around the block cruising, because if I go around the block, I've blown my commitment to myself and I'll go around again. So if I see somebody on the street, I look at them, but I don't go around the block to look at them twice. That's another one of the ways I use the principles of the program toward my other compulsive areas. No matter what, I don't have that first cigarette; I don't go to the park; I don't go around the block. And I talk about all this stuff that goes on with me with the people around me. I'm open with my feelings and my behaviors, and that has been real freeing for me.

After being sober a couple years, I was volunteering at a recovery house and the director came to me and said, "We really like what you're doing. Have you ever thought about doing this for a living?" To me, it was another God shot. He asked if I would consider going to school, if they would pay me to go, and then would I work there? And I said, "Yeah, that would be wonderful. Let me think about it." I went home, and I thought about it. I talked to my sponsor, and I realized that I had missed a lot of opportunities in my life. Next day I said, "Yeah, I'll go to school." So I did. Three years later, I only have one more class to finish. I took it easy. At first, I was afraid. My sponsor said, "Bernie, you're not responsible for anything except showing up and doing your best." That made it easier. I had to be there and be there on time and do the best that I could — whether I passed or failed didn't matter. So I showed up and did my best and it was cool; I enjoyed it.

If I just show up and do what I need to do, and stay clean and sober, things really move smoothly for me. Anyway, they offered me a position and I've loved it. I've been here three years now and couldn't have dreamed of doing anything better. On the twenty-seventh of this month I'll be five years sober, and I'll be in Rio on vacation. It's wonderful having sobriety and this life.

BURT

I bought a new Volkswagen, got a German Shepherd named Bruce, and a pup tent, and I took off. That was in '67. . . . We did so many drugs in those years. If you talk to somebody about the MDA summer, they know it was the summer of '69.

My childhood was abusive. My parents shouldn't have been together. There was a lot of screaming and manipulating. My mother was a pill junkie. My father would tell me to go talk to my mother, because I could handle her and he couldn't.

There were enormous amounts of screaming and yelling — and craziness. I'd come home and my mother would have slit her wrists and she'd be arranging herself on the couch with the vomit and wine and blood. I'd come in and I'd think she was dead and she'd open her eyes and say in a whisper, "Call the doctor." And I'd say, "I don't know the number." And she'd say, "The number is, blah blah blah. Tell your father you found me." That happened more than once. The whole thing was always like that, so I shut down. I knew I was useless by the time I got to high school. I didn't know how to relate; I was terrified of all my classmates — totally terrified.

My father had a heart attack in 1949, when I was six, and he was never the same after that. When I was eight or nine, my mother went in for shock treatments, and my father put me in an orphanage. I was only in the orphanage a few months 'cause I kept running away. I was a throw-away kid.

I was in a couple of mental hospitals before I was eighteen. You see, by the time I went to high school, I had no social skills at all. My whole life was this hurricane going on at home and I had no way to cope, so I went into the hospital. That started a lifelong pattern of running. It was the best I could do. There are many people with backgrounds not as bad as mine who end up on towers with shotguns shooting people.

I got away from home very early and was out on my own in San Francisco when I was eighteen. I got a job and started making a success of myself. Then the 1960s came along; they were built just for me — drugs and all the complete escapism.

I didn't regard myself as having a problem because drugs were part of what everybody did. At one point, I dropped some acid, looked out over San Francisco, and thought, What am I doing going to this job that I hate, that I have to take drugs to be able to cope with? What am I doing here? I'm leaving. And I did. I bought a new Volkswagen, got a German Shepherd named Bruce, and a pup tent, and I took off. That was in '67.

Eventually, I ended up on Laguna beach, and I stayed there for ten years. I should have known that Laguna was going to be made for me because Timothy Leary had moved there the week before. I became a waiter and a bartender, and I spent a lot of time on the beach. We did so many drugs in those years. If you talk to somebody about the MDA summer, they know it was the summer of '69. Drugs were very much a part of our culture, but I didn't do drugs the way other people did them. I got very paranoid on grass; I got paranoid on all of it, but on the heavy drugs I'd sit there and cry.

While in Laguna, I got into a thing with macrame and plants and suddenly started making a lot of money. I opened a shop, a plant boutique. Macrame was a big item, and I was making a lot of money. But, in order to make the business go, I had to stay loaded on uppers.

The Big Crescendo to Mahler's 8th
and Suddenly I Was Totally Sober

Then I fell in love and gave up my own business, my own identity — everything, to be taken care of. We had a house in the mountains, a house at the beach, a house in the desert. Mark was a very upwardly mobile person; I was more of a kind of kick-back person, so I took care of the house up in the mountains. It was a gorgeous showplace, a redwood and glass house. I had my cats, and dogs, and my roses, and vegetables, a new Cadillac convertible, a new MG, and I didn't have to work. I dabbled at school a little bit and got into some of the most unhappy times of my life.

One day I was sitting alone in the living room, in this gorgeous living room. It was snowing outside, and I had the inside lights off and the outside lights on, and we had some special lights just to catch the snowflakes as they came down. I was smoking some grass, taking some uppers and some Valium, drinking Wild Turkey out of Rosenthal crystal glasses, and looking out at the lights playing on my new Cadillac convertible. Mahler's 8th was playing, the fireplace was going, reflecting on all the glass. It was beautiful, I mean, the most perfect surroundings. And I took a hit of amyl to get off on the big crescendo to Mahler's 8th, and suddenly, I was totally sober. Flat. It was like everything was taken away, and I was just there alone.

I remember thinking, I don't know what I'm doing alive. I have absolutely no purpose. I had done everything, including sell my soul to somebody I didn't like; I did everything I knew to be happy, and I was so unhappy. I knew I would have to change. I knew right then I was going to have to leave the whole thing. Within a year I did.

When I got into the relationship with Mark, what I thought was, I had this shitty childhood and this is my reward. I didn't know there was another side to that coin. I don't think anybody does unless they go through it. I lost my identity in that relationship. I remember him yelling at me when he finally realized I was leaving, "You'll find out what it's like to get out there on your own." And I thought as he said that, Have I come this far? I'm the guy that got out on my own at eighteen; what am I doing in this situation?

As part of the divorce settlement, I got a little house in Palm Springs. I was living down there when I met this incredible man, Bob, who was as neurotic as I was. He was also an alcoholic. He eventually ended up in the program. I hated people; I hated everything. I was totally alone, totally lonely, even with this relationship. He was all I had and it wasn't working out. He and I split up, and I got sick one weekend and was crying and ready to pack it all in, and he said, "You've lived your life on the edge for so long, you've used up all your resources. Why don't you try the program? What have you got to lose?" And so I did.

To My Surprise, He Died

All of a sudden, there were people who understood me. I embraced AA totally. I was an "AA Nazi" for years: two, three meetings a day, every day for the first three years. In the second year of my sobriety, Bob got sick. He was one of the first people to ever be diagnosed. They called it GRID. We weren't together, but we weren't apart yet either. I thought it was one of his power plays; he loved to be the biggest victim. He was six-foot-six and a hunk and an actor and gorgeous, and he could play it to the hilt. To my surprise, he died.

After he died, I went into a period of total denial. I convinced myself that because I hadn't gotten sick when he did, I probably wasn't going to get the bug. A few years later, I tested positive. I decided that it hadn't done anything to me, so it didn't matter.

Over the subsequent years, I started getting very fatigued. I used to have ups and downs a lot, but now I wasn't coming back up. I can trace it as far back as '85. I remember going to Paris for the first time and dragging around. Finally, I went to a doctor specializing in AIDS and ARC. He made me look at the fact that I was positive and that I had a virus that would probably kill me. I mean, that's what the statistics are at this point. That's at least a realist's way of looking at it. Unless something comes along, people die. My T-cells were down to 300, and I hadn't faced it.

I don't think I could have faced it if I hadn't been in Alcoholics Anonymous. I used the program. At least you get a sense of being powerless, you get a sense of having the wisdom to say "I can't do anything about this."

I'm Forty-Six and All My Old Friends Are Dead

I went to a shrink too. I'm on anti-depressants now because what I did was stuff all my worries. Plus, I only have a few friends left. I'm not being dramatic; that's the truth. Between alcoholism, AIDS, and a few crazy ones who killed themselves, I've lost forty, fifty people. I'm forty-six years old and practically all of my old friends are dead. So I stuffed a lot of that. I was in an enormous clinical depression. I still think I haven't dealt with it totally. I mean, it's really just dealing with one's own mortality, whether it happens today or fifty years from now.

There is that thing in AA that states that we should practice these principles in all of our affairs. AA is not about drinking and using; it's about learning how to live while being powerless over alcohol. HIV fits right in there. There comes that point when you have to surrender, to say, "Okay, I've got it." The program helped in that respect. I knew there was a process to let go. I knew that at a certain point in anything, you have to let go of attempts to control; you have to surrender; you have to cast your fate to the wind.

I'm still in the middle of a big depression. I can't say my life's changed, yet. If you're looking for one of those stories where a guy walks along and is suddenly transformed by a bolt of lightning, that's not me. I never have learned that way. I've always been a slow learner.

The Only Problem with AA Is that It's Full of Drunks

Anyway, back to my story. November of '81, I was gradually getting angrier, lonelier, more withdrawn, and I started to have a nervous breakdown. My ex-lover said, "Try the program for thirty days." I walked in to my first meeting, and it was home. It was the first group of people who ever understood me. And I understood them. I thought, Well, if that means I'm an alcoholic, that's what I am.

They have a saying around AA that the only problem with

AA is that it's full of drunks. And I started seeing that some of these people were, you know, not gods. I started seeing that some of the people who hung around the program all the time were saying the same things year after year. It sounded good when you were brand new, but it sounded really stupid after being there awhile. My sponsor was one of the great AA Nazis of LA, and he said that therapy was just for people who couldn't admit they were alcoholics. One day recently, I realized what a vicious jerk he was.

Well, I think a person like myself needed that AA Nazism at first. I needed to just do it — do what I was told, do what the book said, take it very fundamentally. I needed that. Nevertheless, I started seeing that some of the people I originally thought were so profound, were not changing. I knew I needed more than AA.

I knew a guy in a support group that I'm in who's been sober five or six years. When he was diagnosed, he went to a meeting and talked about how upset he was. An old-timer came up to him and said, "This is an Alcoholics Anonymous meeting, we don't get into that." So he left the program, totally. Coincidentally, somebody asked me to lead a meeting, and I had a choice of topics to pick from. One of the topics was issues in sobriety other than alcohol and drugs. That's the topic I chose, and I told them the whole story of my friend and how wrong I thought that was. I also told them that I had been diagnosed HIV positive. This was one of those West Hollywood husband-hunting meetings. But I'm glad I did it. I said, "I'm positive, and I couldn't have dealt with it without the program." Pretty soon, half the people in the room were sharing that they were positive.

I'm constantly amazed. On one hand, the gay LA community is doing an enormous amount to help itself. I'm very proud to be part of it, on both sides of the fence: I received help and I've given it; I've given money and I've taken it. On the other hand, I was dating a guy and as soon as he found out I was in the hospital for suspected pneumocystis, he couldn't even call me. Totally cut it off. You meet a lot of people who will not deal with

AIDS yet; they just won't. I have a good friend who just died 'cause he wouldn't deal with it. He wouldn't go get the test, so he died of pneumocystis. Nobody dies of pneumocystis anymore, unless you let it go so far.

So I did my bit. I think that AA is the place for everything — including AIDS. The two are very compatible. AA is supposed to be a program for living. The word *alcohol* is mentioned in the First Step and the Twelfth Step — that's it. The rest of the Steps are all about living. And living is everything. Some AA members use excuses to say, "We're not here to talk about AIDS." Well, what are you here to talk about? Talk about your life.

Are You Still Sober?

I got loaded two weeks ago. I didn't exactly go out and get loaded, but it's close enough for me: I smoked three tokes off a joint. It was during a sexual situation. Maybe that invalidates this whole interview. I'm still processing and I'm still working on that. I finally told people. I called up my baby, my sponsee, and said, "As far as the rules go, I went out. I can't sponsor you anymore." He asked, "What'd you do?" And I said, "I had three tokes off a joint." He said, "You know, that's almost disappointing." My upbringing in AA was such that I had to tell people. Anyway, it was an isolated situation, probably because I told all the people I didn't want to tell. That was the deal I made with myself.

I know that in the context of the program you change your sobriety day, but I'm not about to throw away seven and a half years. I've been around the program seven and a half years; I've had three tokes of a joint in seven and a half years. I don't feel like I'm two weeks old and brand new, 'cause I'm not. I will go in, and I will pay lip service to that, because those are the rules. Besides, you sound pretty ridiculous defending your position, saying, "Well, I'm really still sober." So I've given in to that; I understand what's going on with that. And I knew that when I did it.

When you get to be seven, eight years sober, people all look at people they've known from the beginning, and if they haven't seen someone for a while, the question always comes up, "Are you still sober?" I ran into a guy, we started talking, and he said, "You still sober?" I said, "Well, I had three tokes two weeks ago." And then he told me that he had too, and that he didn't change his sobriety date. He didn't tell anybody; that's the way he handled it. Whatever the other ramifications were, it wasn't worth it to me to always be wondering if I was lying to people. That's just the way I am. I believe that keeping this a secret would pretty much assure that I would relapse.

My friend Jim told me that he was very upset about my using. We've been sober since we've known each other. And now he says he has to look at himself. Yesterday was his seventh sober birthday. He asked me, "All I want to know is, are you out or are you in?" I knew exactly what he meant. I said, "I'm in."

I have a feeling that this three tokes might really have taken me out had it not been for the fact that I shared it with my support group at APLA [AIDS Project Los Angeles]. In the course of the support group, the psychologist said, "Maybe any of you, if you feel the desire to drink and use, can use each other to call." And I said, "Why would they want to; they're not alcoholics?" And they all looked at me, and they said, "Well, you can't do it when you're HIV positive. If you have AIDS particularly, you can't drink and use." And I didn't know that. As soon as I heard that, I thought, Oh, here's yet another reason to stay sober.

Deep Clinical Depression

My depression was hard to spot because the symptoms of depression overlap the symptoms of alcoholism; one is isolation. I was isolating more and more, getting completely like I was before I got sober. I stopped going to meetings; I didn't want to talk to people; I wasn't eating; I wasn't sleeping. It was worse than I thought it was. I had no idea what was going on. Then my doctor wanted me to see a psychologist. They told me later they were thinking of hospitalizing me; I was that far gone. I was in a deep clinical depression, and maybe I have been all my life. They put me on anti-depressants. I didn't know about anti-depressants, and I said no at first, but then they explained them. They aren't mood altering. I've never felt any physical effects from them.

I've been in therapy off and on for all my life; every once in awhile, I'll be in therapy for a couple of years. This is the first time it's ever worked, the first time I've ever understood what a therapist does — and what I do.

I think the program helps my therapy work too. Actually, it's very funny. You see, I originally came from an AA group where therapy was frowned upon. But because of AA, I was able to finally develop at least a modicum of trust in another person, and I think you have to have that to finally trust the therapy process and the people involved. AA really helped me to learn trusting.

I remember when I first got into *A Course in Miracles* and asked, "I'm looking outside the program. Is this a slip?" And my sponsor said, "Go read exactly what it says. It talks about improving our conscious contact with God. Step Eleven. It doesn't say how; it just says to do it."

But you see, I had had this other sponsor. I just understood, just now, that *that* sponsor was abusing power. Isn't that funny and sad? He was just like my parents. He put me down; he put everybody down. That's part of the reason I backed off from AA. It may be necessary for me to go back to AA for a while, just to fully understand that I'm wrong about AA. I have a bad feeling about AA because of him and people like him.

This friend of mine was telling me, "If you go back to meetings, it's not a big deal, but if you do go back, you don't have to do it the way we did it. We did it as Nazis, rigid and judgmental. There are lots of people in AA who are open and flexible. They were there when we were there; we put them down. They're probably still there, doing just fine."

I shared at this meeting not long ago where there were a lot of what I would have generally called West Hollywood twinks and I dismissed them as that. Well, these kids were just sweet, and one of them came up to me and he put his arm around me, and he said, "Burt, you're a very wise man." And I just said, "Eddie, no I'm not. I'm not a wise man. Wisdom has nothing to do with it." He said, "But you don't understand. We heard you tonight and you know a lot of things." And I thought, Yeah, I suppose so; I can understand that. But the truth is, as far as I know, knowing never kept anybody sober — unless it was knowing how to ask for help. That's a form of humility, I think. And I've still got that; it's still there. For that, I'm very glad.

CHAPTER SEVENTEEN

Parents with AIDS

NOLAN

I'd have these insane thoughts of how bad it was. I'd remember Lori being home with the two kids, and there'd be $10 left in the house. If it was a choice between milk and Pampers, and my high, you know, "I'm sorry kids," and I'd take the last dollar she had. What was really scary was the lights were gettin' turned off and the eviction notices were comin'. The life that I had lived growin' up, and everything that I hated so much as a kid, was happening to me as an adult, and now happening to my kids.

I come from an alcoholic family. My mother, stepfather, and older brother died of the disease. I have two brothers who are in recovery. I also have two brothers who are still active. I was born in Brooklyn; my parents were on welfare. I was raised in poverty. What I remember most about my childhood was the constant moving, every two years or so, because of not paying the rent. I remember having the electricity and gas turned off. We never settled in one place, and every two years we went to a new school and had to make new friends. And with the alcohol and the inconsistency of life, there was a lot of violence. There was no flow to my life; everything about it was very choppy. Even my memory is choppy. I still have difficulty sometimes piecing it together.

My brothers were all locked up in jail. There was really no father in the house. And this was the view that I had of life as a child. The kids I hung out with all came from similar backgrounds — poor, usually alcoholic or very dysfunctional families. I didn't understand any other way of living. This was the way it was. I remember a tremendous amount of fear because I'd come in from school and I didn't know if my mother was gonna be drunk or sober, if she was gonna be happy or mad. There was a lot of tension, a lot of fear in my childhood.

The only time in my childhood that I ever got any attention was when my older brothers came to kick my ass. They were pretty much the father figure in my life. My mother was also very abusive at this time. I was the youngest child, and by the time I showed on the set, she really didn't have anything left to give. Her alcoholism had really progressed. When she was drinking, there was a lot of physical abuse. She beat me with belts, iron cords, whatever.

I remember when I was about eight, standin' on the corner of Broadway and West Fourth Street in Brooklyn and making the realization that there was nobody there for me, and I have to do everything myself. So at twelve, I was drinking. By the time I was thirteen, I was shooting dope, taking pills, smoking pot. I stopped goin' to school and lost interest in anything. I always felt different than everybody else and isolated. Never, never measuring up. I grew up with a lot of shame, a lot of guilt, and by the time I was sixteen, a pattern had already set in — to cope by drinking and taking drugs. That was the way I dealt with it. I had few friends. I didn't socialize well. It was always just two or three friends and my brother Jackie. That was basically the extent of my world.

Living with Dad on Long Island

When I was about fifteen, my mother found drugs in my pocket and she sent me to live with my biological father, who lived out on Long Island. I lived with him for three years, and I did well. I did well because I was out of the alcoholic environment. The pressures out on Long Island were a lot less than they were in the city. I got into sports and that seemed to take the edge off a lot. I really enjoyed it out there; I really did.

At the end of my junior year I didn't have enough credits to finish my senior year on time, so they were gonna hold me back a year. My father's wife didn't want to keep me that extra year, so they sent me back to the city. I felt totally rejected and I was afraid to go back into the city. As soon as I got back into the city, the old pattern set up. I took up the drinkin' and the drugs, and I didn't go to school anymore. By the age of eighteen I was really into heavy use of drugs. I got into a crowd, it was the '60s.

I got married at nineteen. I got married 'cause she looked good on my arm. She got pregnant and we had a son. That lasted a year, and then she basically threw me out. I haven't seen my son in nineteen or twenty years.

It was just another bad card that was stacked against me. That's how my view of life was, you know: I always got the shit end of the stick; I was the product of my environment; God always gave me bad cards, impossible cards to play. That was my thinking.

Meanwhile, I made no effort to hold a job. My drug habit got out of hand, and I started doin' burglaries and robberies. I made a run like that for about two years. I was gettin' arrested, but the court system in '69 was pretty quick. They'd get you in and get you out, and you wouldn't have to spend much time in jail. But then they arrested me for a robbery in a factory and what they did — and I see now it was a blessing — was they tried to clear their books of all the robberies they had pending or outstanding, and they hooked me up with them all. Anything that involved a white, six foot male, they charged me with. So they charged me with like thirty robberies, plus the one that they caught me for. They gave me a package deal.

Eventually, I got a five-year sentence to a narcotic addiction control program. Basically it was a jail, but they had social workers and therapists. I did time in what they called a rehab with the same mode of thinkin' as I had in jail. I didn't want to look at myself; I didn't want to grow up. In the place, out of the place, in jail, out of jail — I just continued to use.

As far as I was concerned, I was an addict, and I was gonna die that way. From the time I was eighteen to the time I was twenty-seven, I was constantly in and out of jails and rehabs. It took its toll. My mother died when I was twenty-seven years old, and I started wondering, What the hell is my life gonna be like? So I made a promise to myself that I would stop using the drugs and get a job. I met my present wife in a rehab in Manhattan, and we got together. We had no money, no nothin', and we just hooked up. I was still drinkin' and smokin' pot on occasion, but basically, I stayed away from the drugs. Occasionally, I would do drugs, but I was just really into drinking.

My wife, Lori, got pregnant with my daughter, and that's when my drinkin' really got out of hand. I was constantly blacked out, constantly in fights, and I was getting arrested again. I really didn't understand this, 'cause I thought I had put that behind me. Now, however, my arrests were not crimes of property; they were assaults — physical crimes. And it confused me. I started makin' attempts at recovery. At that point, my brother Ricky went to AA and sobered up.

I Didn't Want to Give Up Drinking

I had tried goin' to AA. Basically, the reason I went to AA was not so much to really stop drinking, but to keep Lori off my back, or to keep jobs. I really didn't want to give up drinkin' My daughter Suzie was born and she was slow developing. The realization that there was somethin' wrong hit me and my drinking really progressed. The way I handled any kind of stress or difficulty in life was to run, you know, run to a bottle, run to a drug. When we discovered that Suzie was retarded, my attitude was Suzie was a burden. I loved her, but I used to sit in the bars and think, How am I gonna deal with this? Another bad card in my life, you know. I was really feeling alone. How do I deal with this? Who cares? Then Lori got pregnant with Matthew, and I was really scared, 'cause I didn't know if we were gonna have another retarded baby.

Once, we took Suzie to Mt. Sinai Hospital to have some genetic testing done, and there was an old nun sittin' there. I was very bitter and beaten, and she said to me, "Oh, oh what a beautiful little baby. What a beautiful little girl." Suzie was just startin' to walk then, and I looked at her, and I just said to her, "Yeah, and she's retarded." She grabbed me by my arm and said, "Son, God must love you very much to give you a special child like that." At that point, it didn't have any big impact, but a lot of times since I have thought about that. I realize what a blessing she is.

What happened was, after Matthew was born I was working at a bowling alley, and I got in with this guy who was dealing coke and pot. I wasn't drinking at the time when I got this job. I made a couple AA meetings and had stopped drinkin', but I was smokin' pot with Lori, and I thought this was the way I was gonna do it. But before I knew it, I got into the coke. I was never one for snortin' coke, you know, so I got into IV use of cocaine. I got into dealing it for about a year and four months. I picked up the drink again and the coke, and that's the way I believe I got the AIDS virus. It was during that time, because prior to that I hadn't used IV drugs for maybe five years.

A Choice Between Milk and Pampers and My High

That was seven years ago. Matthew was just born. He's seven now. What I didn't realize was that the coke was just accelerating my bottom. See, the bottom that I hit was not about what I had done or the places I had been. It was the way I really started feelin' about myself. I'd have these insane thoughts of how bad it was. I'd remember Lori being home with the two kids, and there'd be $10 left in the house. If it was a choice between milk and Pampers, and my high, you know, "I'm sorry kids," and I'd take the last dollar she had. What was really scary was the lights were gettin' turned off and the eviction notices were comin'. The life that I had lived growin' up, and everything that I hated so much as a kid, was happening to me as an adult, and now happening to my kids.

The self-loathing and self-hate really started to fix into me, and I became aware of it. Prior to that, I could always suck my stomach in and put some kind of actions together, some kind of hustle, and pull myself out. Now I just didn't have that ability anymore.

And there was constant fighting with Lori. I became physically abusive, and she got the protection orders to keep me out of the house. I was working for $60 a day, drinking seventeen hours a day, and every night, after sittin' in the bar till it closed, I was putting a pistol to my head and hating myself 'cause I didn't have the courage to pull the trigger. I vividly remember the conflict of knowing that all I had to do was squeeze that trigger, and then not havin' the courage to do it. I felt worthless.

Through the grace of God, I came out of a bar in Bay Ridge, and two guys from the program pulled up. They were my recovering brother's friends. They were just passing by and they called me over. They knew me and asked me what I was doin'. All I could do was cry. They took me to detox. I went to detox with no hope of recovery. I went there out of fear of dying.

Kings County Detox...I Was Safe

The only detox available was Kings County, which is in a black neighborhood, and it's basically black people who go there. My ego said, I'm not goin' there. The racial lines were always large in my life. But I went to the Kings County detox. I remember being in the detox and looking out and not wanting to leave — not wanting to face this world and this life. I felt like I was in a cocoon; I was safe. After that, they made arrangements for me to go to South Beach Rehab out in Staten Island. I had to wait a month for the bed, and I didn't want to drink, so all I did was meetings. I didn't say nothin' to anybody; I just went to meetings, and I stayed at the meetings until they had the bed open. At the rehab, I still had no hope and no sense of what recovery could be like. The thing that happened, I guess, is that I took suggestions from people. Maybe for the first time in my life I just got humble enough to allow another human being to help me.

They told me about a halfway house that was located on the Bowery and I went for the interview. It frightened me. See, I didn't want to be there. I thought I was better than that. I was gonna go back with Lori, but Lori was actively smokin'. My counselor suggested I not do that and I listened. But while waiting for the bed at the halfway house, I had to stay in the Salvation Army. My counselor figured if I'd go back with Lori I'd never make it to the halfway house, which was probably the truth. And so I went to the Salvation Army and stayed there for three and a half weeks.

He Was Aware of My Anger and My Cowardice

The only relief, the only sense of comfort that I got was in AA meetings; I was amazed at this. I was just amazed that I had this sense of belonging. You know, it didn't happen overnight, but it happened in a fairly short time. And I got a sponsor. The amazing thing about it is that this man knew me better than I knew myself. Fifteen years prior to that he had been through exactly what I was going through, and probably more. He was brutally honest; he didn't hold back the punches. As my relationship with him progressed, I understood a lot more, and what he said to me was that I didn't know how vulnerable and how dangerous I was when I first came to the meeting rooms. He was aware of it; he was aware of my anger, and he was aware of my cowardice, of my inability to stick. The pattern of my life was that I ran when things got tough. And he would say things to me like, "Nolan, I don't know who the fuck you think you are, but all you are is a drunk." A lot of the things he said to me, I really didn't like, but I was forced to listen because of the pain in my life and my recalls were just so horrendous.

I Was Blessed with Sober Feet

During this time I had flashbacks of my life. I would catch a memory of wakin' up in the morning and throwin' up in the toilet bowl, just throwin' up and throwin' up and sweat comin' over my body and laying on the cold tiles in the bathroom and lookin' up and there's my little two-year-old daughter, Suzie, with a smile on her face, and that's her daddy on the floor with puke all over the place. I remembered things that I did, a guy I shot in a bar one time. I'd just go crazy. I just didn't think I was worth it. I'd remember all the women I slept with, wakin' up in hotel rooms with this God-awful loneliness and bein' disgusted.

I remember, one time I woke up and I looked at this woman, and said, "Who the fuck are you?" She said to me, "Who the fuck are you?" But I thought, This is really probably my soul mate; she is in the same boat I am. Usually what I do at that point is I run. I get up, get my clothes, and get the fuck out of there, but this time we went down for breakfast. She was just as frightened and as confused at her behavior as I was. And I talked to her, and we realized that we're sick people.

So I'm now livin' in a halfway house in the Bowery. What's happening to me at this stage is that I'm just becoming more aware of what alcoholism is about. I have a safe place to go now, and I'm witnessing the degradation and humiliation of alcohol, and I'm talking to some of these guys. I can talk to them for hours. I realized that I couldn't have had a seven word conversation with my neighbors in Brooklyn, yet I can stand here and talk to these guys for hours. Something was basically wrong in my life, and I saw AA as my answer.

What I was amazed at was the stories that I heard in the rooms. Yet these people seemed to be happy and pretty content with their lives as long as they weren't drinking. That was basically my first year and three months of my sobriety. The only thing I could think good about myself was the fact that

I wasn't drinking. It was a daily struggle for fifteen months. You know, some people walk into the rooms and they have an easy time with losing their desire to drink. I didn't. I wanted to drink every day. But what happened was, somehow on a mental level I started listening to what was being said, and I got into good habits. My sponsor told me I was blessed with sober feet.

The friendships that I made early in my recovery have nurtured and enriched my life. But I wasn't aware of how important they would be at that point. I thought people were just gonna be in and out of my life. The people in the rooms that I made friends with in the beginning of my recovery are still there, and it's four and a half years later. And we've grown closer and much tighter. I can depend on these people, you know, with no shame and no fear. I trust them. That was new in my life.

My recovery in AA has been a struggle. I had a brother, Marty, who died of AIDS three years ago. My sister just died of cancer five months ago. And through all that, there's been somebody there for me. I was amazed that I could deal with these situations and not fall apart. And, deal with the separation from Lori and the kids.

I Had a Dependent Need for Women

On the advice of a sponsor, because Lori was still active, I did not go back to her and the kids. He asked me to look at my track record. I'd made attempts at recovery before, and every time I went back with her, I picked up. I used her and her addiction as an excuse. So he suggested that I not go back. I had a dependent need for women, and he was keen; he was aware of it. And you know, I didn't like it, but I'd gotten that far on his advice and his suggestions, so I tried it.

I stayed away, and I learned a lot about myself by not going back. I learned that I was equipped to live life by myself, that I didn't need a woman in my life. And I didn't need the alcohol and the drugs in my life. I could go to work every day, I could clean my house, I could pay my bills, and at the same time, support Lori and the kids with whatever money I had. And it gave me a great sense of feeling good about myself.

I had to take my dependencies to the rooms of Alcoholics Anonymous. I had to allow myself to be wrong, allow people into these deep dark secret feelings. When I was angry, I didn't have Lori to make passionate love to, and when I was frightened and insecure, I didn't have her to mother me. I had to deal with it; I had to turn to people and learn how to trust on a larger scale. That's exactly what I did. By taking these risks, I allow people into my life, and I allow myself to feel concern for other people. I have become sensitive to other people in my life. So all of a sudden, I got this great hope of this thing called recovery.

I think of that little eight-year-old kid on Roosevelt and Broadway, and I think of myself today, and I know my life is a miracle. 'Cause that eight-year-old kid never left me. A lot of my emotions and a lot of my motivation as an adult stem from that little kid. I heard in the rooms that you have to raise this kid; you have to nurture him; you have to give him the love and support that was denied him back then.

We're Threefold: Mental, Physical, Spiritual

The way I treat myself is the way I treat the world at large. And lately, I've been able really to reach out to people on a deeper level than I had ever imagined existed. I'm able to do that because I'm able to do that with myself.

The process that I've learned in the rooms of Alcoholics Anonymous has helped me in dealing with my virus. I believe there is no difference between alcoholism and AIDS. Both of them could kill me. I don't think one is stronger than the other. Both of them cause me mental and physical torment, and both of them affect me spiritually. The way I view alcoholism and AIDS is, they're gonna attack me in three different areas: physically, mentally, and spiritually. The whole time that I spent in jail, I did a lot of reading on different religions, different cultures, and basically, I got into an Eastern type philosophy about life. I believe that we're threefold: mental, physical, and spiritual. The ideal is to keep the three in balance, which is just an ideal, something to strive for.

I'm pretty happy, today, with where my recovery has taken me. I'm not financially well-off. I don't have much prestige, much recognition in my life, but when I go to bed at night, I'm really happy with the person I am. And I'm happy with the opportunity afforded me in AA to reach out and give of myself, to broaden my horizons, and to open my mind and my heart to new ideas and new people. I'm almost overwhelmed with it. Dealing with AIDS, I've found a lot of AA people who really care. They have that gift of giving of themselves. A stranger walks into their life, and they readily accept me and offer me hope, encouragement, love, and understanding. I can accept that today. I can accept love in my life, and I can accept sharing in my life, because I feel I have enough to give in return.

Living with Lori and the Kids Again

By another strange twist of fate, I'm back with my wife, Lori. I had, in the course of being separated for four years, thought I was gonna get a divorce. I didn't believe Lori could ever stop smoking pot. Lori's an addict, and our attitudes and our view of life were conflicting heavily. There were a lot of arguments, a lot of bitterness, and I had conditioned myself for the finality of a divorce.

When I got sick, Lori asked me to come back. I thought about it, and I made the decision to come back, basically because I felt very needy. In order to get better, I felt that I needed somebody there for me, and I needed the kids. I had a lot of problems with this decision, a lot of guilt. I felt very selfish. But I can afford myself that right to be needy. Our relationship is not the best, but we're workin' on it.

Focus on Healing

I was diagnosed at the end of July with pneumocystis. I'm a carpenter, and I was workin' on loft renovations in Manhattan when the fatigue got to the point where I couldn't even put in a full day's work. After five, six hours of workin', I'd be really pooped. I'd be out of it. I went to one of the city hospitals, and they couldn't find anything wrong with me. At that point, I knew I had it. My brother Marty had died from AIDS, and he was treated at St. Vincent's, and I figured the West Village, you know, they really had to be up on it. I went into the emergency room; my temperature was 105 degrees, and they treated me for pneumocystis with intravenous pentamidine. They did a sputum analysis and it came back positive pneumocystis. The strange thing about it, I had no fear. My concern was with Lori and the kids. In my recovery from alcoholism I had pretty much made peace with myself and God. I had no fear of dyin' anymore. I started lookin' at death, not as the end, but as a continuation of life. I don't view it as the end of something; I view it as the beginning of somethin' new.

I remember an incident happening: I couldn't eat, I was nauseous, I just finished throwin' up, and I was layin' down. I cleared all the thoughts out of my head and got a feeling of peace. I said to myself, If this is what dying is about, this ain't bad. Then my ex-boss came up to see me, and I got a great sense of gratitude that people cared about me. Here I am, I'm sick, I've got the dreaded AIDS, and people came up to see me. It was a great feeling. After he left, I started thinking how much I had to live for, that I didn't have to die if I really didn't want to.

The support I got from people in AA was great. I'd make a phone call and people would be up to see me in an hour. I began to know how much I meant to people. People who I didn't consider myself close to, but who had heard me share in the rooms, would tell me, "You don't know how much you've helped me." That's when I began to think, I'm not ready to die; I've got too much livin' left to do. On a mental level and on a spiritual level, I started gettin' into a healing type frame of mind. And then I got better. I mean, I was in really sad shape when I left the hospital; I was 128 pounds. When I got out, I got into eating and resting and building. And slowly but surely I started puttin' on weight, started feelin' better, started gettin' into the spiritual part of my program.

I'm fortunate because I got two kids in my life, and they give me so much to hope for. I wake up in the morning, I hug them and I give them a kiss. These are the things that are important to me: my kids, my family, my friends.

I asked my friends not to let this change anything, to treat me as they treated me before. And they pretty much do. I'm a regular guy; I've just got AIDS. My fear was that people would feel sorry for me, overcompensate, and rob me of dignity as a human being. But it hasn't happened. Some people are still as obnoxious as they always were; they don't allow me to feel different.

The Twelve Steps Has Become a Way of Life

To me, AIDS is a blessing because it's made the Twelve Steps real in my life today. Now I see AA and the Twelve Steps not as a program of recovery, but as a way of life — an honest way of life. Like the Ten Commandments being the way of life for Moses' people, the Twelve Steps has became a way of life for people like me. Since AIDS, I'm more aware of the quality of my life. My values have changed. Now, it's the daily thing of being there. It's allowed me a lot more time to relax. I'm a lot more aware of stresses in my life. I'm more aware of my environment and the effect it has on me. And because I'm able to be more gentle with myself, I find that I'm more gentle with other people. I'm not so critical anymore; I'm not so rigid. If somebody, especially somebody in recovery, went outside my perception of what the Twelve Steps meant, I didn't have the flexibility to adjust to it. So I would build a wall. In my life, today, there's no need to build walls anymore.

I have a sense of peace, calm, and serenity. Dealing with AIDS, I don't know what's gonna happen. They're talking new drugs, they're talking this, they're talking that, but that's not really my concern. My focus is living with it today. I'm not allowing the fact that I have AIDS to disrupt my spiritual growth. I'm not allowing it to be a burden, be another bad card in my life. I accept it for what it is. It's not that damning disease that only gays and drug addicts get. I know I got it from my lifestyle, and I knew I was at risk, but it doesn't make me a bad person. In a lot of ways I have a lot more to give than most people because a lot of the fears that people try to hide behind are not with me anymore. And I don't feel the need to hurt and attack other people just because I'm fearful. That's just a great release of a lot of stress, a lot of tension.

There's a lot worse things than havin' AIDS. One of them is being drunk. You know the other one is probably stickin' a needle in my arm.

A Loving, Forgiving, Gentle God

Growing up Catholic Irish, God was always an ominous force. He was all powerful, always judging, always ready to come down with his terrible swift sword. My entire life, I always had this cloud of impending doom hangin' over my head. I never felt He was the one to turn to in times of struggle, crisis, or pain. I never got comfort from Him. What I knew in my life was guilt. When I felt guilt, then I knew there was a God. When I was eighteen, nineteen, twenty, I got into the search for God. There's always been that emptiness, that void in my life, and somehow through all the confusion of the drugs and the alcohol, I recognized the need in myself for a God. But I couldn't accept the God that I was raised with; I just knew it had to be a different way. My God didn't have the need for vengeance. Today, I am in touch with a very loving, forgiving, and gentle God.

I remember the first time my sponsor asked me to pray. I was really angry and bitter, sittin' in a meeting, and I recognized that if I didn't lose this bitterness, this anger, that I was gonna drink again. I was living in a halfway house. I went to my room, got down on my knees, looked up, and I asked, "God, just please take away this anger and this bitterness from my heart." I remember kneeling there with this great fear that Jesus Christ was gonna walk into that room and strike me dead. But when I got up and it didn't happen, I was a little relieved. I got in the habit of praying, of talkin' to God. No big change took place in my life. There was still a lot of the anger and bitterness, but over the course of the constant praying, it started to lift. I started to be able to laugh again, started to enjoy other people's company. It's been a slow thing, but the God in my life is very real now. He's as solid and as substantial as this table, and I'm as sure of it as I am of myself.

So I don't see God as that ominous force anymore. I see Him as a light and I see Him as love. I see a piece of Him in everybody I meet. I see Him within me and within the things that I'm able to do today, like care about other people. I believe with every fiber in my body that we're His children. I look at my relationship with my son, and I see him make mistakes, all right? And I see my relationship with my God, and I see myself make mistakes. And I see that I'm allowed to make mistakes. My son can make a mistake, but that doesn't diminish my love for him. I can make a mistake, and that doesn't diminish God's love for me.

We Huddle Together Against a Frightening Storm

Sometimes it's easy to feel alone and isolated; it's easy to give in to that. It's easy to believe that you're worthless and that's why you got AIDS. It takes strength and courage to say, "No, I'm not worthless." That takes strength and courage, because you're swimmin' upstream. So we huddle together against a frightening storm, and somehow we manage, a day at a time, to live with our AIDS and with our alcoholism. The truth of the matter is, they stack the odds against us, they label us, and if we believe them, we lose. My entire life, the church, my family, schools, the courts, they told me I was no good, and I believed them. It's like a self-fulfilling prophecy. Today, I don't believe them. I'm a caring, decent human being. AA has given me a sense of decency about myself.

ALICE

...God carries me through each and every day. He guides me. I still suffer the pain of being molested as a child. I didn't know how to deal with it for all those years. But when my son died of AIDS and I was diagnosed with HIV, I knew things had to change. I had to face reality.

Things started to be what I would call dysfunctional when my father, who was in the service, ended up staying in Germany. My mother wanted to come back here to Chicago; she didn't like it there. So she brought my brother, my sister, and me here to Chicago to stay. Then she met this man and she ended up living with him. He was a child molester. The first thing that happened that I remember was my mother's boyfriend sent her out to the store with the other two kids, and he made me take a bath with him and perform oral sex. Really horrible things went on. That was the beginning; I was five years old. He also abused my brother and sister. My mother was using drugs and alcohol, and so was he.

My father came back to get us I'd say maybe three years later. Then we had to stay with him in hotels while he was trying to get settled, trying to get organized with a job. My mother finally got tired of the life she had with her boyfriend too. He physically abused all of us, including my mother. He beat us pretty bad, and my mother had plenty of black eyes and a broken nose, and you know, the whole thing. So my mother ended up running away from Chicago. By that time, she had two other children, Lisa and Helen, so she left all of us with my dad, and she went to hide from this man. My father was a practicing alcoholic. He had a job all the time, but we still were always kinda fending for ourselves. I started abusing alcohol when I was thirteen years old because I didn't know any other way to take the pain away. I also used drugs — speed, downers, various things — anything that helped me not to think about anything.

I ran away from home several times. I'd end up running away to an older couple's house that used drugs and alcohol, and

357

I'd stay there until I couldn't stay there anymore. It'd be back and forth for me. And I was suicidal. That was because of the sexual abuse that had happened. I just couldn't deal with it. I still hated the person for it. I didn't feel very good about myself at all. I wasn't proud of myself, that's for sure.

We didn't have any affection or love in our family. Nobody was there to hug you or tell you how much they cared for you. It was really rough for me. My parents were always drinking, and my mother was also an addict, so you know there wasn't any love. My sister ended up being like the mother and taking care of everybody. She was the oldest. She still does to this day.

When I Was Sixteen, I Got Pregnant with Mary Ann

I kept using and drinking, and then when I was sixteen, I got pregnant with Mary Ann. For a while there, I wasn't drinking or anything. I straightened out for a little bit. I worked for a while in a factory, and for the sake of my daughter, I tried to straighten up and do things normal. Soon, I ended up going back out and drinking and using drugs again. Things just didn't really get any better. Then I met somebody and he married me. That only lasted about eighteen months. I was still drinking while I was married to him. So I went my way and ended up moving back in with my father.

About a year after that, I ended up in a treatment center for alcoholics. They found me one night, almost dead, according to the alcohol level that was in my body. It probably was the trauma from the divorce and everything, the marriage breakup. I stayed in treatment for five weeks, and after that, I tried to stay straight. It worked for about maybe five to six months. Then I was back to using and drinking again. Then I had Betty Lou, my second child. I continued to drink, and there wasn't really much of a break in between my relationships with men. None of them ever really worked out.

In 1986 I met the father of Elizabeth and Jonathan. That's

when I started using intravenous cocaine. Then things really went downhill for me, 'cause he was beatin' me up a lot, and I was doin' a lot of horrible things to get high, including prostitution. I never paid my bills; we always owed money. There was hardly ever anything to eat. My kids ended up goin' over by my dad's. Things got bad then. My husband was incarcerated last May, and I had my son, Jonathan, in June. It ended up, well he wasn't doin' real well health-wise, and I found out in December of '88 that he was infected.

Around that time, I decided to become abstinent from alcohol and drugs. I went through a lot of hell watching my little boy suffer the way that he did. It was hard for me to see all that they did to him in the hospital. To feed him they had to put a central line in him that goes directly to the heart. They first diagnosed him as having AIDS because he had something that caused diarrhea. His diarrhea was very, very chronic. They couldn't do anything about it. They checked several different things and just couldn't do anything for him. He was runnin' high temperatures, up to 105 degrees. His heart rate was extremely high. It was really incredible how he endured all that he did. Finally, I had seen enough suffering. When the doctors had done all they could, they asked me to make a decision: keep trying to sustain him, or put him on morphine and let him go peacefully.

I thought about it and about a week later God gave me the courage to let him be free of all pain and suffering. He hung in there for a full week from the day that he started the morphine. I spent all my time with him. I spent nights and I played with him. I strolled him around in the hospital and pretended like we were taking walks outside. I talked to him, telling him how much I loved him. I let him know that I cared about him a great deal.

The last day before he passed away I got a call that he was in a critical state. My pastor, from the church that I attend, brought me to the hospital. We got there about three in the afternoon. When I got there, I picked him up and he was really limp. I said, "Mommy's here and I love you," and his eyes opened up enough to see me. I held him, and we played some lullabies for him so he'd be peaceful. About seven o'clock that night he started to breathe hard. By about eight o'clock he passed away in my arms. I watched him go. There were some horrible things about watching him pass away. I try not to think about them too much. There was this green fluid that came from his nose and his mouth; it was real hard for me. But at least I knew then he was at peace with God. I held him for a while longer; I probably stayed there for about forty-five minutes, just holding him. Then the nurses came to give him a bath.

He passed away on February 17. After I went through that and finding out that I am HIV positive, I decided that it was time to live and do right things with my life. Ever since then, I've been actively involved in a church life, and I've been involved with treatment. I just finished an intensive outpatient drug and alcohol treatment program two weeks ago, and now I go once a week. I found HIVIES, and I go to NA and AA meetings too. I'm tryin' to get some counseling for all of us together as a family group.

How Truly I Love Them

There are nights and days that I cry about AIDS and I'm afraid because I don't know what tomorrow's going to bring. So I feel sad that if there isn't any cure found, I'm gonna have to leave my children behind. I'm afraid for that because I truly love them and we're so close.

Right now I'm dealin' with a lot of the suffering and pain from Jonathan's death and the fear I have for myself. I'm just taking it one day at a time like they say, and it seems to be workin' for me. I feel good about myself even though I know I have this illness. I'm proud of myself today, and I'm respected by a lot of people that I wasn't before. It feels good not to be sick all the time. I'm not wakin' up with headaches. I just feel good.

The kids are also proud of me. We can do things together

and enjoy one another. We go to the zoo and to the parks. Sometimes we just get together on the floor and wrestle and play. I'm a huggable person, so a lot of times I'll tell them, "Everybody get together, we're gonna hug." We have a lot of affection here in my house. I guess I enjoy that with them because that's somethin' that I never had as a child. They're really lovable too. Mary Ann's been active in Girl Scouts this past year; she got lots of awards from school. She's always been a high honors student. They're gonna go to day-camp this summer. So a lot of positive things are happening, and I'm grateful for that. I'm just happy that I'm alive today and takin' good care of myself and the children. The best thing that helps me is the counseling — to talk about it — and all the meetings. Because without those, there isn't any other way. And of course, God carries me through each and every day. He guides me.

I still suffer the pain of being molested as a child. I didn't know how to deal with it for all those years. But when my son died of AIDS and I was diagnosed with HIV, I knew things had to change. I had to face reality.

I see a private counselor for the abuse. She talks to me about everything. She's a real close friend. She's also godmother to one of my daughters. I can open up and talk about everything. Yeah, it's helping me, and I'm grateful for that 'cause I need to talk about it.

AA, NA, and HIVIES. I Take the Kids to Meetings.

I go to AA and NA and HIVIES. And I seek out more meetings, different meetings. As I go along, I see what I like and what works for me. I have to get the proper care for the children before I can do certain things. If there's not an open meeting, well, I can't go. I have to wait and see what's available.

I take the kids to meetings. It's good for them, because Mary Ann and Betty Lou are at an age where they need to talk about it too. When I was growin' up, nobody talked about anything. Everything was, "Shut up, don't say anything." So I talk about things. I'm real open with them. I talk about, you know, strangers and what can happen to them — sexual abuse. I tell them that it can be your best friend's father, whoever, just watch for those things. So we talk openly here in my house about those issues.

I'm okay today and I'm happy. I'm grateful; I'm responsible; I have this apartment; I have plenty of food; I take care of this place. I'm proud of that. It's important for me to do these things. I know that's always what I wanted in my life. With all the problems that I had growing up in a dysfunctional family, I didn't know what was normal.

It's really amazing how things happen. I got involved with a man who I ended up using intravenous drugs with; he ended up incarcerated. Now I see that as a gift from God; if he was still here, I probably would've died from using. So you know, I was asking for help, and the Lord heard me. Everything just fell into place and I'm real happy today. I'm proud of myself, my father's proud of me, and my family is proud of me. Before, you know, I had to hang my head, and I was ashamed of myself. I'm not today. Life is really beautiful.

As far as this illness is concerned, I've started to accept it. It was just something that happened, and I don't feel any blame. I don't try to figure it out. I just live with it each day. I have a lot to be grateful for. I have three beautiful, healthy daughters, and they help me through a lot of things. I just look at them and know how precious they are. They're beautiful; they're smart; they're good kids. And I'm gonna keep on doin' the same things that I've been doin', the right things.

I am the first one in my family in recovery. Everybody else is still practicing. So I'm quite a miracle. I'm grateful for it, you know. Earlier in my recovery, I thought I could go get something to drink and nobody would know. A lot of people think that. Now I know better than that. And I don't even really want it today. I am tired of it. I really am tired of it. I crave a cigarette now and then, but that's as far as it goes. I'm not smoking cigarettes anymore either.

I think the most important thing is that just because you test positive doesn't mean that's the end. There's a lot to live for, a lot to be grateful for. An individual can do a lot with his or her life. You don't have to throw your hands up in the air and say, "Well, that's it." It's not over. I'm just starting to live; that's where I am at today. I see how beautiful the world is, and life.

THE TWELVE STEPS OF ALCOHOLICS ANONYMOUS*

1. We admitted we were powerless over alcohol — that our lives had become unmanageable.

2. Came to believe that a Power greater than ourselves could restore us to sanity.

3. Made a decision to turn our will and our lives over to the care of God *as we understood Him.*

4. Made a searching and fearless moral inventory of ourselves.

5. Admitted to God, to ourselves, and to another human being the exact nature of our wrongs.

6. Were entirely ready to have God remove all these defects of character.

7. Humbly asked Him to remove our shortcomings.

8. Made a list of all persons we had harmed, and became willing to make amends to them all.

9. Made direct amends to such people wherever possible, except when to do so would injure them or others.

10. Continued to take personal inventory and when we were wrong promptly admitted it.

11. Sought through prayer and meditation to improve our conscious contact with God *as we understood Him,* praying only for knowledge of His will for us and the power to carry that out.

12. Having had a spiritual awakening as the result of these steps, we tried to carry this message to alcoholics, and to practice these principles in all our affairs.

---

*The Twelve Steps of A.A. are taken from *Alcoholics Anonymous*, 3rd ed., published by A.A. World Services, Inc., New York, N.Y., 59-60. Reprinted with permission.

Other titles that will interest you...

The Color of Light
Daily Meditations for All of Us Living with AIDS
by Perry Tilleraas
Drawing from a wealth of spiritual and philosophical resources, these meditations offer hope and comfort to us all. We can find positive thoughts to encourage us, and a place to take time to reflect on our priorities and values. 400 pp.
Order No. 5056

AIDS
The Drug and Alcohol Connection
by Larry Siegel, M.D. and Milan Korcok
The authors cover a broad range of AIDS-related issues and discuss the roles of chemical dependency and health care professionals in working with people with AIDS. Includes an important section on the positive impact recovery can have on people diagnosed with AIDS. 128 pp.
Order No. 5072

The Twelve Step Response to Chronic Illness and Disability
Recovering Joy in Life
by Martha Cleveland
Martha Cleveland has sensitively interpreted the Twelve Step program for use in dealing with the emotional pain often felt by those who are chronically ill. Living the Twelve Steps can aid us in finding spiritual strength, humility, understanding, emotional stability, and peace of mind. 160 pp.
Order No. 5477

For price and order information, please call one of our Telephone Representatives. Ask for a free catalog describing nearly 1,500 items available through Hazelden Educational Materials.

HAZELDEN EDUCATIONAL MATERIALS

1-800-328-9000   **1-800-257-0070**   **1-612-257-4010**
(Toll Free. U.S. Only)   (Toll Free. MN Only)   (AK and Outside U.S.)

Pleasant Valley Road • P.O. Box 176 • Center City, MN 55012-0176